The Plays of Beaumont and Fletcher

To my dear Father

The Plays of Beaumont and Fletcher

Sexual Themes and Dramatic Representation

Sandra Clark
Birkbeck College

HARVESTER
WHEATSHEAF

New York   London   Toronto   Sydney   Tokyo   Singapore

First published 1994 by
Harvester Wheatsheaf
Campus 400, Maylands Avenue
Hemel Hempstead
Hertfordshire, HP2 7EZ
A division of
Simon & Schuster International Group

© 1994 Sandra Clark

All rights reserved. No part of this publication may be reproduced, stored in a retrieval system, or transmitted, in any form, or by any means, electronic, mechanical, photocopying, recording or otherwise, without prior permission, in writing, from the publisher.

Typeset in 10/12pt Ehrhardt
by The Midlands Book Typesetting Company

Printed and bound in Great Britain
by BPCC Journals and Reference Books Ltd, Exeter

British Library Cataloguing in Publication Data

A catalogue record for this book is available from the British Library

ISBN 0-7450-1569-7

1 2 3 4 5   98 97 96 95 94

Contents

Preface		vii
Notes on editions		ix
Introduction	*The Beaumont and Fletcher Partnership: Reputation and Collaboration*	1
Chapter 1	*The Price of Virtue: Chastity Plays*	24
Chapter 2	*Gender*	53
Chapter 3	*Misogyny and Manhood*	78
Chapter 4	*Sex and Tyranny*	101
Chapter 5	*Courtship and Marriage in the Comedies*	128
Conclusion		153
Notes		160
Bibliography		184
Index		195

Preface

This book has evolved over a period of several years during which I have been on the lookout for signs that there were other people in the world who shared my interest in Beaumont and Fletcher. Increasingly, I have seen such signs, though I am still surprised that there are not more of them. As I suggest in the book, there are several current theoretical trends, which, if nothing else, ought to prompt people working on the literature and culture of early modern England to look at Beaumont and Fletcher's plays anew; I hope, of course, that there is something else, even if, at the moment, there are plenty of people more interested in theory than in plays.

I want first to thank David Atkinson, who has been involved with this book at several stages and in many ways; I am also grateful to Graham Handley and Jan Cole for various forms of help and kindness. Probably no one could have entirely eliminated the traumas involved in coping with material prepared on several different word-processing systems, although I had supposed that this might be one of the roles of Central Computing Services in University institutions; but in this respect David Clark did much more than anybody else.

Note on editions

I have where possible quoted the Beaumont and Fletcher plays from the Cambridge edition, *The Dramatic Works in the Beaumont and Fletcher Canon*, General Editor, Fredson Bowers, (Cambridge, Cambridge University Press, 1966-). There are to date 8 volumes. For plays not available in this edition I have used *The Works of Francis Beaumont and John Fletcher*, eds. Arnold Glover and A.R.Waller, 10 vols, (Cambridge, Cambridge University Press, 1905-12).

Abbreviations

ES	E.K.Chambers, *The Elizabethan Stage*, 4 vols (Oxford, Oxford University Press, 1923)
JCS	G.E.Bentley, *The Jacobean and Caroline Stage*, 5 vol. (Oxford, Clarendon Press, 1956)
JEGP	*Journal of English and Germanic Philology*
PMLA	*Proceedings of the Modern Languages Association*
RORD	*Research Opportunities in Renaissance Drama*
SEL	*Studies in English Literature*
SQ	*Shakespeare Quarterly*
SS	*Shakespeare Survey*
Shares	Cyrus Hoy, 'The Shares of Fletcher and his Collaborators in the Beaumont and Fletcher Canon', *Studies in Bibliography*, 8-9; 11-14, (1956-61)
Works	*The Dramatic Works in the Beaumont and Fletcher Canon*, General Editor, Fredson Bowers, 8 vols (Cambridge, Cambridge University Press, 1966-)

    Vol. 1   *The Knight of the Burning Pestle*, ed. Cyrus Hoy
              The Woman Hater, ed. George Walton Williams
              The Coxcomb, ed. Irby B. Cauthen, Jnr
              The Captain, ed. L. A. Beaurline
    Vol. 2   *Cupid's Revenge*, ed. Fredson Bowers

	The Scornful Lady, ed. Cyrus Hoy
Vol. 3	*Love's Cure*, ed. George Walton Williams
	The Noble Gentleman, ed. L. A. Beaurline
	The Tragedy of Thierry and Theodoret, ed. Robert K. Turner, Jnr
	The Faithful Shepherdess, ed. Cyrus Hoy
Vol. 4	*The Woman's Prize*, ed. Fredson Bowers
	Bonduca, ed. Cyrus Hoy
	The Tragedy of Valentinian, ed. Robert K. Turner, Jnr
	Monsieur Thomas, ed. Hans Walter Gabler
Vol. 5	*The Loyal Subject*, ed. Fredson Bowers
	The Humorous Lieutenant, ed. Cyrus Hoy
	Women Pleased, ed. Hans Walter Gabler
Vol. 6	*Wit Without Money*, ed. Hans Walter Gabler
	The Wild-Goose Chase, ed. Fredson Bowers
	A Wife for a Month, ed. Robert Kean Turner
	Rule a Wife and Have a Wife, ed. George Walton Williams
Vol. 7	*Wit at Several Weapons*, ed. Robert Kean Turner
	The Night Walker, ed. Cyrus Hoy
	The Two Noble Kinsmen, ed. Fredson Bowers

Introduction

The Beaumont and Fletcher Partnership: Reputation and Collaboration

(i)

The aim of this introductory chapter is to provide various kinds of contexts which will illuminate the dramatic handling of subject matter central both to human experience and to Beaumont and Fletcher's dramaturgy: sexuality. My starting point is the acknowledgment that the representation of sexuality in those plays has been considerably responsible not only for their huge popularity for much of the seventeenth century but also for their subsequent striking fall from critical favour. The first part of this assertion may seem more obviously true than the second; but I would argue that those theatrical strategies which the dramatists deployed in constructing and developing sexual situations form the basis of their dramaturgy more generally, and that it is the nature of this dramaturgy and its aesthetic which, by contrast with those of Shakespeare, has led to the critical marginalisation of a huge and influential corpus of plays, at least since the time of Coleridge.

The focus of the remainder of this book is quite narrow, but in this chapter it is broadened in order to provide the subject with more shape and definition. I want first in fairly general terms to survey the fortunes of Beaumont and Fletcher's critical reputation, and in doing so to consider the politics of this reputation at its various stages. By politics, I mean the interest-serving practices and ideologies according to which the value and significance of the plays was defined at any particular time. It is necessary to explore not only how reputations change, but why; and the factors relevant to answering the second part of this question might also shed light more broadly, for example on the interrelations of drama and society in the seventeenth century, and on what is now often known as the Shakespeare 'myth'. Behind this examination of the history of Beaumont and Fletcher's reputation lies the implication that its current condition is worth more scrutiny; and a justification for this may be found by looking again at Beaumont and Fletcher's handling of sexuality in the light of certain current critical attitudes and preoccupations, in particular the reaction against liberal humanist readings of Renaissance texts and the connections drawn – often, but not exclusively, by feminists – between sexual themes and power and authority. An examination of the gradual disappearance from critical scrutiny (and historical prominence) of the Beaumont and Fletcher plays after the end of the seventeenth century highlights the ways in which the liberal humanist construction of Shakespearean dramaturgy, particularly by Coleridge and his successors, has been inimical to Beaumont and Fletcher's reputation. By contrast, a consideration of the reputations of both the plays and the collaborative partnership in the seventeenth century will show how these reputations were created and the part played in this creation by their association with royalist politics; it will also suggest that this part, though significant, need not be seen as foreclosing on the plays' own potential for offering a wider range of political meanings.

(ii)

The Beaumont and Fletcher canon is currently defined as consisting of about fifty-three plays,[1] primarily those published in the Second Folio of 1679 but also including *Henry VIII*, *Sir John Van Olden Barnavelt*, and *A Very Woman*;[2] and perhaps another half dozen, now lost, could have been attributed to one or both of these playwrights.[3] Yet nowadays students of Renaissance drama, familiar with the work of Marston, Middleton, Webster, and so forth, are unlikely to have read even four of them. The extraordinary invisibility of so vast a corpus is of course a reflection of its critical neglect, which is to an extent a twentieth-century phenomenon.[4] For although Beaumont and Fletcher's reputation had begun to decline before the end of the seventeenth century, texts continued to be available; in the eighteenth and nineteenth centuries each there were three collected editions, but since the Glover and Waller edition of 1905–12 there have been no complete works until the as yet unfinished Cambridge edition, which began to appear in 1966. More significantly, perhaps, only six plays, *The Knight of the Burning Pestle*, *The Maid's Tragedy*, *Philaster*, *A King and No King*, and, by virtue of their Shakespeare connection, *The Two Noble Kinsmen* and *Henry VIII* have ever appeared in cheap paperback editions. By comparison with the annual flood of scholarly writing on Webster and Middleton, that devoted to Beaumont and Fletcher is but a trickle.

Some twentieth-century critics, uncomfortably conscious of the discrepancy between the evaluation of the Beaumont and Fletcher plays in their own time and in ours, totally abandoning any attempt to historicise this phenomenon, have lapsed into expressions of surprise and even revulsion at the implied low quality of seventeenth-century taste. 'No English dramatists before or since have had so extraordinary an influence',[5] is one characteristic response, while another influential critic mentions with a shudder how the Beaumont and Fletcher style retained pre-eminence 'for an appalling number of years' after their deaths.[6] 'If they do represent their times, then the simple answer is, so much the worse for their times' is the dismissive comment made by the author of *A Study of Elizabethan and Jacobean Tragedy*, who allows that *Philaster*, one of the most popular and successful plays by any writer in the seventeenth century, is just about worth 'a very quick reading through'.[7] A recent account of Jacobean tragicomedy which is alive to several new kinds of critical perspectives on literature begins by noticing that 'of all the oddities of this hybrid genre, the most prominent . . . remains the striking discrepancy between the aesthetic inferiority of many of the plays and their undoubted historical importance', and then proceeds to dismiss the validity of critical studies of Beaumont and Fletcher deriving from 'the text itself' because they can only be 'ultimately defeated by the plays' artistic mediocrity'.[8]

Rather than attempt any head-on confrontation with such views, I prefer to begin by trying to suggest some factors, other than the purely aesthetically evaluative, that might account for them. The influence of Coleridge has been profoundly significant for later Beaumont and Fletcher criticism, and makes a good place to start. Coleridge was sufficiently interested in the plays to borrow Lamb's copy of the 1679 Folio which he annotated in the margins, as he did with his own copy of the 1811 *Dramatic Works of Ben Jonson, and of Beaumont and Fletcher*. Although there was much to be appreciated in the plays, especially their lyrical qualities, Coleridge found them in many respects morally offensive, he disliked their politics, and his veneration for Shakespeare as a god-like genius led him to a wholesale devaluation of Beaumont and Fletcher's work by comparison. To him even the most likeable of their characters appeared bespattered with 'filth', and he noted with horror 'how many of the Plays are founded on rapes – how many on unnatural incestuous passions – how many on mere lunacies', and in their work more generally 'the minutiae of a lecher'. 'Shakespeare always makes vice odious and virtue admirable, while Beaumont and Fletcher do the reverse – they ridicule virtue and encourage vice: they pander to the lowest and basest passions of our nature', he asserted, and he found particularly objectionable the fact that although they imitated Shakespeare extensively, 'in every play, more or less', they were shameless enough to 'miss no opportunity of sneering at the divine Man, and sub detracting from his Merits'. The contrast with Shakespeare extended to politics, and where Coleridge constantly applauded him for his divine and timeless impartiality, the only one who could give 'the permanent Politics of Human Nature', he formed the view of Beaumont and Fletcher as 'the most servile jure divino royalists', and in a much-repeated phrase 'high-flying, passive-obedience Tories'.[9] Coleridge was of course writing in the aftermath of the French Revolution with which he had in youth been idealistically sympathetic, although his political opinions were modified in later years. Wallis (with some justice) accuses him of 'stout Tory prejudices'. His desire was to see his own beliefs reflected in Shakespeare, and this encouraged him to create a polarity between Shakespeare and Beaumont and Fletcher and to extend his critique of their political excesses to their moral laxness and decadence. Hazlitt and Leigh Hunt, like Coleridge, took the expression of absolutist beliefs by Beaumont and Fletcher characters as evidence of the playwrights' personal politics; Hunt was especially censorious of the way they had sold their birthright 'for the mess of loathsome pottage of the praise and profligacy of the court of James I'.[10]

The spectrum of critical opinion on the politics of these plays has always been broader than Coleridge's much-quoted views suggest, yet to the present day some critics have continued to see Beaumont and Fletcher as more or less what Margot Heinemann forthrightly calls 'royal slaves';[11] Marco Mincoff, for example, refers to Fletcher's 'rabid propaganda of absolutism' in *Valentinian* and *The Loyal Subject*.[12] J. F. Danby, in a subtle and influential book, traced the development of a 'Cavalier mentality' in their work in which loyalty to the monarch constituted an absolute value requiring no debate.[13]

Yet the royalist bias which has been used to account for the popularity of the plays in the Restoration was not evident to critics of that period; and this is not because their criticism can be written off as the apologetics of royalist theatre where absolutist beliefs constitute part of an invisible ideology. Flecknoe, the earliest of the Restoration theatre historians, thought Beaumont and Fletcher 'excellent in their kind' but guilty of faults against decorum by their 'irreverent representing Kings persons on the Stage, who shu'd never be represented but with Reverence'.[14] Rymer, who in *The Tragedies of the Last Age Consider'd* (1678) chose to discuss three of Beaumont and Fletcher's tyrant plays, *Rollo, A King and No King,* and *The Maid's Tragedy*, as 'The choicest and most applauded English tragedies of this last age' (with *Othello, Julius Caesar* and *Catiline*), followed the same line. The plays, and particularly the representations of rulers, failed on grounds which, though apparently aesthetic, are also by implication political: they are indecorous. 'All crown'd heads by Poetical right are Heroes',[15] says Rymer. The killing of the king in *The Maid's Tragedy* is indecent, because performed by a woman, but not politically abhorrent. The king is not in any case responsible for the tragedy because his commands could with honour have been disobeyed; Amintor's situation expresses not a heroic dilemma but his own unworthiness. Dryden agreed with Rymer on this matter and thought Fletcher at fault in that he gave neither to the king in *The Maid's Tragedy* nor to Arbaces in *A King and No King* 'the qualities which are suitable to a monarch'. And although he allowed that Fletcher was faithful to history in showing Valentinian as 'an effeminate, voluptuous man', none the less 'he has forgotten that he was an Emperor, and has given him none of those royal marks which ought to appear in a lawful successor to the throne.' He concludes that Fletcher should not have depicted Valentinian at all if he could not avoid making him vicious.[16] In fact, far from seeing the plays as absolutist texts Flecknoe, Rymer and Dryden consider them if anything subversive of absolutism.

One assumption on which the criticism of the Restoration was based was that some of the Beaumont and Fletcher plays did not deserve their vast stage popularity in view of such lapses in decorum as their representation of monarchs as both legitimate and morally vicious. The idea that Beaumont and Fletcher's tragedies might have political significance was certainly around, but the forms which it took do not suggest that they were regarded as royalist texts; in fact, if anything, the opposite. The debate still continues as to whether Charles II actually did ban *The Maid's Tragedy*, as Langbaine said, because he was offended by a scene in which a king was killed by his mistress.[17] Waller rewrote the last act, incriminating Evadne less ambivalently than did Beaumont and Fletcher, and allowing the King to repent and survive. Rochester wrote what is in effect a depoliticised version of *Valentinian* (1685), in which the ethical dilemma of the husband wronged by his ruler is played down and the ruler's corruption takes the form of sexual irresponsibility only, and is not related to disorder in his country. In Thomas Scott's tragic version of *A Wife for a Month*, retitled *The Unhappy Kindness: or a Fruitless Revenge*, by contrast, tyrannical behaviour of the ruler is much stressed and the victimised husband is made to hold back from revenge because he cannot contemplate killing his sovereign.

Now the orthodoxy is that Beaumont and Fletcher's texts are aesthetically almost worthless in comparison to Shakespeare's, and politically abhorrent as well; while it would be a folly to attempt totally to overturn these assumptions, there is evidently some profit to be made from questioning them. Wallis began to do this in *Fletcher, Beaumont and Company: Entertainers to the Jacobean Gentry* (1947), and proposed that far from being servile royalists they in fact demonstrated 'a distaste for the theory and practice of absolutism'.[18] More recent books by Finkelpearl and Bushnell,[19] informed in different ways by the current trend to repoliticise Renaissance drama, support the view that Romantic assumptions about the politics of these plays were mistaken and need to be reread against the historical conditions in which they were formed. Recent studies – some, but not all, from a new historicist perspective – of the operations of power in the early modern period and of the functioning of theatre as a cultural practice in relation to this power, have created a climate appropriate for the re-evaluation of representations of authority in the Beaumont and Fletcher canon, especially when read in conjunction with accounts of the politics of gender in the Elizabethan and Jacobean theatre.[20]

It is perhaps surprising that the attention directed at perceived unorthodoxies in Beaumont and Fletcher's treatment of women and sexuality, not only by Coleridge, but from Flecknoe and Rymer on, has not alerted more twentieth-century critics and readers to consider whether their representation of the politics of gender might not be worth a new look. Rymer disapproved of the indecorum with which some of the female characters were handled; he thought Edith in *The Bloody Brother* 'more like some Minx in an alley, than any character for tragedy'.[21] Flecknoe's criticism, more morally based, was of 'that witty obscenity ... like poison infused in pleasant liquor' that dangerously permeated the plays.[22] Coleridge elaborated on Flecknoe's views in his many references to the indecency of the female characters, and many critics of our own century follow this line. At one time accusations of prurience, licentiousness, cynicism, and so forth tended to be focused on Fletcher, and utilised as a means of distinguishing between the respective contributions of the two playwrights. Thus Gayley, in *Francis Beaumont, dramatist: A portrait*, while attributing to Beaumont all portraits of 'the maiden of pure heart whose love is unfortunately placed too high', saw Fletcher's hand in comedies of intrigue, 'especially in sections of plot that are carnal, trivial, or unnatural'. Oliphant, similarly, asserted that 'in the Beaumontesque plays we do not find nasty scenes and nasty people wholly unnecessary to the plot wantonly introduced as is too often the case with Fletcher'.[23] Though the moral terminology may be modified later in the century, the underlying tone is the same. Philip Edwards's paradox about Fletcher being 'a moral writer with highly immoral tendencies' implies distaste; Robert Ornstein so dislikes Fletcher's 'ethical frivolity' that he discusses *The Maid's Tragedy*, which he takes seriously, as if Beaumont alone wrote it.[24] Efforts have been made to rehabilitate Fletcher, even to redefine his attitudes to women as more 'politically correct' than Beaumont's; but it is hard to be entirely convinced by the arguments of Nancy Cotton Pearse, the thrust of which is indicated by the subtitle of her book *John Fletcher's Chastity Plays: Mirrors of Modesty*; and the statement of L. C. Knights that 'the only thing Fletcher took at all seriously was a decent freedom for women'[25] derives from attitudes to the relationship between author and text that many now find questionable. Finkelpearl's valiant efforts on Fletcher's behalf also rest on some shaky premises.[26]

But more damning to any serious exploration of the achievement of Beaumont and Fletcher than either accusations of objectionably absolutist politics or frivolous prurience has been the long tradition of unfavourable comparison with Shakespeare. Dryden's strictures were of course seminal, and Coleridge again highly significant; Lawrence Venuti, in an important article on Massinger's reputation which has many ramifications for Beaumont and Fletcher, regards Coleridge, with Eliot, as responsible for the 'valorization of bourgeois individualism in romantic and modern critical discourse' which has resulted in the prioritising of Shakespeare and the playwrights whose work lends itself to this way of reading over those whose work does not.[27] The central reason he gives for the marginalisation of Massinger's work, much of which, of course, forms part of the Beaumont and Fletcher canon, is that 'his texts do not conform to the individualistic assumptions of bourgeois critical discourse, namely, unconstrained intentionality, organic unity, and illusionistic response';[28] these assumptions have offered the basis for what, until recently, has proved the dominant mode of reading Shakespeare's texts, but they are even more inappropriate to the work of Beaumont and Fletcher than they are to Massinger. It is hardly necessary to illustrate unfavourable criticism of the Beaumont and Fletcher plays on grounds of their fragmented and discontinuous dramaturgy, the 'factitious' or meretricious aspects, the evasion of 'great questions', the 'bankruptcy of the tragic vision', their lack of profound human values in comparison with Shakespeare.[29] Coleridge's organic metaphor (echoed in Eliot) epitomises the issue:

> The latter (B. and F.) you will find a well-arranged bed of flowers, each having its separate root, and its position determined aforehand by the *will* of the Gardener – a fresh plant, a fresh volition. In the former [Shakespeare] an Indian fig-tree ... – all is growth, evolution, γένεσις – each Line, each word almost, begets the following – and the Will of the writer is an interfusion, a continuous agency, no series of separate acts. Sh. is the height, breadth and depth of Genius. B. and F. the excellent mechanism, in juxtaposition and succession, of Talent.[30]

Two particular issues arise here, the manner of Beaumont and Fletcher's dramaturgy, especially in its lack of the organic unity and moral profundity to be found in Shakespeare's, and the fact that the collaborative nature of their work presents a formidable obstacle to any attempt to account for its valued features as the inspired creation of individual genius. This is not the place for an account of Beaumont and Fletcher's dramaturgy; but what needs to be stressed is that even descriptive accounts of it, like Eugene M. Waith's groundbreaking *The Pattern of Tragicomedy in Beaumont and Fletcher*, cannot avoid contaminating aesthetic with moral categories. Waith's discussion of the rhetorical mode of their theatricality is often brilliant, but his underlying adherence to the notion of illusionistic response to drama as the proper response leads him to regard the strategies he has identified as characteristic of Beaumont and Fletcher with suspicion and implied disapproval. Of *The Maid's Tragedy*, for example, he observes that an effect of the dramatists' 'manipulation of character and plot' is 'that the spectator comes to relish the very means by which his emotions are appealed to'. Again and again he notices how the handling of situation is such as to challenge and surprise the audience, and elicit the maximum emotional response. 'The renunciation of meaning', he acknowledges is 'one of the strategies by which Beaumont and Fletcher achieve their superbly calculated succession of dramatic moments', but he cannot accept that play with meaning, or theatrical effects which draw attention to themselves, can be legitimate aesthetic activities.[31] Donohue in *Dramatic Characters in the English Romantic Age* analyses *Philaster* most acutely to demonstrate the playwrights' 'emotional manipulation' of the audience, illustrating the effects of such characteristic tactics as the withholding of explanatory information, the presentation of 'immediate and absolute response to events', and the dichotomy between the heard (one character's speech) and the seen (the other's silent reaction); but his responsiveness to theatricality, to the potential for meanings as created in the theatre by the interaction between actors, text, and audience, is vitiated by the underlying implication that this dramaturgy is somehow only second-best: 'What probably disturbs us most ... is the evident posturing of the Fletcherian character.'[32] I would argue that this sort of critical discomfort with Beaumont and Fletcher's techniques of characterisation arises from their resistance to humanist reading, as Belsey defines it in *The Subject of Tragedy*. Discussing the dramatic speech, particularly in the form of soliloquy, of 'the precariously unified protagonist of Renaissance drama', she writes:

> Since the subject of the enunciation always exceeds the subject of the utterance, the 'I' cannot be fully present in what it says of itself. It is this gap which opens the possibility of glimpsing an identity behind what is said, a silent self anterior to the utterance, 'that within which passes show'. The project of humanist criticism is to fill this gap.[33]

The discovery of this 'selfhood', this illusion of a personal consciousness, an individuality, within Shakespeare's characters has been the bedrock of much Shakespeare criticism, at least until very recently; but Beaumont and Fletcher's characters are rarely susceptible to this kind of analysis. It is not easy to identify 'real' selves, for whom an inexpressible subjectivity can be constructed which will unify the fragmented utterances of the speakers in the play. The speeches, therefore, 'mean' what they say; there is no elusive 'real meaning' hidden behind them, of which the text itself is only a set of incomplete signs, requiring the reader or audience to fill in the gaps. Hence, the characters seem to 'posture'; that is, to adopt attitudes not natural to them, because they have no 'nature'.

The problems attendant on extricating the criticism of Renaissance drama from the claims and premises of a humanist theory which has (or has had) more to offer for Shakespeare studies than for those of other dramatists of course affect many playwrights other than Beaumont and Fletcher. But the problems resulting from dramatic collaboration are peculiarly theirs. Not that they were the only playwrights to operate in this way; far from it.

Bentley in fact reckons that between 1590 and 1642 half of all the plays written by professional dramatists were collaborations, and of the 282 plays mentioned in Henslowe's diary the proportion is more like two-thirds.[34] But in the history of collaborative playwriting in Renaissance theatre the Beaumont and Fletcher partnership was unique, and consequently the politics of collaboration bears far more significantly on their work than on that of any other writer or writers of the period. Modern attitudes to artistic autonomy tend to downgrade collaborative enterprise and find more intrinsic interest as well as aesthetic authenticity in the inspired creative efforts of individual genius. As a recent Marxist critic of Renaissance theatre, Walter Cohen, puts it:

> Modern suspicion of collaborative art reflects a bias in favor of bourgeois values like originality, individuality, projection of personality, and aesthetic unity, a set of ideals, in short, that was rarely paramount in the public theaters [of the Renaissance].[35]

In discussions of the Beaumont and Fletcher plays this distrust of collaboration as an authentic mode of artistic production is expressed through the idea that collaborative works cannot achieve the highest artistic standards, and that culturally privileged kinds of writing are essentially beyond their reach. Thus Ian Fletcher feels that a good tragedy cannot be written by two playwrights together 'since it demands that the artist himself submit to that solitude';[36] and A. R. Humphreys, in his account of the authorship of *Henry VIII*, delimits its potential for success according to the humanist standards of aesthetic autonomy:

> If it becomes apparent that two authors shared the play, then one may content oneself with finding in it the qualities of an impressively devised stage diversion, suitably furnished with splendid acting parts and notable speeches in the presentation of a colourful era of English history, and the prospect of defining some deep symbolical or conceptual unity may be dismissed as a will-o'-the-wisp.[37]

Even Cyrus Hoy, who has done more work than anyone on the textual problems of the collaboration, sees the crucial issue purely in terms of humanist aesthetic, as 'how satisfactorily the multiple dramatic visions have fused into a single coherent one.'[38] Seen from another angle, this is as much as to say, as Jeffery Maslen does, that 'the collaborative project in the theater was predicated on erasing the perception of any differences that might have existed ... between collaborated parts.'[39] This very erasure is what Hoy's work is attempting to undo.

Undoubtedly these strongly-rooted post-Romantic notions of authorship and literary creativity have contributed greatly to the critical neglect of this large collaborative corpus. Not only do they promote concepts of integrity, unity, dramatic coherence, profundity of vision, and so forth, which are then found lacking in the Beaumont and Fletcher plays, but they also tend to demote the genre of tragicomedy/romance to which so large a proportion of the plays belongs.[40] Tragicomedy itself, when approached descriptively, can often be seen to possess generic features which are inimical to the idea of unity or dramatic integrity (in an aesthetic sense) as a controlling structural principle, for example, the tendency to operate in terms of the scene as a unit of action, the 'playing with aesthetic distance', the manipulation of the audience's narrative knowledge for the creation of effects of shock and surprise.[41] The ability of these plays to provide their audiences (and readers) with pleasurable surprises is frequently mentioned in the tributes which preface the First Folio, many of which also remark upon the unique quality of the Beaumont and Fletcher collaboration; indeed collaborative practice may well have been a factor in the evolution of the Beaumont and Fletcher dramaturgy, particularly in its reliance on 'strong scenes'.[42] Significant for my general topic of the handling of sexual themes is the fact that many such scenes take the form of some sexually significant situation, developed through such devices as tests, trials, and ordeals, often involving role-playing.

(iii)

The detailed exploration of these situations is, of course, to come later in the book. Having briefly considered the politics of the reputation of the Beaumont and Fletcher plays in our own century, I want now to locate them in contexts of their own time in order to reflect on the relationship between their reputation at its height and in its depths. It is convenient to return to the issues surrounding collaboration, since they were significant in various ways for the politics of the plays' reception in the seventeenth century.

As a method of literary production, collaboration had little prestige during the Renaissance period, and particularly not in the world of theatre where, with certain exceptions, no one involved in the writing or production of plays enjoyed high social status. The title-pages of printed plays often obscured the fact of collaborative authorship, and playwrights themselves contributed to the uncertainty over the authorship of many texts. Jonson who, admittedly, was unique in his concern for the authenticity of his published texts and for the creation of his own image as an author who owned them as intellectual property, worked jointly with a number of other writers on plays for the professional theatre in the earlier part of his career, but he ensured that none of them was included in his Folio of 1616. In fact, despite Jonson's efforts in other directions as a self-publicist, much of this work would be unknown to us now were it not for entries in Henslowe's *Diary*, since the playwright himself did not choose to preserve it. In his address to the readers for the printed text of *Sejanus* he notes that he has specifically weeded out parts contributed by a collaborator to the stage version.[43] Massinger, Fletcher's second most important collaborator, whose hand Bentley has found in nineteen plays of the Beaumont and Fletcher canon,[44] referred to some of his collaborations as 'those toyes I would not father' in a verse letter to his patron, the fourth Earl of Pembroke,[45] and he evidently was less concerned to get his collaborations recognised than the unaided plays he collected and corrected for publication. His important contributions to the Beaumont and Fletcher Folios are nowhere acknowledged in the prefaces and prefatory poems, though they were certainly known.[46]

Although attitudes to authorship were changing in this period it was still unusual for plays to be regarded as literary texts. Confusion over the attribution of their authorship was rife,[47] a state of affairs partially reflected on the title-pages of the ten Beaumont and Fletcher plays which appeared in quarto form before 1647. Five of these were not attributed to any author even though they were printed within Fletcher's lifetime; quartos of the 1630s *Cupid's Revenge* (1630), *The Maid's Tragedy* (1630) and *The Knight of the Burning Pestle* (1635) were each attributed to both playwrights. This does not of course signify that the authorship was unknown, only that the meaning of the contents of a title-page was very different in the seventeenth from in the twentieth century. Prologues and epilogues are notoriously misleading as to the number of authors involved in the writing of a specific play, and often seem to have been composed more with an eye to publicity than to accuracy. Playwrights' names were not routinely attached to the titles of their work; in the records of the Revels office of plays performed at court the playwrights' names tend not to appear, and casual playgoers in letters and diaries rarely mention playwrights by name. In the controversy surrounding what is now probably the most notorious of the collaborations, *Sir John van Olden Barnavelt*, no writers are named, and in fact no external evidence for the play's authorship has ever been discovered.[48]

Since the relationship between a playwright and his text was still so fluid it is not surprising that when Humphrey Moseley brought out the First Folio, consisting of thirty-four play-texts, *Comedies and Tragedies Written by Francis Beaumont and John Fletcher Gentlemen. Never printed before, and now published by the Authours Originall Copies*, he was able to manipulate the facts of authorship to his own advantage. But what is noteworthy is the way that he transformed collaborative authorship from a commercial workshop practice into a unique spiritual partnership. This was partly achieved by the suppression of Massinger's contribution, which was in fact considerably greater than Beaumont's, to the plays included in this edition, many of them written after Beaumont's death. Yet Moseley had not included texts previously published, among them many of the most popular plays of the collaboration, which shows that he had great – and evidently justified – confidence in the existence of a real market of readers for the plays. Massinger's collaborative work was certainly known, not least to the ten members of the King's Men whose dedicatory letter opens the volume, since some of them would have been directly responsible for commissioning him to do the work.[49] He had died, at the height of his fame, in 1640, fifteen years after Fletcher and twenty-four after Beaumont, but only his friend, Sir Aston Cokaine, recorded any unease with Moseley's dealings. As his poem to Moseley and his co-publisher Humphrey Robinson suggests, Cokaine was concerned for the truth, and for fairness to all parties:

> In this large book of Plays you late did print
> (In *Beaumonts* and in *Fletchers* name) why in't
> Did you not justice? give to each his due?
> For *Beaumont* (of those many) writ in few:
> And Massinger in other few; the Main
> Being sole Issues of sweet *Fletchers* brain.[50]

But Cokaine's real interest was less in justice to Massinger than in the myth which Moseley's volume sought to foster and promote, of Beaumont and Fletcher as what, in another verse letter to his cousin Charles Cotton, Cokaine called 'our *English* Polestars'. Many of those who wrote verse-tributes for the Folio celebrated the collaboration between Beaumont and Fletcher in similar terms. Although Fletcher's greater contribution to the collaboration was acknowledged by the higher proportion of tributes addressed solely to him, the overall stress is on the mutuality of the partnership. Beaumont and Fletcher were called 'Parnassus biceps', 'potent wits', 'twin-like brains', 'great pair of authors', 'two voices in one song', 'renowned twins of poetry'; 'they lived a miracle', asserted Shirley in his fervent preface. One of the most metaphysical tributes is by Sir John Pettus:

> How Angels (Cloyster'd in our humane Cells)
> Maintaine their parley, *Beaumont–Fletcher* tells;
> Whose strange unimitable Intercourse
> Transcends all Rules, and flyes beyond the force
> Of the most forward soules . . .

More prosaically, Sir George Lisle describes the unique mutuality of the partnership:

> Behold, here's FLETCHER too! the World ne'er knew
> Two Potent Witts co-operate till You;
> For still your fancies are so wov'n and knit,
> 'Twas FRANCIS FLETCHER or JOHN BEAUMONT writ.

Jasper Maine begins his eulogy with an apostrophe:

> Great paire of Authors, whom one equall Starre
> Begot so like in *Genius*, that you are
> In Fame, as well as Writings, both so knit,
> That no man knowes where to divide your wit.

He ends by distinguishing the nature of this collaboration from that of the more mundane working relationships:

> Nor wrote you so, that one's part was to lick
> The other into shape, nor did one stick
> The others cold inventions with such wit,
> As served like spice, to make them quick and fit;
> Nor, out of mutual want, or emptinesse,
> Did you conspire to go still twins to th' Press.
> . . .
> And the Presse which both thus amongst us sends,
> Sends us one Poet in a paire of friends.[51]

There were modified views of the actual nature of Beaumont and Fletcher's working partnership in circulation, such as the much repeated idea that the over-fertile Fletcher needed to submit his rampant fancies to Beaumont's more sober judgement;[52] this of course took no account of Fletcher's predicament once Beaumont's critical eye was unavailable. It is evident from many studies of collaborative playwriting in the period that the system was extremely flexible and could operate in a variety of modes. Hoy's attribution studies show all manner of ways in which the composition of a play could be divided between two, three, four, and maybe even more playwrights. In a few examples, chosen at random, he discerns the following divisions: in *The Beggar's Bush*, Fletcher writes Acts III and IV, Beaumont II, and part of V, Massinger I and the other part of V, including the first half of a scene where Beaumont takes over in the middle. In *The Coxcomb* Beaumont and Fletcher each wrote separate scenes in every act, except for V, which was written by Beaumont, and there were three scenes (I,vi, II,ii, and III,iii) which they apparently wrote together; and while each was largely responsible for a separate strand of the plot, it was Beaumont's job to tie everything together. In *The False One*, by contrast, Fletcher writes Acts II, III, and IV, and Massinger I and V.[53] Gurr is no doubt right to call *Philaster* 'the end-product of an extraordinarily ingenious exploitation of the collaborative process',[54] but it may be wrong to assume that collaboration generally operated rigidly or mechanically.[55] Be this as it may, however, the image of the Beaumont and Fletcher collaboration promoted in the First Folio was a novel and potent one. Moseley says he had considered publishing Fletcher's plays on their own, but decided against it: 'Since never parted while they lived, I conceived it not equitable to separate their ashes.' This, of course, flies in the face of fact, as Moseley knew, but the myth outlived the reality. Aubrey's well-known account of Beaumont and Fletcher's shared life of romantic poverty, and of the 'wonderful consimility of phansey' between them, participates in it:

> They lived together on the Banke side, not far from the Play-house, both batchelors; lay together: had one Wench in the house between them, which they did so admire; the same cloathes and cloake, &c. betweene them.[56]

The First Folio, then, exists as a monument to a new image of authorship, but this is by no means its only significance for the politics of the plays' reception after the playwrights' death. The very timing of the production was also a part of its meaning. Moseley had been planning it for a while, perhaps since 1641 when the Lord Chamberlain forbade the printing of some sixty of the play-texts owned by the King's Men, including twenty-seven of the Beaumont and Fletcher canon, without their consent. R. K. Turner thinks this entry likely to have been made after Moseley had obtained from the King's Men the right to print these particular plays.[57] The Folio appeared in the middle of the Civil War, when the theatres had been closed for four years, and the fortunes of the Royalist cause were at a low ebb. Moseley was a publisher of good repute, consistently associated with publications of Royalist sympathies[58] and the Folio itself was clearly a propagandist work. Most of the commendatory poems were written by Royalist supporters who presented themselves as sensitive patrons of the arts in contrast with their philistine opponents and reiterated with mournful echo their common theme, that the plays stand as monuments to good times past. Thomas Peyton even questioned whether writing a eulogy of Fletcher might not in the present context be a subversive act, likely to 'raise a discontent / Between the Muses and the [Parliament]' (the rhyme-word to be supplied by the reader). James Howell, writing from prison, imagined the reactions of the dead poets, Shakespeare, Chapman and 'grim Ben' to the current crisis, and concluded that only Fletcher could have done it justice:

> Yet none like high-wing'd FLETCHER had bin found
> This Eagles tragick-destiny to sound;
> Rare FLETCHER'S quill had soar'd up to the sky,
> And drawn down Gods to see the tragedy.
> (Glover and Waller, I, xxvi)

Analogies between the decline of poetry, the closure of the theatres, and the fall of the King abound; Beaumont and Fletcher are implicitly assimilated to the royalist cause. In a confident hyperbole Roger L'Estrange identifies the curative power of Fletcher's work with the life-giving rays of the majestic sun, and the suppression of the stage is equated with that of the monarchy in this 'the worst scene of time' (Habington). It is worth noting how these verses implicitly accord the Beaumont and Fletcher plays the status of poetry, of texts that will reward reading; they are not ephemeral productions created to satisfy commercial considerations but a 'library of man' (Grandison). Thomas Stanley in his tribute points out the irony that the prohibition of plays on stage has actually ensured their continued existence in a more permanent form:

> They that silenc'd Wit
> Are now Authours to Eternize it;
> Thus Poets are in spight of Fate reviv'd,
> A Playes by Intermission longer liv'd.
> (Glover and Waller, I, xxvii)

In his prefatory letter to the readers Moseley asserts his desire to present them with a complete and authentic corpus of work: 'And as here's nothing but what is genuine and Theirs, so you will find here are no *Omissions*; you have not onely All I could get, but All that you must ever expect.' These statements beg many questions, some of which surface openly later in the preface, but they reinforce the sense, created by so many aspects of the Folio, that this production represents a milestone in the history of drama as a cultural formulation.

The Folio, brought out at a very specific historical moment, establishes Beaumont and Fletcher as royalist icons. But any account of the history of their reputation and reception requires the consideration of how far this image reflects a political reality that was true throughout the seventeenth century, and how far its meaning is likely to be transformed in circumstances other than those of the 1640s. This is particularly important since so much significance has been attached subsequently to Beaumont and Fletcher's royalist connections. It has to be remembered that a text's significance is not constant, but rather a matter of continuous negotiation with its audience, and this is especially the case for plays. It is clear that at certain moments in the seventeenth century the plays were closely identified with royalist values; but it is not clear that the point of first production was one of these. In the case of *The Faithful Shepherdess*, for example, the royalist possibilities of the play were more evident in the 1630s than they had been in 1608–9. The uses to which the writers and their texts were put after their deaths are obviously outside their control.

The dramatists became popular, even in some views legendary, in their own, or, at least Fletcher's, lifetime; their work was performed at court from 1611 onwards. They may have been collaborating together as early as 1605, on *Love's Cure*,[59] even if *Cupid's Revenge* (1607–08) represents a truer start to their literary partnership.[60] Fletcher's work was well thought of by other writers, including Jonson, before *The Faithful Shepherdess* was published (?1609), and Webster in 1612 named them with Jonson,

Chapman, Shakespeare, Dekker, and Heywood, all older writers, as men whose work he admired.[61] The associations with the Court are undoubtedly very strong in the 1620s and 1630s; Wallis notes that of 114 plays performed at court between 1615 and 1642, forty-six were by Beaumont and Fletcher, as compared with sixteen by Shakespeare.[62] In the season of 1621–22, six of their plays were performed, including an old favourite, *The Coxcomb*, as well as the latest work, *The Wild-Goose Chase*. In 1623, *The Maid in the Mill*, then a new play, unusually had three court performances within three months. In 1624, *Rule a Wife and Have a Wife*, also new, had a performance in November 'for the ladys', and another six weeks later, 'upon S^t. Steevens night, the prince only being there'.[63] In the season of 1630–31, ten of the twenty-one plays performed at court, an unusually large number, were of their work.[64] Throughout the 1630s there were court performances, usually of two or more of the plays every year, and a particularly notable revival of the hitherto rejected play, *The Faithful Shepherdess*, in the 1633–34 season. There is no record of any performance of this play since its notorious failure in 1608–9, but on this occasion it was put on under the auspices of Queen Henrietta Maria, who provided costumes from the pastoral play, *The Shepherd's Paradise*, by Walter Montague, which she and her ladies performed at court the previous year, to the displeasure of William Prynne. Davenant wrote a new prologue for *The Faithful Shepherdess*, flattering the royal couple and complimenting the Queen almost as if she were the play's presenter. There were settings by Inigo Jones. The next winter season saw a large-scale Beaumont and Fletcher revival with performances of *Beggars' Bush*, *The Coxcomb*, *The Loyal Subject*, *Love's Pilgrimage*, *The Spanish Curate*, *A King and No King*, *The Bloody Brother*, and *A Wife for a Month*. But a poignant note is struck by the entry in the court records for the monarchy's last season:

> On Twelfe Night, 1641, the prince had a play called The Scornful Lady at the Cockpitt, but the King and Queene were not there; and it was the only play acted at court in the whole Christmas.[65]

These performances were, of course, given by the King's Men, with whom the work of the two playwrights had been associated since 1609–10; *Philaster* was probably their first play for this company, and though a few subsequent pieces may have been written for the Boys' companies,[66] Fletcher's attachment to the King's Men became exclusive at least after the deaths of Beaumont and Shakespeare in 1616, and perhaps from 1613 when Beaumont probably retired from the stage. One outcome of this long and important association was the First Folio itself, dedicated as it was to the fourth Earl of Pembroke by the ten surviving patented members of the King's Men. The question arises as to whether another outcome of this connection, and of the close association with the Court which it represents, was a political prescriptiveness in the plays themselves. Could a King's Man ever be less than a fervent royalist?

Royal preference alone would not have accounted for the plays' high reputation and they were also popular and frequently performed in the commercial theatre, as the title-pages testify. Even the King's Men were heavily dependent on their income from commercial performances and plays that would fill the Globe and the Blackfriars.[67] Though they were put on at the Globe as well as at the Blackfriars there seems no reason to question the generally accepted view that they appealed to a social and perhaps an educational elite, but this fact need not have specific implications for their politics.[68] Shirley's well-known eulogy, in his Folio preface, of 'the authentic wit that made Blackfriars an academy' locates the plays' appeal within a narrow social spectrum, in its references to 'the hopeful young heir' and 'the young spirits of the time, whose birth and quality made them impatient of the sourer ways of education', but in this it is not unlike Sidney's *Apologie for Poesie*, or, of course, the humanist educative texts in which tradition the *Apologie* stands. It is, however, very unlike an analogous preface, that of Heminges and Condell to the Shakespeare First Folio; the King's Men address this volume simply 'to the great variety of readers, from the most able to him that can but spell'. This is not to say that the politics of such an audience would necessarily have been homogeneous or class-determined; Martin Butler's work on the Caroline theatre convincingly explodes what he calls 'the myth of the Cavalier audience',[69] and illustrates the intense participation of a drama, previously written off as conformist and compromised, in the complex politics of its age.

That the Beaumont and Fletcher plays engaged with controversial and political issues has often been proposed, even by those who do not, like Coleridge, regard them as uncritically reflective of absolutist orthodoxies. Early critics like Thorndike, Gayley, Upton, and Baldwin Maxwell[70] all drew attention to topical references in the plays which were critical of James I, his court, and his politics. Tucker Brooke's comment about the 'abnormally low quality' of kings and rulers has been followed up in numerous books and articles, particularly recently.[71] Leech remarked on the 'element of open debate' in many of the plays which explore kingship and authority. In the last few years, in a study of Fletcher's tyrant plays, R. Y. Turner has made a case for 'his full imaginative engagement with the threats of unopposable power',[72] and Finkelpearl has devoted a book to the fullest exploration yet of the plays as politically involved. In one instance, the play *Sir John van Olden Barnavelt*, Fletcher and Massinger specifically set out to dramatise an issue of immediate controversial interest: the execution of the Arminian Barnavelt on a charge of state treason took place in Holland only three months before their play was staged, probably at the Globe, in the teeth of objections from the Bishop of London. It is likely that Fletcher and Massinger (with

Field) had recently written another play on a similar subject, *The Jeweller of Amsterdam*, but tantalisingly nothing survives of this other than an entry in the Stationers' Register much later.[73] No other play stages a topical situation in this way, yet several have been considered to offer political comment at various levels of directness on topical issues. For example, Upton's claim, elaborating on Gayley's observations of more than sixty years ago, that *The Woman Hater*, now regarded as one of the earliest collaborations, is not an unsuccessful *juvenilium* in the Jonsonian 'humour' school but a Marstonian satire on 'the crimes and follies of the court of James I',[74] is endorsed by Finkelpearl; he reads it as a risky and sophisticated comment on court dissoluteness with 'the ring of specific, personal satire'.[75] The play's shifty-toned prologue, in which the authors disclaim 'the ordinarie and over-worne trade of jeasting at Lordes and Courtiers, and Citizens', may well deserve to be read as a signal of secret meanings, in the light of the hermeneutics system Annabel Patterson has taught us to identify in texts of this period.[76] Recent work on *The Faithful Shepherdess* in the light of the politicisation of seventeenth-century pastoral has offered new readings of that play which challenge the formerly accepted view of pastoral as a genre outside the reach of politics.[77] *The Loyal Subject* has long been a favourite with searchers after topical material. Appleton asserts that 'without question ... [it] contains some explicit political comment', and reference to the recently executed Ralegh seems highly possible.[78] The most recent editor of *The Noble Gentleman*, Beaurline, traces a network of significant references to topical and controversial subjects in the play, especially the Arabella Stuart affair, and the rapid rise in social status of the favourite, George Villiers, by 1623 Duke of Buckingham. Such instances could be multiplied.[79]

Philaster and *The Maid's Tragedy* may both have been the objects of censorship. *Philaster* exists in two early quartos (1620, 1622) with certain striking differences; J. E. Savage some years ago argued that the first (and inferior) quarto was an authorised version of the (authentic) second quarto constructed to satisfy a censor's demands, but the play's two most recent editors, Turner (1966) and Gurr (1969), do not accept this as an explanation of the variants.[80] None the less Gurr found reason to state firmly, if debatably, that '*Philaster.* like no other play in which Fletcher was concerned, but quite like *The Knight of the Burning Pestle* and *The Woman Hater*, involved itself with contemporary issues.'[81] Articles by Adkins (1946) and Davison (1963) explore the play's treatment of the relationship between rulers and subjects, and Gurr sees a close connection between Dion's challenge to the King's hyperbolic assertion of absolute authority in IV,iv and a specific clash between Sir Edward Coke and James I in Parliament in 1608.[82] *The Maid's Tragedy* also exists in two early substantive quarto texts with numerous variants; none of the play's recent editors or textual critics has considered the possibility of censorship to account for some of them, although Clare, locating the play in the context of the King's known fear of tyrannicide and the censored play, *The Second Maiden's Tragedy*, makes a convincing case for some judicious pruning of the first quarto (*c.* 1610) by George Buc, Master of the Revels.[83] Bowers, some years back, remarked that the play deals with 'an extremely ticklish subject', though he thought this subject, royal absolutism, handled 'so as to avoid giving offence'.[84] Presumably, since *The Maid's Tragedy* was performed more than once at court, this must have been the case for James I, yet Restoration readers of the play clearly found it insufficiently orthodox,[85] and recent studies have uncovered many signs of sceptical demystification in the play's representation of the institution of monarchy,[86] such that Finkelpearl, in his summary of them, states that 'it remains one of the greatest mysteries in Jacobean censorship that much more severe action was not taken against *The Maid's Tragedy*'.[87] *A King and No King*, sometimes grouped with *Philaster* and *The Maid's Tragedy* as part of a kind of trilogy,[88] has also proved open to readings in terms of a critique of royal absolutism.[89]

Even in one of the Folio tributes Fletcher's representation of royal authority had been regarded as didactic rather than flattering. William Habington praised him for his moral art in the private but more importantly in the public sphere:

> Thou didst frame governments, give Kings their part,
> Teach them how neere to God, while just they be;
> But how dissolv'd, stretcht forth to Tyrannie.
> How Kingdomes, in their channell, safely run,
> But rudely overflowing are undone.
> (Glover and Waller, I, xxvi)

That Habington's interpretation is worth taking seriously is suggested by the fact that a few years before the publication of the Folio, in 1640, he had himself written a tragicomedy, *The Queen of Aragon*, twice performed at court, in which challenging political issues concerning the basis of the ruler's power are directly faced. The performances were organised by no less a figure than the Earl of Pembroke, Habington's uncle, and Butler describes the main argument of the play as 'radically new, and potentially revolutionary'[90] in the way it distinguishes between rule based on the consent of the people and on the inherent authority of a legitimate monarch. Although there is, of course, no implication of any political heterodoxy in Habington's lines, his assessment of Fletcher may be read as something more than flattery.

The meaning of the surreptitious and interrupted performances of Beaumont and Fletcher plays during the Civil War may be debated: two tragedies, *A King and No King* and *The Bloody Brother*, were unsuccessfully attempted (in 1647 and 1648), and a comedy, *Wit Without Money* (in 1654).[91] Obviously the plays were chosen because they were popular, and presumably symbolised pre-war values; though the tragedies in our own century can be made to yield anti-absolutist meanings, these would not then have been appropriate. But, as has been shown, a variety of Restoration readers did not regard the Beaumont and Fletcher plays as totally orthodox in their representations of the monarchy, and adaptors often found it necessary to simplify and refocus ethical dilemmas involving the behaviour of kings in order to suppress disquieting ambiguities. The Royalist appropriation of the plays in the 1630s and 1640s was not terminal.

(iv)

This study of sexual themes in the plays of Beaumont and Fletcher has been undertaken according to certain premises both about the nature of meaning in drama and the ways in which it is profitable to discuss such themes in a dramatic text. By acknowledging what has been called 'the artificial, constructed (and ideological) nature of dramatic representation',[92] I want to recognise meaning as produced rather than inherent, and, in the theatre especially, the outcome of interactive processes, which operate within specific social and cultural contexts. The materiality of the theatre as a social institution must be taken into account, despite the difficulties and unanswerable questions that will arise. The problem is not so much the ongoing disagreement about the social constitution of theatre audiences in the seventeenth century as the way in which the Beaumont and Fletcher plays shaped and responded to audience expectations. After early attempts which were not at the time successful they very rapidly became popular and influential; increasingly the playwrights catered for audiences familiar with their dramaturgy, and were thus able to capitalise on this familiarity by playing with expectation in a variety of ways. The close relations between playwright and audience were enhanced by another factor: the long, and for many years exclusive, association between the plays and the company who owned and performed them, the King's Men. In detail what this signified for the meanings of the plays as created in performance is irrecoverable, but it constitutes a gap in our understanding of the plays' reception which must be registered. In his account of the Amintor/Melanthius scene in *The Maid's Tragedy* Rymer, who unlike most modern critics was familiar with the play on stage, gives his readers a timely injunction: 'We may remember (how-ever we find this Scene of *Melanthius* and *Amintor* written in the Book) that at the Theater we have a good Scene Acted.'[93]

Dramatic representation is socially conditioned; it serves interests and can be instrumental in reinforcing ideologies. Representations of sexuality and gender relationships in drama of this period particularly are now scrutinised for their ideological content; many feminist critics are concerned to reveal how the drama, in relation to which women had anyway extremely marginal roles as producers and consumers, operated sometimes to challenge but often to endorse a patriarchal construction of sexuality. My account of how the Beaumont and Fletcher plays engage with themes of sex and gender is informed by a range of current debates in these areas. I hope to demonstrate an awareness of the differences between late twentieth-century constructions of sexuality and those of the early modern period, and I am concerned with meanings that would, as far as it is possible to say, have been culturally accessible to the plays' original audiences, as well as with those that might not have been.

Recent studies of Shakespeare and Renaissance drama have been almost hyper-aware of their own theoretical positions and critical procedures, particularly where the dramatic representation of sexuality has been concerned, in part because many of them are shaped by some kind of political agenda, such as that acknowledged by Valerie Traub at the end of an article protesting against 'the erasure of erotic difference' in recent work on homoeroticism in Shakespeare; she defines the 'radical project' of which she sees her own work forming part in the following terms:

> Persons of all erotic persuasions – and I stress this is not solely the task of erotic minorities – can renegotiate the terms by which desire is understood, setting into critical motion the various contingencies that structure arousal and foster erotic satisfaction.[94]

While I can sympathise with such a project my own aims are differently directed and perhaps more circumscribed. In a study of the representation of sexuality in whatever medium the words 'erotic' and 'desire' are unavoidable; but since I regard it as questionable whether the analysis of eroticism can be satisfactorily undertaken without recourse to psychoanalytic theory[95] I want to focus my attention rather on the dramaturgy by means of which sexual themes in the Beaumont and Fletcher plays are articulated than on the implications for the meanings of sexuality to be derived from these themes as such. It hardly needs saying that such a distinction will not always be able to be rigidly observed.

I want also to argue that these plays, scrutinised in the light of new work on sexuality in the Renaissance theatre, retain more of what Stephen Greenblatt calls the 'social energy'[96] originally encoded in them than their critical neglect would suggest. Perhaps some will feel that his view of the aesthetic forms in which this energy manifests itself, 'the capacity of certain verbal, aural, and visual traces to produce, shape, and organise collective physical and mental experiences ... associated with repeatable forms of pleasure and interest' and his stress on the capacity for some of these forms to 'survive at least some of the constant changes in social circumstance and cultural value that make ordinary utterances evanescent' runs disturbingly counter to the accepted postmodern notion of all reality as socially constructed and historically contingent. It may even seem that the history of the decline in the reputation of the Beaumont and Fletcher plays since the seventeenth century is testimony to a change in cultural value so great as to suggest that any social energy in the circulation of which the plays were originally involved can no longer be traced. I hope to demonstrate that this is by no means the case; and my demonstration is based on a belief that, although, for example, systems of gender-difference and concepts of the feminine and the masculine are socially constructed, it is not impossible to recover either the operations of these systems and concepts from the textual traces of their period or something of the 'illusion of life'[97] created by their articulation in the Beaumont and Fletcher plays.

That gender questions in the plays may repay study is further indicated by evidence that women were perceived as a significant component of the Beaumont and Fletcher audience, though some of it must be treated with caution.[98] Moseley's preface in the Folio, for example, singles out the requirements of a female readership, when he justifies his exclusion of texts already in print in rather disingenuous terms:

> It would have rendered the Book so voluminous, that *Ladies* and *Gentlewomen* would have found it scarce manageable, who in Workes of this nature must first be remembered.

Various of the Folio tributes refer to the plays' particular appeal for women; but those which stress the exemplary quality of the plays' sexual morality, like Henry Harington's lines which credit Fletcher with an ability to reform prostitutes coming to the theatre to meet clients, are clearly written with an eye to defending the stage against Puritan objections. On the other hand the claims made, for example, by Lovelace, that women might respond in gender-specific ways to characters such as Bellario, Aspatia, or the Scornful Lady, or might be particularly susceptible to tragicomic pathos, seem worth entertaining. Prologues and epilogues, usually written for revivals of the plays after the playwrights' deaths, sometimes address women's interests, like the prologue to *The Woman's Prize*, perhaps composed for the court performance of 1633:

> Ladies to you, in whose defence and right,
>   *Fletchers* brave Muse prepar'd her self to fight
> A battaile without blood, 'twas well fought too,
>   (The victory's yours, though got with much ado,)
> We do present this Comedy . . .
>
>   (*Works*, IV, 15)

Partnership: reputation and collaboration

A prologue to *The Woman Hater* written by Davenant, probably in or before 1638 but published in 1648, also addressed to women, apologises for the sexist content of the play which is described as atypical of its author, here assumed to be Fletcher (although Beaumont was responsible for most of the play):[99]

> His Muse beleev'd not, what she then did write;
> Her Wings were wont to make a nobler flight;
> Sor'd high, and to the Stars, your Sex did raise;
> For which, full Twenty yeares, he wore the Bayes.
> 'Twas he redem'd *Evandra* from her scorne,
> And taught the sad *Aspacia* how to mourne;
> Gave *Arethusa's* love a glad reliefe,
> And mad *Panthea* elegant in griefe.
>   (*Works*, I, 236)

Fletcher's image as the woman's champion, which Coleridge was at pains to counteract,[100] has not, of course, been reflected in modern criticism, at least until recently.[101] Rather, there has been a long tradition of disquiet with the plays' treatment of women and sexuality, from Flecknoe and Rymer onwards. Flecknoe's comment about their indecorum ('seldom representing ... an honourable woman without somewhat of *Dol Common* in her'[102]) expresses a sentiment to which many a bosom has returned an echo. While acknowledging the behaviour of many female characters as unconventional, critics have rarely attempted to explore the sexual dynamics of the plays within which it is articulated. Their own patriarchalist assumptions tend to occlude wider perspectives. While my account of the plays will not offer a sustained search for readings that resist patriarchal ideology, it is shaped by a sense of how such ideology has functioned to close off possibilities. Equally, the disclosure of the structures and operations of patriarchal power within the text,[103] though not my principal objective, cannot be ignored. However it is important to acknowledge that plays in the theatre can give pleasure without necessarily commanding the audience's full ideological assent, and at the same to recognise that the conditions of theatrical regulation under which Beaumont and Fletcher operated created many challenges for playwrights responsive, as they were, to the social energies of their time, which often called upon resources of delicacy and tact and strategies of indirection to negotiate.

Chapter 1

The Price of Virtue: Chastity Plays

Central to many representations of sexuality in the drama of Beaumont and Fletcher's period is the notion of female chastity, often handled as the site of a struggle for possession between men, a perishable commodity whose market value can all too easily be ruined. The social and moral meanings attached to chastity were in a state of flux at this time; the values accorded to asceticism in the Middle Ages, and to celibate life in Catholic culture were no longer accepted in Protestant England where the strong reaction in Elizabeth's reign against the monastic ideal was accompanied by a rise in prestige of the institution of marriage.[1] None the less, female chastity as constructed in discourses of love in the Neo-Platonic and Petrarchan traditions retained a strong influence in imaginative literature, where a male lover might achieve spiritual connection with divinity by means of his service to the idealised beauty of a chaste woman. Such a notion of chastity implicitly denies female sexuality and the materiality of the female body; the beloved's beauty is spiritual, an outward reflection of inner perfection, 'That inward sun in thine eyes shineth so', as Sidney puts it.[2] The tensions created for the lover who cannot separate spiritual from physical desire are articulated in some sonnet sequences, especially, of course, *Astrophel and Stella*; elsewhere, the sonnet discloses masculine anxiety that the chaste beloved may relinquish her role as passive object of desire and seek active expression of her own power.[3] The awareness that chastity could constitute a source of power potentially threatening to men was always inscribed in the concept; the popularity of the virgin-martyr figure reflects one way of handling this awareness.

In R.B.'s *Apius and Virginia*, (1567), for example, Virginia begs her father to kill her rather than let her become mistress to the corrupt judge, Apius. The power of her virginal appeal is acknowledged by Apius, who is totally overcome by his desire for her: 'I rule no more, but ruled I am, I do not judge but am judged/By beauty of Virginia';[4] and her death empowers her father to proceed to the overthrow of Apius.

But in Elizabethan England the developing cult of the Virgin Queen, centred on her 'combination of femaleness and physical autonomy'[5] foregrounded the issue of chastity and power in a new way. Berry notices how, in the entertainments presented to the Queen by those courtiers who especially promoted her cult, the Earl of Leicester, Sir Henry Lee, and Sidney, the 'combination of erotic innuendo' with 'compliments to the Queen's decision not to marry' creates a paradox 'whereby Elizabeth's chastity was often represented in implicitly sexual terms, as a state of physical autonomy rather than physical virginity'.[6] Her celibate state is identified, not with asceticism and abnegation, but with self-sufficiency and power over her own body, a body whose privacy she refused to subordinate, even to the need of the state for a successor. In the Ditchley portrait, commissioned by Lee to commemorate her visit to his house in 1592, she is depicted standing on a map of England; Stallybrass reads in this an allusion to the *hortus conclusus*, the walled garden, the territory totally sealed off from invasion, which functions to symbolise the Queen's virginity just as, reciprocally, her virginity symbolises her country.[7] Accordingly, female chastity, while not sacrificing its spiritual meanings, accrues others from the realms of the social and political. Lyly in *Euphues* acknowledges how Elizabeth's success as a ruler derives from the deployment of her virginity both to take on but also to transform aspects of patriarchal power:

> What greater mervaile hath happened since the beginning of the world, then for a young and tender maiden, to govern strong and valiaunt menne, then for a virgin to make the whole worlde, if not to stand in awe of hir, yet to honour hir, yea and to live in spight of all those that spight hir, with hir sword in the sheth, with hir armour in the Tower, with hir souldiers in their gownes ...[8]

This virgin, though potentially capable of a warrior's power, prefers to conceal it when asserting her authority. But the virgin-warrior, a common type in literature of the period, is often an equivocal figure, androgynously chaste like Belphoebe in *The Faerie Queene* or sexually ambivalent like Moll Cutpurse in *The Roaring Girl*. Depictions of the armed virgin can often disclose the anxiety this paradoxical image arouses.[9]

The image of the autonomous virgin is countered by that of the woman whose chastity belongs not to herself but to her (male) kinsfolk. In literature of this period, the meaning of female chastity is regularly defined through the notion of woman as a property category.[10] A woman's chastity may be in the gift of her father or some other male relative to bestow on a suitor who can make a good return for it; when the woman chooses to take charge of her own body, as does Annabella in *'Tis Pity She's a Whore* or the Duchess in *The Duchess of Malfi*, she may be usurping a masculine prerogative. Fathers guard their daughters, brothers their sisters, and husbands their wives from the predatory sexual attentions of rival males who would make illicit use of them without paying the proper price. 'Zounds, sir, you are robb'd ... you have lost half your soul', Iago tells Brabantio (*Othello* I, i, 86–7), when announcing Desdemona's secret marriage. Othello thinks in similar terms when he wishes to deny the possibility of Desdemona's infidelity: 'He that is robb'd, not wanting what is stol'n / Let him not know it, and he's not robb'd at all.' (III, iii, 348–9). Collatine in *The Rape of Lucrece* is rhetorically accused of responsibility for the rape of his famously chaste wife: he is 'the publisher / Of that rich jewel he should keep unknown / From thievish ears, because it is his own', and Tarquin is motivated initially by a spirit of competition, 'envy of so rich a thing / Braving compare', to obtain what belongs to a rival. In *The Revenger's Tragedy* Castiza's chastity, ardently desired by Lussurioso, is the symbol of her family's honour, a 'crystal tower' (IV, iii, 2) which must not be scaled and entered, 'the very emblem of the inviolable boundaries of the family'.[11]

No doubt this view of chastity, and the double standard of sexual morality which is a concomitant of it, is closely related to the social and economic need to guarantee the legitimacy of heirs and preserve the bloodline within a family;[12] this need rationalises patriarchal rights over the bodies of the female family members, and also finds its justification in the view of the female body as, in Bakhtin's term, 'grotesque'. For the grotesque body 'the stress is laid on those parts of the body that are open to the outside world ... the emphasis is on the apertures and the convexities.'[13] Woman's body, the weaker vessel, might then be seen as notoriously leaky, dangerously prone, through its orifices, both to let out what should be kept in and to admit of foreign invasion;[14] hence, the imperatives for premarital chastity of women, and for wifely monogamy. A wife's fidelity guaranteed not only the legitimacy of offspring but also her husband's virility; if he was incapable of satisfying her, the propensity of her 'unstanched'[15] body for sexual pleasure would impel her to look elsewhere. According to Petruchio in *The Woman's Prize*, if the husband does not employ more continual labour then a Gally [slave] 'on appeasing his wife's desires she will 'spring more leakes / Then all the fame of his posterity / Can ever stop againe' (III, v, 120–1). The identification of the chaste female body as a watertight vessel is implied in the use of the sieve motif in portraits of Queen Elizabeth; this use derives from the legend of the vestal virgin Tuccia, whose ability to carry water in a sieve over a distance proved her virginity.[16] In many plays, of which *'Tis Pity She's a Whore* is a notable example, the female body is an important locus of meaning, and may be represented, in Susan Wiseman's words, 'as an ethical, financial, spiritual, amatory, and psychological territory'.[17] Such centralising of female chastity is not peculiar to tragedy, and similar claims could be made, for example, for *A Chaste Maid in Cheapside*, *The Roaring Girl*, *The Dutch Courtesan*, as well as for a large number of plays in the Beaumont and Fletcher canon.

In fact, explorations of chastity appear in plays of all genres, from all periods of the canon, and although it has sometimes been seen as a preoccupation of Fletcher's,[18] it features in a form that was to become characteristic in the one play regarded as solely Beaumont's, *The Knight of the Burning Pestle*,[19] and is central to *Philaster*, in which Beaumont had a large hand. Situations of trial or testing are regularly devised whereby a woman's chastity may in some sense be proven, vindicated, or demonstrated, and the dramatic modes evolved to display an interior essence exemplify that peculiar theatricality for which these plays were in their century so admired and have subsequently been so denigrated. Some of these situations, which have wider ramifications for the politics of sexuality, will be discussed in other chapters;[20] here I focus on plays involving trials and ordeals of continence which function primarily to prove a woman's chastity and assert its value. This assertion is sometimes reinforced by a secondary test of male sexual desire, which exonerates it from the charge of being aroused by wantonness. In these plays, the meanings of chastity are defined primarily in ethical and spiritual terms; the social and economic discourses in which the meanings of chastity also circulate are largely excluded.

The focus on chastity in the Beaumont and Fletcher plays illuminates the extent to which their treatment of sexuality more broadly was shaped by an awareness of the contradictions in traditional accounts of womanhood. Many plays display the clash between, on the one hand, the medieval celebration of virginity and the neo-Platonic or Petrarchan idealisation of woman's chaste beauty as a channel for man's spiritual connection with divinity, and on the other, misogynistic premises traceable to the classics and endorsed by St Paul and the early Church fathers, according to which women were inherently weak and more prone to sin than men, their beauty culpably responsible for arousing male desire. The meanings of chastity for the English nation in the sixteenth century had been considerably extended and enriched through the cult of Elizabeth as Virgin Queen, and her memory during the reign of her successor often invoked nostalgia for a lost golden age of virtue, temperance, and chivalric idealism.[21] The model which Elizabeth supplied for the concept of chastity as strength and self-sufficiency constitutes the conceptual framework for the major chastity play in the canon, Fletcher's *The Faithful Shepherdess*.

The Faithful Shepherdess is by no means the first of the plays to handle this subject. Though the date of composition is not certain, it is in all probability around 1608–9 and was preceded by *The Woman Hater*, *The Knight of the Burning Pestle*, and possibly also *Love's Cure* and *Cupid's Revenge*.[22] But it serves to begin with because it provides a schematic and formal display of what were to emerge as seminal chastity motifs, or 'theatregrams', as Louise George Clubb calls them,[23] 'compositional structures that are to a theatrical text roughly what *narremes* are to a narrative'. The play was an ambitious experiment that failed at the time, as the prefatory matter to the first quarto edition, undated but probably published in 1609,[24] makes clear. Fletcher's superciliously phrased preface 'To the reader' assumes that the play was too clever for its audience, and in this he seems to have been correct; for although it was condemned by 'a rout of nifles', as Chapman called them,[25] who had mistaken notions of what pastoral tragicomedy should be, *The Faithful Shepherdess* came into its own some twenty years later, when it was revived at court and then at the Blackfriars Theatre in 1634, the same year that a third quarto was published, and Milton's masque, *Comus*, which draws on it,[26] was performed. Four years later it was translated into Latin by Sir Richard Fanshawe.[27]

The play is significantly influenced by Spenser in its pastoralism and its handling of sexuality, but owes the formality of its organisation and action to Guarini's *Il Pastor Fido* which Fletcher imitates closely;[28] but he borrows the intricately interwoven series of relationships between Arcadian shepherds and shepherdesses in order to shift the conceptual emphasis. Guarini's complex plot is entirely shaped by the generic requirement to achieve a happy ending from a potentially tragic situation, exactly reversing *Oedipus Rex* so that the Faithful Shepherd's discovery of his true parentage saves his life, redeems his country from a curse, and fulfils the oracle by allowing him to marry a woman he had previously thought destined for someone else. The apparently misplaced desires of the characters are redirected by a series of marvellous reversals and good is born of evil. The moral design of Fletcher's play operates to exemplify not the workings of divine providence but the power of chastity, and the foregrounding of this quality sets the play apart from its source.

The characters are arranged in a hierarchy, from the most to the least chaste. At the top of the scale is Clorin, the shepherdess of the title; she is loved hopelessly by Thenot but has pledged herself to lifelong celibacy in memory of a dead lover; her virginity empowers her, not in a quasi-androgynous way, like Belphoebe's, but mystically; this is represented by magical skills and an affinity with natural forces, embodied in a satyr, the god of the river, and a priest of Pan. The absent Pan is a moral and benevolent deity, father of the flocks and preserver of the chastity of his pastoral worshippers. Clorin's authoritative virginity enables her to strengthen and cure the weaker characters debilitated by lust. At the next level is Amoret, who is loved chastely by Perigot; their temperance enables them to postpone the sexual fulfilment at which they aim until after a formal ceremony. But Perigot is also loved by the sensuous Amarillis who plots to get him for herself. The lowest of the four women is the opportunist Cloe, who lives for pleasure and attempts to give herself to any of the shepherds who are available. At the base of the hierarchy is Clorin's antithesis, lust polarised against virginity, the Sullen Shepherd, a solitary figure brutalised by insatiable desire which is expressed not in Comus-like revelry but in isolating and self-destructive promiscuity. He is

> One that doth wear himself away in loneliness,
> And never joys, unless it be in breaking
> The holy plighted troths of mutual souls;
> One that lusts after every several beauty
> But never yet was known to love or like.
> (I, ii, 197–201)

From the interrelations of these characters emerge those motifs that characterise the handling of sexual themes in so many of the Beaumont and Fletcher plays: the chaste woman doubted, belied, or slandered by a man; the chaste woman who, unrecognised by the man she loves is wounded by him; the chaste woman who enacts for a man the role of wanton as a kind of aversion therapy; the polarising of women who can and cannot control desire. The triangular situation between Amoret, Perigot and Amarillis exploits three of these motifs, the relationship of Clorin and Thenot the fourth. The motifs can be read as Spenserian moral allegory, as ways of distinguishing love and lust, but they also function to define aspects of male sexuality and its relation to female desire.

With the assistance of the Sullen Shepherd, Amarillis transforms herself into the shape of Amoret to win Perigot's love, literalising the male construction of female sexuality as desirable when passive and threatening when active. Amarillis is not promiscuous: 'To thee / I am only fixt and set', she tells Perigot; all she wants is to enact her desire. In the play's gradations of temperance she is contrasted with Cloe whose desire is indiscriminate:

> ... From one cause of fear I am most free,
> It is impossible to ravish mee
> I am so willing.
> (III, i, 211–13)

Yet Amarillis's desire for Perigot is also culpable; in the play's terms her attempt to persuade him to make love to her by urging that desire is natural to all women is libertinism which arouses him to violence.

Amoret, like her prototype in Books III and IV of *The Faerie Queene*, is the virgin without desire, and attractive to Perigot because she does not attempt to requite his desire for her. But when Amarillis, her *alter ego*, takes over and actively offers herself to Perigot he is so horrified that he first threatens to kill himself and then to kill her. Amarillis runs off, and when Perigot comes upon the real Amoret he wounds her, leaves her for dead in the forest, and then unable to tolerate actively expressed female desire, prepares to kill himself. At this moment Amarillis reappears, repentant, confesses to her shape-shifting, and offers to demonstrate it by temporarily reverting to the form of Amoret to order. This enables a re-enactment of the wounding scene, when Perigot sees the real Amoret, forlorn and rejected, believes her to be the role-playing Amarillis, and repeats his expression of anger. This representation of male fears of female sexuality is never translated into terms of Perigot's consciousness; but when he finds himself unable to wash away Amoret's blood he realises this means she is innocent. In Clorin's sacred bower, where she has been taken for healing, he is reconciled to her. From their last exchanges it is evident that Perigot's violence is the fault of Amarillis alone:

> Perigot. My deare deare *Amoret*, how happy are
> Those blessed paires, in whom a little jarr
> Hath bred an everlasting love, to strong
> For time or steele, or envy to do wrong!
> How do you feele your hurts? alasse poore heart
> How much I was abusd, give me the smart
> For it is justly mine.
> Amoret.   I doe beleeve.
> (v, v, 109–15)

Masculine insecurity about female chastity is thus naturalised; so too are the extreme means required to allay it.[29] Perigot's violence is conditioned by the explicit and even masculine idiom of seduction used by the disguised Amarillis ('Still thinkst thou such a thinge as Chastitie, / Is amongst women? Perigot thers none'), which contrasts with his own Petrarchan idiom of chaste flames and lovers' service which is his own style. It may be, as Kathleen McLuskie suggests,[30] that this exchange of sexual styles, wittily reversing theatrical conventions of wooing, serves to neutralise the scene's potential for engaging the audience's emotions; such theatrical strategies were to become characteristic of Beaumont and Fletcher's dramaturgy, but perhaps the audience had not yet learnt how to read them.

But the play's perspectives on sexuality shift constantly and in a scene between Clorin and Thenot, the shepherd who loves her, Fletcher wittily deconstructs the idea that a man has a right to expect a woman to be chaste. Clorin is pledged to virginity and must cure Thenot of his love. By what appears to be a paradox, her method of achieving this is to pretend to offer herself to him. Thenot like Perigot, and a dozen other Beaumont and Fletcher male characters similarly disconcerted by displays of female sexual desire, is repelled and outraged; he begs her to return to her familiar and unthreatening role of the obdurately constant woman, and when she resists repudiates her and all her sex in a direct equation of female sexuality with sin:

> Thou art of women's race, and full of guilt.
> Farewell all hope of that sex.
> (IV, v, 92–5)

Clorin remains briefly onstage alone at the end of the scene to ensure that the audience will read her behaviour correctly:

> Blest be yee powers that gave such quick redresse,
> And for my labours sent such good successe.
> I rather chuse, though I a woman bee,
> He should speake ill of all than dye for me.
>
> (IV, v, 92–5)

Her awareness that her play-acting of sexual eagerness will instantly cure Thenot's desire for her problematises the assumptions underlying Amoret's ready forgiveness of Perigot's repeated violence towards her; because Clorin is all-powerful and all-knowing, and the audience is in complicity with her motivation, Thenot's response is rendered comic, almost an automatic reflex which calls into question the premise on which it is based. Like Perigot, he is never disabused; Clorin's chaste fidelity to her dead lover thus acquires an extra dimension of authority. Perigot's moral revulsion at what he takes to be Amoret's unvirtuous behaviour is to an extent subverted by the audience's privileged knowledge of the true situation, but the violence, and also the repeating of the wounding, precludes an ironic reading. In fact, Perigot's bewilderment loads the second wounding with a heavier emotional freight than the first; he convinces himself that he is killing the false Amarillis to vindicate the true Amoret:

> Was any man soe loath to trust
> His eyes as I, or was ther ever yet,
> Any so like, as this to Amoret,
> For whose deare sake, I promise if ther bee
> A living soule within thee, thus to free
> Thy Body from it.
>
> (IV, iv, 157–61)

Clorin and Amoret may be the more virtuous in that men believe that they are the opposite but women's chastity can never be taken for granted. None the less, chastity when distinct and excluded from the claims of sexuality is, legitimately, power. The play's last scene shows Clorin in her bower, surrounded by those she has assisted, blessed by the priest, adored by the satyr who remains alone onstage with her at the end and begs to be allowed to do her service:

> Shall I stray,
> In the middle Ayre and staye,
> The sayling Racke or nimbly take,
> Hold by the Moone, and gently make
> Suit to the pale Queene of the night
> For a Beame to give Thee light?
>
> (V, v, 244–9)

The final tableau of the virgin with the satyr at her feet enacts the conquest of lust and appetite by chastity; Clorin is a maiden queen who with the assistance of the priest and the satyr controls and harmonises life in the forest.

In the light of this play's strong Spenserianism it is tempting to see in Clorin an image of the dead Queen, and recent critics have read Fletcher's revamping of Guarini as a conscious effort to politicise the pastoral play. The older view of pastoral tragicomedy as apolitical, even especially attractive on account of its 'political blankness or blandness',[31] has been considerably revised in recent years;[32] James J. Yoch's account of Renaissance tragicomedies as plays that 'illustrated for their audiences right rule of the self and, by implication, of the body politic'[33] is extremely persuasive. In *The Faithful Shepherdess* Fletcher has clearly reworked his source text to enhance the female roles and in particular to create a central role for an active woman, making Clorin both a high-ranking shepherdess[34] and also a priestess who celebrates the cult of Pan, 'Thou that keepest us chaste and free, / As the young spring'. The play's Spenserian qualities have been remarked on by all its critics, and Clorin's role recalls Belphoebe's; the style in which her virtues are celebrated is also reminiscent of the praise of Eliza in *The Shepheardes Calender*:

> Brightest faire thou art devine:
> Sprung from great immortall race
> Of the Gods: for in thy face,
> Shines more awfull majesty,
> Then dull weake mortalitie
> Dare with misty eies behould.
> (I, i, 59–64)

> Thou devinest, fayrest, brightest,
> Thou most powerfull mayd, and whitest,
> Thou most vertuous, and most blessed,
> Eyes of Starrs and Golden Tressed.
> (V, v, 238–41)

The meaning of her chastity, which is distinguished from Amoret's as Belphoebe's is from Britomart's in *The Faerie Queene*, is defined in the opening scene. In its stress on the civilising power of this quality, it has a humanist inflection which distinguishes it from other representations of chastity elsewhere in the canon. In a wood as full of shadows, illusions, and nightmarish fantasies as the wood of Athens in *A Midsummer Night's Dream*, Clorin reflects on the source of her ability to see the truth and to subdue the wild creatures:[35]

> What greatnesse or what private hidden power,
> Is there in me to draw submission,

From this rude man, and beast? . . .
. . . sure there is a power
In that great name of virgin, that bindes fast
All rude uncivill bloods, all appetites
That breake their confines.
(I, i, 103–5; 124–7)

It may be pulling the text too far in one direction to suggest, as Finkelpearl does, that the play's nostalgic evocation of a glorious past when the 'shepherds' and 'shepherdesses' of the court lived in a state of temperance and harmony under the sway of the Virgin Queen constitutes a 'plea . . . for England's moral regeneration';[36] yet qualities like these may well have been attractive to court and audiences in the 1630s. Certainly a recognition of them should dispel the illusion that in his handling of chastity in *The Faithful Shepherdess* Fletcher was merely 'paying lip service to a virtue that actually left him rather cold'.[37]

Several of these chastity motifs recur in plays written within a few years, either side, of *The Faithful Shepherdess*, though in no other is the focus so confined to this single subject. The most significant of these are the collaborative plays, *Cupid's Revenge* (c. 1608), *Philaster* (1609–10), and *The Maid's Tragedy* (1610–11), but the motif of threatened injury to a woman to test her fidelity appears first in Beaumont's solo play, *The Knight of the Burning Pestle* (1607).[38] Finkelpearl[39] is right to draw attention to the curious passage between Jasper and Luce in Act III where he decides while she is asleep to threaten her with death as a test of her love for him. A correct reaction (readiness to die) will prove that his rapturous vision of her as 'a love without the faults of women, / And greater in her perfect goods than men' (III, i, 59–60) is not an illusion. Jasper, like Perigot and Thenot, requires the reassurance that his lover is without what he sees as women's failings (which, of course, would not be failings in men). The lyric intensity of his soliloquy marks it off stylistically from its context, but the mood of the scene is soon broken by the commentary of the Citizen's Wife, who fails to accept the situation as romance convention and sends for the Watch to arrest Jasper. Momentarily, however, Jasper can be seen in Finkelpearl's words as one of 'the strange "heroes" of Beaumont and Fletcher's most famous romances, where the pulling out of a sword against a helpless and usually loving woman is a frequent gesture'.[40] There are major differences between this and similar scenes in the romances, in that there the women are often in transvestite disguise,[41] and they are partners in the action, ready to accept wounding and even death on their lovers' behalf. However, in these plays the sexual woundings can be read in terms of an equation between active female sexuality and guilt; this reading is enhanced by the addition of the disguise motif, and by the important fact that the woman loves the man without hope of return.

Urania in *Cupid's Revenge* and Aspatia in *The Maid's Tragedy* both die virgin in plays where much of the action is directed by the sexual power of a harlot figure whose role is more significant; in *Philaster* Bellario/Euphrasia pledges her life to celibacy in the service of Philaster and Arathusa, who will marry and perpetuate the joined dynasties of Sicily and Calabria. The disguise also symbolises the woman's self-containment and separation from the corruption of court life; this corruption is largely represented in sexual rather than social or political terms, and tends to be epitomised in the figure of a licentious woman, Bacha in *Cupid's Revenge*, Evadne in *The Maid's Tragedy*, or Megra in *Philaster*. In Urania and Aspatia, sexual desire is re-channelled into desire for death; in both plays the romantic convention of the epicene girl-page who devotes her life to the quasi-chivalric service of her lover/master is reinterpreted through a reading of chastity as self-denial, even frustration. In *Cupid's Revenge* a negative account of chastity as the denial of natural impulse is explicit; the efforts of Hidaspes, the Duke's daughter, to eradicate the worship of Cupid and to pull down all his 'erected obsceane Images' result in the destruction of the entire ruling family. But in Bellario/Euphrasia, however, the most fully developed of the three transvestite roles, the play's tragicomic shaping enables a positive portrayal of female sexuality in the main female character, Arathusa, and upholds a romantic reading for this role.

In *Cupid's Revenge* Urania's cross-dressing serves two purposes: to escape her wicked mother's marriage plans for her, and to deny her identity as potential heir to the throne. It is a denial of both sexual and political rights, and also of the power of her lascivious mother, Bacha, who has been Prince Leucippus's mistress before becoming wife to his old father. In the last scene she is wounded shielding her step-brother Leucippus from an assassin's knife; she loves Leucippus, but also intends that he should inherit the throne. Urania's chastity constitutes a rejection of courtly corruption; her rustic speech and simple manners are additional signifiers of it.[42] She reveals her identity, and thus her sex, only when she is dying. Leucippus displays to the assassin a handkerchief stained with her blood, an equivocal token conflating chastity with sacrifice, but alluding to the blood-stained fabric which denotes virginity. Urania is not pledged to virginity as Hidaspes originally was, but believes herself unworthy to marry Leucippus because of the reflected shame of her mother's sexual misbehaviour. Her self-sought death is not a glorification of chastity, but another example of the operation of Cupid's revenge like the death of Hidaspes earlier in the play. Chastity, figured as virginity, is not a stable and self-sufficient condition as it is for Clorin in *The Faithful Shepherdess*; rather it is conceived in terms of 'a phase of social transition'[43] beyond which the unfulfilled women Hidaspes and Urania are unable to pass.

In *Philaster*, Bellario's role as page to Philaster shares many similarities

The price of virtue: chastity plays

with Urania's, but discloses a different vision of virginity. Bellario too loves a man from whom she can expect nothing in return, and this fact, along with her gender-identity, is withheld from him until the closing moments of the play. She too is wounded, but actually at the hands of the man she loves rather than in his place. This wounding, though far from fatal, is in fact more significant than Urania's; this is partly because Bellario's is a major role, the true nature of which is not fully revealed to the audience until the closing moments of the play, but also because the wounding figures as part of a complex nexus of meanings relating the motif of blood-shedding to love. It is an element in a triangular situation involving Arathusa, who will marry Philaster, uniting herself, like Amoret in *The Faithful Shepherdess*, to the man who has hurt her. Philaster wounds Arathusa in a jealous rage, believing her to have been unfaithful to him with Bellario, who functions as their go-between. He himself has been wounded, by the notorious 'country Fellow' in his misconceived attempt to defend Arathusa. Her wound is not severe and no one expects her to die; since she willingly accepted, even invited, Philaster's sword thrust, it is a kind of sadistic literalisation of the Petrarchan metaphor of love's wounds. In the next scene Philaster finds Bellario asleep in the forest and wounds her, again, as his soliloquy makes clear, as a token gesture:

> Sword, print my wounds
> Upon this sleeping boy. I ha' none I think
> Are mortal, nor would I lay greater upon thee.
> (IV, sc. vi, 23–5)

Bellario has acted as Philaster's substitute in his role as go-between; and Philaster believes the page to have acted out, rather than simply retelling his master's message of love. Now the master acknowledges his identity with his servant by marking him with wounds identical to his own. All three characters are now united in a visibly signified blood-bond; Bellario and Arathusa, equally innocent victims, accept their wounds as tokens of love. But the dramatic interest is focused largely on Bellario's wounds. The courtiers take her (ignorant, of course, of her gender) for Arathusa's attacker; in a sacrificial gesture devised, like Urania's, to shield her lover, Bellario admits to the crime. But Philaster overhears the false confession and steps forward to claim the guilt for himself. He takes the page in his arms and weeps, displaying Bellario's wounds to the bystanders as emblems of innocence and priceless virtue:

> You hard hearted men,
> More stony than these mountains, can you see
> Such cleere pure blood drop, and not cut your flesh
> To stop his life? To bind whose bitter wounds,
> Queenes ought to teare their haire, and with their teares

Bath um? Forgive me, thou that art the wealth
Of poore *Philaster*.

(IV, sc. vi, 116–22)

The paradox in Philaster's final words, addressed to Bellario, suggests that the prince has finally recognised his true source of strength. But of course the closure of the romance denouement, in which, through the union of true prince and princess, the union of two kingdoms is also achieved, excludes the page, now a redundant third party. For the virtuous heroine, Arathusa, virginity is merely 'a phase of social transition', now concluded; not so for Bellario, who in the play's closing moments is required to make yet another gesture of self-abnegation, breaking her vow of silence over her identity in order to vindicate Arathusa's chastity. The threat of her ambiguous sexuality now permanently removed by this disclosure, she is permitted to enter into a permanently triangular relationship with Arathusa and Philaster. This version of chastity does not refigure either the self-sufficiency and power of Clorin or the displaced sexuality of Urania; though it is nearer to the perpetual virginity vowed by female saints, it is obviously compromised by Bellario/Euphrasia's admission of love for Philaster. This image of the chaste woman is ultimately one of pathos and unfulfilment.

In *The Maid's Tragedy* the triangular situation of two women, is reworked with a distinctive stress on the barren and even deathly quality of chastity in the transvestite woman. The man, Amintor, is again a jealous lover, but this time his jealousy is justified. Evadne, for whom he has deserted Aspatia, has on their wedding night confessed herself to be the King's mistress. Aspatia, a bitter and grieving victim, models herself not on self-sacrificial pages but on betrayed and suicidal women of antiquity such as Dido. Absent for the main part of the play, she reappears only in the last scene where her male disguise, like Urania's, creates the circumstances for a pathetic and self-sacrificial death scene. Pretending to be her own brother come to revenge her dishonour on Amintor, she challenges him to a duel. Amintor eventually perceives her suicidal intention, after he has wounded her to death; as in *Philaster* and *Cupid's Revenge* receiving wounds equates with receiving love:

> What dost thou meane,
> Thou canst not fight, the blowes thou makst at me
> Are quite besides, and those I offer at thee
> Thou spreadst thine armes, and takst upon thy brest
> Alas defencelesse.

(v, iii, 101–5)

The triple wounding scene is refigured when, before Aspatia can reveal herself, Evadne enters 'her hands bloody, with a knife'. The blood belongs to the King whom she has just murdered, but it signifies as a love-token;

she has killed her former lover in revenge for the dishonour he has done her, and comes to claim Amintor's love. When he repudiates her, she kills herself. As in *Cupid's Revenge* chastity functions in the construction of a negative view of female sexuality, a view polarised between the powerfully active and threatening appetites of Bacha and Evadne on the one hand, and the powerless and unfulfilled victims Urania and Aspatia on the other; like Ophelia's recourse to madness, it is the desperate act of a suppressed woman, whose voice cannot be heard until she speaks from an outsider's position.[44] The Amoret/Amarillis duality is reworked in the polarised female images of lustful temptress and chaste maiden.

In plays which centre on marriage rather than courtship, female chastity remains an issue, but explored in terms of continence and constancy rather than of the preservation of virginity. The ordeal by wounding is replaced by trials of other kinds. The assumption that chastity is the pre-eminent form of virtue in women, and precondition for all the rest, continues to be taken for granted,[45] and is perhaps even more central to the representation of women where it is not identified with virginity. A married woman's chastity signifies in social and political as well as personal terms; and the ordeals to which married women are subjected in some plays are imposed, not by the husband, but by the head of state. Such ordeals may constitute a damaging attack from which the woman, though proven chaste, does not emerge unscathed. Zenocia in *The Custom of the Country* is threatened with enforced submission to Count Clodio exercising his traditional *droit du seigneur* before her marriage, and obliged to flee the country; she has many further sufferings to endure, and is brought almost to the point of death before Clodio renounces his right to 'the barbarous custom practis'd in my country', symbol of his absolutism, and subjects his own desires to the rule of law. In *Valentinian* Lucina, although accepting the Augustinian view of virtue as a quality residing in the will rather than being a material possession, still sees herself as having no choice but suicide after her rape by the Emperor. There is no authority to which she can appeal to regulate the Emperor's behaviour. 'Justice shall never heare ye, I am justice' is his answer to her threat to expose him. Her husband accepts the corollary to this absolutism, that her continued existence after the rape would call into question not only her own honour but also his own and that of his descendants:

> When they read, she liv'd,
> Must they not aske how often she was ravished,
> And make a doubt she lov'd that more than wedlock?
> Therefore she must not live.
> (III, i, 242–5)

Once dead, however, she is indisputably 'the best and worthiest lady'. In dying, she reclaims her own body and reconstitutes her virtue in a way that no other means can achieve.[46]

In two contrasting plays, the tragic *Thierry and Theodoret* and the tragicomic *A Wife for a Month* the situation of the tyrant who intervenes in a marital relationship is worked out so as to provide a trial of continence for the wife, which she survives. In both cases he attempts to prevent a newly married couple from consummating their relationship; although this is a trial for both partners, the focus is on the wife and her ability to control her desire. In neither play is sexual timidity at all an issue; they are not based on the assumptions that could make Imogen in *Cymbeline* admirable in the rosy pudency with which she denied Posthumus.

The subverted wedding night, a common situation fraught with erotic tension, features in a number of Beaumont and Fletcher plays. In *Thierry and Theodoret*,[47] Thierry is given a drink which will render him impotent on his wedding night by his mother, Brunhalt, a brutal and tyrannical queen who is jealous of his virtuous wife, Ordella. The assumption is that no normal woman could control her sexual desire at such a time:

> If she have any part of woman in her
> She'le or fly out, or at least give occasion
> Of such a breach which nere can be made up.
> (II, i, 309–11)

Thierry shares this view, and is deeply embarrassed by his inability to 'speak the language of a husband'. He expects Ordella to show if not rage and anger then at least bitter disappointment when he confesses himself impotent, but to his astonishment she accepts the situation without a word of reproach and even reaffirms her love for him. Thierry is so impressed by Ordella's selfless abnegation of her due pleasures that he sees her as Eve before the Fall; together they will exemplify nature's 'first/Justly praisde workmanship, the first chast couple'. In her ability to suppress desire she is more than woman:

> Oh who would know a wife,
> That might have such a friend?
> (III, i, 96–7)

exclaims Thierry; the implication is that a woman who can behave in this extraordinary way is so good as to be virtually identical with a man. Ordella is a shadowy character in the play, largely defined through her role as antithesis to Brunhalt, but perhaps this simplifies her role in terms of the play's handling of sexuality; through her the spectre of a man's inability to satisfy a woman's sexual appetite is exorcised. However, she demonstrates not merely a sexual strength; she even takes on herself the blame for her husband's impotence and in a later test of her fortitude declares herself willing to die so that Thierry may have children by another woman. Ordella's combination of continence and selfless love offers a reassuring account of womanhood: it is evident that this image of a woman who transcends the limitations of her sex in her ability to control desire functions less to idealise women than to assuage a range of male anxieties.

A Wife for a Month[48] provides a fuller and also more complex treatment of female continence. In this later play the representation of female sexuality is considerably less schematic, and the confident characterisation of Evanthe as forthright and witty as well as supremely virtuous exhibits a very different style of dramaturgy. Here the ordeals inflicted on a newly married couple by a usurping tyrant who desires the wife comprise the main action of the play. Evanthe flouts King Frederick by refusing his advances and insisting on marrying Valerio whom she loves. To punish the couple Frederick devises a series of tortures which will demonstrate his control over their sexuality: first he rules that, if they marry, Valerio must die after a month and Evanthe too, unless she can immediately find a second husband on the same condition. The lovers marry nevertheless, and challenge the tyrant's authority by treating death as a fair price for a month which a lifetime of desire can be realised:

> That short month I have to blesse me with her
> Ile make an age, ile reckon each embrace
> A yeare of pleasure, and each night a Jubilee,
> Every quick kisse a Spring . . .
> I will dye old in love, though young in pleasure.
> (III, ii, 29–36)

But for the tyrant the only desire allowed expression is his own; he rules that if Valerio consummates the marriage Evanthe will instantly be put to death, and that if he reveals his reason for abstention he too will die and be blamed as her murderer. Evanthe's situation is thus a much heightened version of Ordella's, and its emotional potential extensively exploited. Not only is Evanthe herself full of erotic anticipation but the dramatic interest of the play is centred on her responses. The action is shaped to build up to the wedding night scene as a high point, providing in its development a degree of emotional complexity. For example, the standard preliminaries of the bride's preparations for bed in the company of bawdy-talking attendants are potentially tragic in mood, while the irony of Evanthe's eagerness to enjoy her husband is undermined by pathos. A strongly sensual undercurrent is produced by the commentary of courtiers and citizens on the tyrant's bargain with the couple, which is public knowledge; the King's fool acts as satirical mouthpiece, normalising a view of female sexual appetite as endlessly voracious:

> With what joy the women run by heapes
> To see this Marriage! They tickle to think of it,

>   They hope for every moneth a husband too;
>   . . .
>   This is a merry world.
>
>   (III, iv, 32–9)

This time chastity is to be tested not in a context which is tragic or in relation to elevated Sidneian values of chivalric loyalty and honour, but in a world of hectic and often comic sexuality. In the wedding night scene Valerio expresses his state of arousal to the audience in fervent asides, yet he must persuade his bride, who does not know of Frederick's change of rules, of the merits of non-consummation. The rhetoric of his arguments against fruition is painfully undercut by the simple formulations of desire; the wit with which the exchanges are managed does not exclude feeling. Evanthe's dilemma is emotionally actualised as Ordella's was not.

> *Evanthe.* Come, kisse me and to bed.
> *Valerio.*   That I dare do,
>   And kisse againe.
> *Evanthe.*   Spare not, they are your owne Sir.
> *Valerio.* But to enjoy thee is to be luxurious,
>   Too sensual in my love, and too ambitious;
>   [*Aside*] O how I burne! – to pluck thee from the stalke
>   Where now thou grow'st a sweet bud and a beauteous,
>   And bear'st the prime and honour of the Garden,
>   Is but to violate the spring, and spoile thee.
>   . . .
>   The happiness of love is contemplation,
>   The blessedness of love is pure affection.
>   Where no allay of actual dull desire
>   Of pleasure that partakes with wantonesse
>   . . .
>   Can ever mix.
>   (III, i, 184–92; 195–201)

In the end Valerio is driven to excuse himself by claiming impotence; Evanthe, after a rueful aside ('T'is hard to die for nothing'), achieves a dignified restraint, and desire is, temporarily, suppressed. She will love Valerio not for 'the pleasure . . . that women aime at' but for his worth. She bids welcome to 'chastity, honour and chastity'.

But this test is soon revealed to have been merely the first of a series. The prolongation of Evanthe's ordeal creates the sense of an almost obsessional need to put chastity through every conceivable kind of test in order to demonstrate that it can have an absolute existence. Misogyny and idealism equally underlie this need: chastity is constructed as exceptional, yet also natural and necessary. In IV, ii Frederick suborns Evanthe's waiting woman, Cassandra, to present her with a more tempting offer: if she will become his mistress he will save her and Valerio too. Using a woman to present the seducer's case for him enables the scene to be shaped as a debate rather than as emotional confrontation; the focus is directed more sharply to Evanthe's responses since Cassandra has no personal investment in being persuasive. She first draws on the argument that if Evanthe consents to Frederick's wishes it may be seen as a 'compell'd necessity of honour' for which she cannot be held culpable, or even as a kind of rape without moral stigma:

> That keeps you cleere, for where your will's compell'd
> Though you yield up your body, you are safe still.
> (IV, iii, 14–15)[49]

Characteristic of Fletcherian dramaturgy of debate, Cassandra rehearses a series of arguments, not as a logically constructed series but as separate and sometimes mutually contradictory positions. She later asserts, for example, that not only is rape physically meaningless, but that in some terms it may be seen to constitute a claim to honour:

> Had Lucrece e're been thought of, but for Tarquin?
> She was before a simple unknowne woman,
> When she was ravisht, she was a reverent Saint;
> And do you think she yeelded not a little?
> And had a kind of will to be re-ravisht?
> (IV, iii, 40–4)[50]

The discontinuity of Cassandra's line of attack evokes the model of a morality play, whereby Lechery tries out every possible inducement and Chastity resists them one by one.

The climax of the ordeal is instituted by a change of focus: Frederick now appears to put the case for himself. By withholding the whole truth of the bargain from Evanthe, he nearly convinces her not only that Valerio has pretended impotence out of fear to lose his own life, but also that he has instigated Cassandra's attempt. The chastity test has modulated into a test of trust; the conceptual framework is less clear, but the excitement of the scene much increased. Evanthe reacts at first with outrage to think of her husband as a coward, but then begins to question Frederick's motives:

> I smell the malice
> It tastes too hot of practis'd wickednesse
> ...
> Shall my anger make me whore and not my pleasure?
> (IV, iii, 183–6)

The terms in which she detects his deception take on an overt religious colour: Frederick is 'a tame Devill' against whom Evanthe will defend 'this little fort you seek ... with chaste obedience to my deere Lord'.

Eventually she discovers the truth from Valerio, that he has dissimulated in an attempt to save both their lives. Her response to this disclosure conforms to the style of paradox that sharpens the whole play's representation of sexual feeling: she is offended. Like Ordella, she asserts her willingness to die; she would have preferred the truth at any price, and she upbraids her husband for his lack of confidence in her love. His self-abnegation has cheated her of a chance to demonstrate her virtue and strength of purpose; not only this, she has been denied an opportunity to inscribe herself in the text of history, like a male hero. The possibility is offered that chastity can constitute a woman's claim to heroism:

> And was not I as worthy to dye nobly?
> To make a story for the times that follow
> As he that married me? What weaknesse, Sir,
> Or disability do you see in me,
> Either in minde or body, to defraud me
> Of such an opportunity?
>
> (IV, v, 34–9)

Valerio like Thierry is overcome by his wife's nobility, in which he sees her not only transcending her sex but outdoing any moral act a man would be capable of:

> Man is a lumpe of earth, the best man spiritlesse,
> To such a woman; all our lives and actions
> But counterfeits in Arras to this virtue.
>
> (IV, v, 71–3)

Valerio's image of commemorative tapestry echoes Evanthe's wish to stand as an example for future times; it suggests the distorting effects created by historical records that obliterate the achievements of women. But the tests which Evanthe triumphantly passes almost redefine chastity out of existence, and its meaning, though implicitly questioned, is never defined. The play evades the truly radical position that a woman's chastity or continence has the same meaning as a man's, although its dramatic situations would have enabled this, but instead the focus is shifted from chastity as such to nobility. So, in effect, he has it both ways: Ordella and Evanthe are irreproachably virtuous in being able to control and suppress their sexual desires even under the greatest provocation, and therefore they are also brave and noble. The nobility they demonstrate is more admirable than anything a man could achieve, but it is achieved on terms peculiar to women.

A Wife for a Month exemplifies one of the ways in which role-play is used as a dramatic stratagem to represent chastity in action, in the Cassandra and Evanthe scene when the women debate the issues like embodiments of

The price of virtue: chastity plays

Lechery and Chastity. That it is a hot-tempered and passionate character like Evanthe, the eager bride, who speaks for Chastity, constitutes a playful variant on stereotypes, which some critics, unable to accept so radical a reformulation of the language of chastity, have found disquieting.[51] Another kind of play with the representation of chastity, also involving the assumption of roles, is the 'pretended wanton' device. The paradigm of this might seem to be the scene from *The Faithful Shepherdess* where Clorin pretends to offer herself to Thenot to make him see that this is exactly what he does not want, but, in fact, there is an earlier use of the motif in *The Woman Hater* (1605–6).[52] Here Oriana, having informed the audience in advance of her intention, pretends to make advances to Gondarino, the woman-hater himself, in the hope of exposing to him the unnaturalness of his misogyny. She initiates the encounter, blazoning her own charms to him,[53] but Gondarino is moved neither by this, nor by her appeal to him to assert his 'natural' masculinity:

> Good my Lord, leave off what you have beene,
> And freely be what you were first intended for,
> A man.
> (III, i, 79–81)[54]

In this instance only, the pretended wanton device backfires; to Oriana's surprise Gondarino later in the scene claims to have been won over by her, and uses her discomfort as the basis of a trick against her. But in three plays written solely by Fletcher, *Monsieur Thomas* (?1610–1613), *The Loyal Subject* (1618), and *The Humorous Lieutenant* (?1619–1625), the virgin's role-play achieves its intended effect.[55]

The most perfunctory version of the motif is in *The Loyal Subject* when two young girls, Honora and Viola, come for the first time to court where the decadent and tyrannical Duke at once sets about seducing them. Court life has already been identified with sexual corruption, which Honora and Viola, up from the country, are determined to resist. So when the Duke makes his predictable advances and challenges Honora to kiss him, his surprise when she does so creates a comic moment. When surprise is followed by revulsion she at once admits that her boldness was only a test and she is delighted that he has passed it:

> Thank ye:
> Upon my knees I pray heaven too may thank ye;
> Ye have deceived me cunningly, yet nobly
> Ye have cozen'd me: In all your hopeful life yet,
> A scene of greater honour, you ne'er acted.
> (IV, iii, 17–20)

Her playacting reveals that, despite appearances, men prefer to recognise women's chastity than follow up their own desires. Both sexes are thus morally vindicated. The Duke testifies to the therapeutic effect of Honora's trick: 'Thou hast done a cure upon me, counsell could not.'

In *The Humorous Lieutenant*, a popular comedy with thematic resemblances to *The Loyal Subject*, the brief episode between the Duke and Honora is expanded to fill up much of the play's main plot and the threat to the virgin's chastity is a significant one; the meaning and place of chastity are examined by means of a setting and structural pattern which juxtapose masculine and feminine values through themes of war and love. Despite its pseudo-classical context, the court of King Antigonus, an heir of Alexander the Great, is evoked in the text with a wealth of Jacobean detail of ushers, perfumed presence chambers, and cork-heeled beauties; its pervasive atmosphere of sexual commerce is heightened by the presence of the court bawd, Leucippe, who is represented at work in her office with two assistants, methodically organising the court's sexual traffic. Celia, a virgin, who makes her entry 'in poore attire', is not part of the court world. But she is desired both by King Antigonus, and his son, Demetrius; she loves the son, who is a prince, despite believing herself too humble for him. While he is away at war, the old king tries to seduce her, but she accomplishes his moral conversion straightforwardly, by an eloquent diatribe against the vanity of aged lust. This King's desire for his subject is not conceived politically; he is acknowledged generally to be a 'good old King' (IV, vi, 26), and his geriatric lust signifies only on a moral level. This encounter functions as a conventional kind of chastity test, since Celia is isolated and socially powerless. But her chastity is displayed to different and more self-consciously theatrical effect in a later scene constructed around the motif of curative role-play. This is at heart a comic scene, yet its affective structure is complex; audience expectations are subjected, not to a consistent process of heightening, but to a series of underminings. At this stage of the play preparations for comic closure are well under way, especially since Celia has now triumphantly overcome the King's attempt on her chastity. None the less there is still space within the play's design for creative exploitation of dramatic tension.

At this point Demetrius, just returned from the war, is sick and languishing because he has been told by his father that Celia has been unfaithful, and is now dead. Celia knows only that Demetrius is sick and she is to cure him. The scene is framed theatrically; Celia is brought to Demetrius's room by a group of lords, all of whom depart except for Leontius, an old soldier and Demetrius's mentor. Unseen by Celia or Demetrius, Leontius remains onstage throughout, his presence and brief asides offering the audience a detached perspective from which to interpret the action. Demetrius is at first astonished to see Celia at all, and then alarmed at the new clothes she wears:

> Demetrius.　　　　　　　The very selfe same *Celia* –
> Celia.　How do ye sir?
> Demetrius.　　　　　　　　　　Only turn'd brave –
> I heard you were dead my deare one: compleat,
> She is wondrous brave, a wondrous gallant Courtier.
>
> [(IV, viii, 42–5)]

The comedy of cross-purposes is enhanced by Celia's equivocal responses to Demetrius's questions:

> Demetrius.　How came you hether *Celia*? wondrous gallant:
> 　　　　　　Did my father send for ye?
> Celia.　　　　　　　　　　So they told me Sir,
> 　　　　　　And on command too.
> Demetrius.　I hope you were obedient?
> Celia.　　　　　　　　　　I was so ever.
> Demetrius.　And ye were bravely us'd?
> Celia.　　　　　　　　　　I wanted nothing.
>
> (IV, viii, 48–52)

Demetrius interprets Celia's speech and changed appearance conventionally, assuming she has become his father's mistress; accordingly, she acts out the role of wanton in which he has cast her. The success of her performance is established when he reacts with outrage; the scene takes on a new configuration, that of the virtuous man repudiating the whore:

> Thou art dead, forever dead; sins surfet slew thee;
> The ambition of those wanton eyes betraid thee;
> Go from me grave of honour; go thou foule one,
> Thou glory of thy sin.
>
> (IV, viii, 85–8)

But the scene does not end at this point: Celia now redirects it to present herself in her former role of virtuous virgin. It is her turn for a display of passionately defensive oratory:

> I am above your hate, as far above it,
> In all the actions of an innocent life,
> As the pure stars are from the muddy meteors:
> Crye when you know your folly: howle and curse then,
> Beate that unmanly breast, that holds a false heart,
> When you shall come to know, whom you have flung from ye.
>
> (IV, viii, 129–34)

Her powerful speech unseats Demetrius's confidence, and she is enabled to sweep out on a note of wounded innocence. Antigonus enters to reassure his son of Celia's chastity, which he claims to have tested on Demetrius's behalf. In a more conventional dramaturgy this would constitute a complete revision of his encounter with Celia, but there must be some question about whether a Fletcher text operates on this basis in the theatre. However, a reader may be conscious of an element of comic paradox about the hyperbolical style of his praise, which recalls the admiration for the nobility of women's chastity spoken by Thierry and Valerio, especially if Antigonus's stance is coloured by its context; this eulogy is spoken by the old king who has himself been cured of lust. He advises his son:

> Since I made a full proofe of her vertue,
> I find a King too poore a servant for her.
> Love her, and honour her; in all observe her.
> She must be something more than time yet tels her.
> And certaine I beleeve him blest, enjoyes her.
> (IV, viii, 169–74)

He exits on this rhetorical flourish, leaving Demetrius to a bewildered soliloquy and the audience to pleasurable anticipation of further role-playing strategies before the young couple are reconciled.

It is impossible to avoid asking whether this regular element of role-play compromises the idealisation of the virtue it is apparently designed to vindicate and support. Since *The Humorous Lieutenant* is generically shaped like a romance, culminating in the revelation of Celia's noble origins as daughter to a king, the pull towards the affirmation of romance values, at least in the play's final act, may counteract any earlier tendency to the destabilisation of absolutes. But the same cannot be said for the similar handling of chastity in a central scene of the comedy, *Monsieur Thomas*.

In this play, the triangular situation of two men, an older and a younger, who are, unbeknown to all, actually father and son, in love with the same woman, reappears; but this time the older man, Valentine, is present (of course, unobserved) during the scene in which the woman, Cellide, plays out her role as pretend wanton. The bond between the two men, who think of themselves as intimate friends, is stressed by this circumstance. Cellide is betrothed to Valentine who is also her guardian; but Francis, who is much closer to her in age, seeing her for the first time, falls in love with her. The echo of *The Two Gentlemen of Verona* (despite the transposal of Valentine's name) is no accident, and the emotional tensions of the central scene are partially created by the conflict between the ties of male friendship and of heterosexual love. Francis has fallen sick of his love for Cellide, as Valentine guesses; in a gesture of self-abnegation he persuades Cellide to visit Francis and attempt his cure by offering her love. Cellide reacts realistically: she is offended, assuming that Valentine has grown tired of her, but agrees to undertake the cure of Francis as a proof of her obedience. When Cellide comes to Francis's bedside she performs the scene without asides like those given to Oriana or Celia to

The price of virtue: chastity plays 47

establish their bona-fides with the audience; but the audience knows she is acting a prescribed role, as the onstage presence of Valentine 'apart' confirms. However, the structure of the action is so convoluted that distinctions between 'pretence' and 'reality' are soon overridden. As Valentine watches Celia's performance he becomes convinced that she is offering herself to Francis in reality. His conviction is a function not of his own gullibility but of Cellide's skill in dissimulation; despite the fact that the situation between the three of them has been engineered by Valentine, it is not his wisdom or integrity that are on trial but Cellide's chastity. The scene invites the question: by being sanctioned to play the role of wanton, is she in fact being licensed to act out woman's true desires? Francis is as quickly convinced by her as Valentine; he reacts with horror, his desire for her suppressed by revulsion for her unchastity. His expressions of virtuous indignation recall Perigot's reaction to the shape-shifting of Amoret/Amarillis:

> *Francis.* Me thinks you are not faire now; me thinks more
> That modest vertue men delivered of you
> Shewes but like a shadow to me, thin, and fading.
> *Valentine.* Excellent Friend.
> *Francis.*   Ye have no share in goodnesse.
> Ye are belyde; you are not Cellide,
> The modest, imaculate: who are ye?
> For I will know: what devill to do mischiefe
> Unto my vertuous Friend, hath shifted shapes
> With that unblemished beauty.
>
>   (III, i, 115–23)

This misconstruction by both men might be read as comic; but, in that it endorses not only masculine anxiety about the reality of female chastity but also a conventional view of the relative strength of male and female virtue, the implications for women are disturbing. Cellide plays the role of 'woman, perfect woman' so well, in apparently betraying the man who loves her and thus conforming to the stereotype of female inconstancy, that appearance and reality become indistinguishable. The text is seen to invite the audience to participate in the men's deception, rather than collude with Cellide in her success. Francis rebuffs her in horror; Valentine, moved by his high-mindedness, resigns to him his own part in Cellide's affections, and leaves the stage unobserved by the others. But the sequence of moral reversals is not yet complete; Francis's display of masculine loyalty so moves Cellide that she confesses her offer of love was only a test, which he has passed in an exemplary way, and she recommends him to preserve the fortress of his honour against future attack:

> Tis like a strong built Castle, seated high
> That draws on all ambitions, still repaire it,
> Still fortifie it: there are thousand foes

> Besides the tyrant beauty, wil assaile it:
> Looke to your centinels, that watch it hourely,
> Your eyes, let them not wander.
>
> (III, i, 167–72)

Cellide's turning of the tables on Francis, and her use of an image more usually associated with female chastity[56] momentarily suggests that male and female chastity may be comparable, but this subversive possibility is not followed up. In a further reversal Cellide as she exits is given her sole aside to the audience, in which she admits to a new-found feeling for Francis:

> O noble young man,
> I love thee with my soule, but dare not say it.
>
> (III, i, 197–8)

Francis remains onstage to soliloquise on his admiration for Cellide; he wishes he could do

> Something for her too
> Though I can never reach her excellence,
> Yet but to give an offer at a greatnesse.
>
> (III, i, 208–10)

Once again, chastity is idealised at the conclusion of a scene which primarily celebrates the outstanding ability of a woman to perform in the roles created for her by masculine constructions of her sexuality. The discontinuous structure of the scene, with its series of sequentially reversing emotional situations, never allows the audience to accept any one position as the truth; each mask is removed only to reveal another beneath it, so that the opposition of truth and appearance is deconstructed. The effect of Francis's brief soliloquy is comically subversive of the notion of closure; in conventional dramaturgy it might be read as the hero's final achievement of understanding, to which he has been progressively educated by the heroine's virtue, but in this context it is only one more moral position, temporarily available but ready to be subverted by the very different representation of sexual manners in the play's other plot.

The last handling of the pretended wanton motif is the most extensive. It occurs in *The Maid in the Mill* (1623), on which Fletcher collaborated with William Rowley.[57] The source for the relevant section of the play is a Bandello novella[58] in which a nobleman abducts the daughter of a miller, rapes her, and hides her away; she is discovered in his house by the Duke of Florence who obliges him to marry her and provide her with a dowry. In the Fletcher/Rowley version there are significant changes: the count who abducts the girl does not rape her, and she turns out in any case to be of noble birth, so that the marriage which eventually occurs, in much the same way as in the source, is not between unequals. Bandello relates without moralising a story in which a wrong done by a powerful man to a powerless woman is righted by royal fiat. Fletcher transforms this into a parable about the power of chastity. This is depicted in two contrasting scenes: in the first (III, ii), Florimel withstands every argument and every trick Count Otrante can devise to persuade her to sleep with him; in the second (V, ii) she tests the nature of his desire for her by pretending to be a prostitute.

The context is that she has been stolen away from the mill where she lives by Count Otrante during pastoral festivities and kept in his country house. The situation of the man enabled by his higher social and economic status to enforce his desires on the reluctant woman recalls Angelo in *Measure for Measure* and the Duke of Florence in *Women Beware Women*, but the emotional temperature of Fletcher's scene is much cooler. Although a social context of sorts exists for the two characters – he is a count, she a miller's daughter – it is a purely formal one appropriate to the pastoral mode of the play, and there is no concern with the kinds of social pressures and tensions that would be required in a realistic setting. Otrante and Florimel are almost as abstract and lacking in social definition as the characters from *The Faithful Shepherdess*. In the first of the two chastity scenes Florimel resists the arguments put from Otrante's position of power, that he will love her longer if she gives herself voluntarily, that he will disregard her low status, that he will protect her if she becomes pregnant; and, with what could be a metatheatrical effect in which Fletcher alludes to his own familiar theatrical practices, she treats him as if his offers were tricks or tests:

> I know ye do but try me, ye are noble,
> All these are but to try my modesty,
> If you should find me easie, and once coming,
> I see your eyes already how they would fright me.
>   . . .
> You are a noble Lord, you pitty poor maids.
>   (III, ii, Glover and Waller, VII, 39–40)

Otrante does not, like Cellide, now reveal his persuasions as a test; instead he answers tersely:

> This cunning cannot help ye:
> I love ye to enjoy [ye]:
>   (*Ibid.*, 40)

and when Florimel calls upon her 'honest thoughts' as a form of divine protection Otrante demystifies this moral blackmail:

> You cannot scape me, yet I must enjoy ye,
> I'll lie with thy wit, though I miss thy honesty.
>   (*Ibid.*, 40)

The scene is structured as usual by a sequence of twists and turns which undermine consistency and disrupt the notion of a progressive revelation, each new situation replacing the previous one. Like Celia in *The Humorous Lieutenant* Florimel is witty and resourceful, and she is not intimidated by the Count's status; intellectually she is his match, so that their encounter can take the form of a debate, one which is conducted entirely on masculine terms. Otrante asks advice of his confidante Gerasto who puts the position that what all women really want is to be subjected to masculine power, and probably to be raped as well. His cynical low-life tone presupposes the collusion of a male audience, if it is to be comic. Instead of violence, Otrante pursues stratagems; he gets Gerasto and the servants to insult Florimel so brutally that she weeps. Then he points out to her what power he has over her reputation: 'Yield now, or you are undone; your good name's perish'd' (*Ibid.*, 44). Florimel's final refusal brings the scene to an ambiguously open ending. By a new tactic, Otrante now admires her resistance, and has Gerasto and the servants praise her honesty as vehemently as they had previously impugned it. But the scene does not follow the pattern of *The Humorous Lieutenant*, where the seducer goes back on his tracks and praises the chastity he has attempted to overcome; Otrante's last move is to assert his power again; he claims authority to define her as chaste or unchaste. By not foreclosing on his situation Fletcher leaves open the possibility of further surprising twists, which only come about when the Florimel/Otrante action is resumed in the play's long final scene where the pretend wanton motif is displayed in its more realistic mode.

The scene opens with Florimel singing bawdy songs to Otrante who initially reacts with pleasure but soon expresses revulsion at her assertive sexuality:

> *Florimel.* You are too cold.
> *Otrante.* I do confess I freeze now,
>   I am another thing all over me:
>   It is my part to wooe, not to be courted.
>   (v, ii, Glover and Waller, VII, 62)

The role-reversal of sexual power relations is overt and comic; like Amarillis or Cloe in *The Faithful Shepherdess*, Florimel takes over the rhetoric of lust and sexual invitation conventionally given to men, extending even Fletcher's usual range of sexual punning:

> What should you do with Maiden-heads? you hate 'em,
> They are peevish pett[ish] things, that hold no game up,
> No pleasure neither; they are sport for Surgeons;
> I'll warrant you. I'll fit you beyond Maiden-head:
> A fair and easie way men travel right in,
> And with delight, discourse, and twenty pleasures,
> They enjoy their journey; mad men creep through hedges.
>   (*Ibid.*, 63)

Otrante resorts to the asides which usually characterise the female response to this predicament, comically inviting the audience to endorse his horror at Florimel's display of sexual aggression. 'How I shake now', he exclaims when she claims to have resorted to 'trade' to satisfy 'such lords as you are'. The scene is broken up when she turns to the audience and exposes her behaviour as a stratagem:

> Pardon [me] Modesty,
> This desperate way must help; or I am miserable.
> (*Ibid.*, 64)

She sustains the role no further and Otrante sees that she is crying; he is about to discover her when closure is postponed by the precipitate arrival of the King of Spain. This necessitates the further concealment of Florimel in a closet, until the King insists on having the closet forced open and revealing her. But whereas in the source the maid could only marry the nobleman when provided with a dowry by the Duke, Florimel makes her own dual claim to Otrante through her chastity and through preserving him from the discredit of rape:

> I do ask you, and I deserve ye;
> I have kept ye from a crying sin would damn ye
> To Men and Time: I have preserv'd your credit,
> That would have died to all posterity:
> (*Ibid.*, 67)

Their union is sealed, then ratified when the King offers to pay Florimel's dowry and her father the miller promises to sell the mill. The play's concluding revelation that Florimel is actually a count's daughter belongs to Rowley;[59] it is totally superfluous to Fletcher's action, even subverting its effect by its conventional gesture towards romance.[60] The pretend wanton motif in this play seems to function in a less ambiguous and compromising way than in *The Humorous Lieutenant* and *Monsieur Thomas* perhaps because it makes its own case without recourse to equivocation or role-play. And Florimel's inability to continue her playacting is done in such a way as to hint, albeit momentarily, at the emotional cost of the deception. The tests and ordeals to which chaste women are subjected in these plays regularly culminate in a eulogy of their extraordinary virtue; in turn, women subject men to moral testing which appears to demonstrate male ability to appreciate the moral worth of chaste resistance over the pleasures of seduction. Chastity is at the same time the normal and proper condition for a woman and also rare and astonishing; in that through the exercise of chastity a woman may, like Cellide or Evanthe, be better than a man, it is also a kind of excess.[61] The plays do not only insist on the preservation of the woman's body for the sole use of a legitimate possessor; the tests and trials of continence acknowledge its value as a supreme form of self-regulation. The plays effectively challenge the common assumption that women are less able to control their appetites than men; these women are by no means the 'leaky vessels' of Middletonian city comedy. But it is conceded that such control is hard to achieve for both sexes. The pretend wanton motif functions to assure men that they can recognise the value of chastity, and also that this recognition does not run counter to their own interests. The theatrical strategies evolved to explore the meanings of chastity are heavily reliant on the contradictions inherent in the concept of role-playing; chastity in these plays may not be a mystery, but the truth of it can be revealed only through dissimulation.

Chapter 2

Gender

The extent to which traditional conceptions of gender were being questioned and challenged in this period has been the subject of debate by historians and literary and cultural theorists of many persuasions.[1] If it is accepted that in a society many of whose members were highly conscious of change and upheaval, systems of gender difference operated as significantly as those of class and status to define the social order, what kinds of evidence are available for the study of contemporary attitudes to gender? Does this period represent a 'liminal moment when gender definitions were open to play'?[2] Or is it rather the case that the hold of medieval and scholastic notions of women and gender was still so strong that a rigidly polarised conception of gender attributes was a more important factor than any other in accounting for attitudes to the position of women in society?[3] One area on which many Renaissance scholars have focused in order to find answers to such questions has been cross-dressing in the late Elizabethan to Jacobean period, both in fictional texts and in fact. It must be accepted that different kinds of cultural manifestations of cross-dressing have different meanings; issues of social status, sexual identity, tradition, religion, law and authority, and so forth arise to varying degrees according to whether the subject is, for example, cross-dressing in carnival, folk drama, or other festive practices, or on the city streets as a cover for criminal activity.[4] But if it is also accepted that what we call society is constructed from an interlocking and interdependent set of cultural practices – the 'fabric' metaphor is almost inescapable – then the significance of cross-dressing in one area, theatre and play-texts, is not entirely separate from its significance in others. The theatre is, of course, an obvious site for the exploration of this topic since cross-dressing of a kind was at its heart, when all women's roles were played by men or boys; and especially when this transvestism was regularly cited in anti-theatrical polemics as a major reason for suppressing the public theatre.[5] According to opponents of public theatre, the spectacle of male actors in women's dress not only contravened a Biblical prohibition against transvestism (Deuteronomy 22.5) but also functioned to incite perverse and lustful desires in those who witnessed it. But almost all plays contained female roles, though sometimes small ones and often few of them, and it is doubtful as to how many of these roles constitute a comment on the debate about gender.

A literal 'debate about gender' certainly existed in print during the Beaumont and Fletcher years; it was conducted both in the general terms set by a formal controversy about women dating back over many decades[6] and in terms of the more specific controversy over masculine women.[7] Beaumont and Fletcher found the whole area of gender differentiation dramatically fruitful, and explored it in a range of plays which can be divided into two groups: first, those where transvestite disguise is a major element in the plot, though handled so as to focus less on the transvestite character's dilemma (as in *Twelfth Night* or *As You Like It*) than on the irony created for the audience through sexual misapprehensions by the other characters; and second, plays not involving disguise but foregrounding questions of gender in situations where normal social constraints, particularly those relating to sexual roles and duties, are, for various reasons, temporarily suspended. In both types of play, characters whose sex is disguised or whose sexual behaviour is in some way compromised or irregular are used to explore relationships between nature, society, and gender; sometimes this definition emerges as the play's main object, sometimes it is relegated to a side-plot. By selecting certain groups of plays for discussion in this way and excluding others I do mean to make the point that gender *per se* is not always an issue in plays where male actors take the women's parts. The argument that gender is always problematic on a stage where all the parts are taken by men, that audiences always read it as 'the unstable product of role-playing and costume'[8] is unconvincing. McLuskie makes a useful distinction for the Renaissance theatre between the requirements of narrative and those of performance:[9] where the former are paramount the actor's sexual identity in the text is a given and his playing a woman's role a convention to which his own private sexuality makes no contribution.

In the narratives of both of these groups of plays, gender identity is an important element, and their plots tend to turn on the discovery or revelation of it; in some of them the true sex of the boy-actor is used in a knowing collusion between playwright and audience to create a further layer of meaning in the play's exploration of identity, but this is not always the case. There is a tendency in some feminist criticism now to substitute ideological for aesthetic evaluation, and to privilege plays which can be shown to challenge or resist traditional patriarchal representations of gender. Concomitantly, there can be a sense of disappointment in the recognition that a text which may promise much in terms of a narrative of sexual disguise or role-play turns out in the end only to endorse 'sexual difference and gender hierarchy'.[10] Simon Shepherd in *Amazons and Warrior Women* is rather dismissive of certain Beaumont and Fletcher plays (which he ascribes to Fletcher) for showing gender identity as biologically determined and not socially constructed, and the boundaries between male and female roles as clearly demarcated and not subject to negotiation. Yet gender issues are treated in a considerable range of plays, from the early *Love's Cure* (*c.* 1605)[11] to *The Sea Voyage* (1622), and in tragic as well as comic and tragicomic modes. The dramatists returned to the subject again and again, and it would be surprising to find that writers so experimental and so often self-referentially concerned with theatrical representation demonstrate no variety here.

My first group of plays features transvestite disguise. Do the playwrights use it, as Dusinberre claims of Shakespeare, to 'explore masculinity and femininity'?[12] If so, what discoveries do they make? What are the forms it takes? And how far do the demands of narrative leave any space for extra meanings potentially created in performance? The most popular transvestite role of the earlier part of the period is that of the girl-page, the young woman who disguises herself as a boy usually in order to gain access to the man she loves. The tantalising ambiguity which is the source of so much of this figure's erotic appeal is at the heart of *Philaster*, one of the most admired of the Beaumont and Fletcher collaborations.[13] The page disguises in *Cupid's Revenge* and *The Maid's Tragedy* are similarly conceived but dramatically more marginal. All three relate to prototypes in Shakespearian romantic comedy, but differ in certain major ways: they are passive and unfulfilled characters whose love is devoted to a man who cannot return it. Urania and Aspatia both die, and Bellario pledges herself to life-long virginity. Their sexual disguise, far from permitting them to test the reactions of others to a 'swashing and a martial outside' (*As You Like It*), or to win a lover, enables them to invite wounding and even death at the hands of their lovers. This alternative treatment of the disguised page derives from Beaumont and Fletcher's other major source, *Arcadia*. It is a common romance motif and the playwrights' representations of transvestism more generally may well relate to such popular texts as *Amadis de Gaul*, Montemayor's *Diana* (also sources for Sidney), or *The Mirrour of Knighthood*,[14] but there is no doubt of Urania's origins from a conflation of two characters in *Arcadia*, the shepherdess, Urania, and Zelmane, who disguises herself as a page for love of Pyrocles.[15] Although Zelmane does not meet her end in the same way as Beaumont and Fletcher's Urania, she is a pathetic and unfulfilled figure, who does not expect any requital from the man she loves, and dies in his arms.[16] In the other tradition girl-pages are attractive through their brave and resourceful behaviour, adopting male disguise in order to follow a lover to war or to face a dangerous journey, to engage actively with the life of a man. By contrast, Beaumont and Fletcher's pages use their disguise to court suffering and death. Their delicacy and pathos is stressed in their juxtaposition with another female character in the play: Urania with her mother Bacha, and Aspatia with Evadne, both of them strong, powerful and sexually active women, and in *Philaster* Bellario is juxtaposed with Arathusa, whom Philaster does love, and with the lustful and vicious Megra. These internal contrasts serve to define the sexuality of the page figures in certain terms: they are docile and submissive beings, whose existence is made meaningful only by the man they love. It was a commonplace of this period that love could make a man effeminate, causing him temporarily to behave in ways proper only to the weaker sex. As Mucedorus in *Arcadia* tells Pyrocles, 'it utterly subverts the course of nature in making reason give place to sense, and man to woman'.[17] The page roles of Urania and Aspatia are assumed only briefly, and with the audience's full recognition of the character's true sex; their known identity as women might have made the page role symbolic of the masculinity they need to imitate in order to behave actively,[18] but, on the other hand, the use to which they put their male disguise stresses both passivity and a feminine sexuality. They die dressed as men, Aspatia by Amintor's hand. Bellario's larger role operates differently since the character is assumed to be male throughout the play.

That the girl-page character in a play might subversively embody the dangerous allure of effeminacy is evident; the combination of his/her multi-layered sexual disguise (boy actor playing a young girl, playing a boy) and his position of subordination both in age and often in rank to the man with whom s/he is in love – a position which might socially duplicate that of the boy actor's relation to a good part of the theatre audience – created a potentially inflammatory socio-sexual dynamic implicitly recognised by those who opposed the stage on account of its employment of boy players who imitated women. This potential might be defused by devices within the play's narrative: the lover could draw attention to the page's 'womanliness' (Viola) or the disguised woman might lament the inconvenience of her 'doublet and hose' as a barrier to the lover's recognition, although of course both devices could operate ambivalently. But if the initial emphasis is on sexual duality rather than ambiguity such that the character is presented prior to assuming the male disguise as an active woman, and is given motivation for the disguise within the terms of the fiction, then the transvestism is less likely to centre on passivity or effeminacy.

A comparison of the transvestite roles in Beaumont and Fletcher with those in contemporary plays by Middleton, a playwright who made regular use of sexually disguised women in his comic plots, helps illuminate the distinctive features of Beaumont and Fletcher's handling of the role.[19] In *No Wit, No Help Like a Woman's* (*c.* 1613) Mistress Low-water in collusion with her impoverished husband assumes the disguise of 'a gallant gentleman' to restore their fortunes; it is a preferable alternative to her only other option – taking a rich lover. Both male and female characters find her sexually attractive in her disguise, but there is no hint of epiceneness. This is avoided partly because Middleton regularly inserts brief scenes between her and her husband to keep the audience firmly in mind of her marital status, and also because of the vigour with which she enacts her male role. This involves the wooing and even wedding of a rich widow, Lady Goldenfleece, who has wronged her in the past. These scenes are broadly comic, especially when Mistress Low-water's bold advances to the widow are so successful that she is glad of the timely intervention of a servant (in fact her own husband) to save her from exposure; but even in the wedding-night scene, when Mistress Low-water refuses to go to bed with her new 'bride', the potential for sexual titillation is avoided. Mistress Low-water's disguise functions exclusively within the world of intrigue, and its moral purpose is always to the forefront both for her and for the audience; no sympathy is invited for the deceived Lady Goldenfleece who has come by her fortune through the usurious activity of her first husband, and the confusion created by Mistress Low-water's transvestism works at her victim's expense. She is firmly within the tradition of the active and resourceful transvestite.[20]

The transvestite roles in *The Widow* (*c.* 1616) and *More Dissemblers Besides Women* (?1622) are differently handled, so as to create a distinctively sexualised comedy with a high degree of titillation in which the ironies of multiple disguise (boy actor playing a girl disguised as a boy, and, in *The Widow*, further disguised as a girl) are consciously exploited. Martia in *The Widow* has disguised herself as a man and run away to escape the elderly undesirable suitor proposed by her father. She is robbed by thieves and rescued, dressed only in a shirt, by Violetta, maidservant to Philippa, a married woman on the look-out for a lover. Both Violetta and Philippa are extremely impressed with Martia's beauty; Violetta lends Martia some cast-off clothes of the elderly Brandino, Philippa's husband, to wear, and Philippa joyously welcomes the disguised girl – 'my husband young again!' Though the audience has never seen Martia as a woman it is evident that they are meant to recognise her sex early on, perhaps in the scene where she appears in her shirt.[21] Her disguise is doubly funny if the audience understands its double nature, both in IV, ii, the comic scene when, dressed in Brandino's clothes, she confronts first one of the thieves who stripped her and then Brandino himself, and particularly in V, i, the play's long final scene, when Philippa, desperate to conceal her new lover from her husband, dresses her as a woman. Martia is just as desirable in women's clothes as in men's, and becomes the focus of the men's lust just as she has been of the women's. Middleton interweaves the prurient fantasies of Brandino and his man Martino who think Martia to be a woman with the equally lascivious imaginings of Philippa and Violetta, who still believe her to be a man. He uses this transvestite figure so as to illuminate the place of fantasy in human sexuality, both for men and women, to whom s/he is equally desirable.

Middleton's play with the dramatic convention of female transvestism is at its boldest in *More Dissemblers Besides Women*, a piece full of disguises, with all of which the audience is in full collusion. But here he is not concerned with the transvestite as an erotic figure; rather, he deconstructs the sexual appeal of female disguise, exposing it as a hollow fantasy. Aurelia's brief attempt at it pleases her lover but is immediately penetrated by her father, who chastises her for immodesty: 'Shame to thy sex, and sorrow to thy father' (I, ii, 213). The comic speed of the father's reaction suggests that the woman-page figure by this time would be immediately recognisable to a theatre audience, since it is only the woman-hating Cardinal whom Aurelia and her lover expect to deceive. Lactantio's mistress, however, passes for a page throughout the play. She deceives the Cardinal, to whom her attraction is clearly pederastic; he calls her

> 'the prettiest servant
> That ever man was bless'd with! 'tis so meek,
> So good and gentle'
> (I, ii, 151–3)

To him, and to the Duchess, who shares his sentimental response, the page is the conventionally pathetic boy, orphaned by a sea-storm, tearful, effeminate, submissive. The absurdity of this stereotype is pointed up by the fact that the page is actually pregnant, and during a farcical dancing lesson goes into labour. In this scene (V, i) the notion of the page as androgyne is bawdily debunked when the dancing master comments on 'his' inability to master male body-language:

> Open thy knees; wider, wider, wider, wider: did you ever see a boy dance clenched up? he needs a picklock ...
> Come on, sir, now; cast thy leg out from thee; lift it up aloft, boy: a pox, his knees are soldered together, they're sewed together: canst not stride?
> (V, i, 188–205)

But, of course, the effect of this scene is to contradict what it appears to assert; the 'natural' sexuality of the girl which cannot be hidden when she attempts to mimic a boy is actually the construction of the male actor. But within the play's narrative the attempts of the Cardinal and the Duchess to deny the strength of human sexuality fail; and nature, comically represented by the page's pregnancy, cannot be repressed.

While some of the Beaumont and Fletcher plays share Middleton's interest in exploiting possibilities of the transvestite for effects of comic irony and for commenting on gender distinction, in general they neither depict the figure in active roles with moral motivation,[22] nor allow for the disguise to function as a transitional stage *en route* to heterosexual fulfilment. They avoid situations with potential for comic or farcical exposure, like the wooing scenes between Mistress Low-water and Lady Goldenfleece, or the dancing lesson in *More Dissemblers*. Instead, the transvestite's true sex and identity tend to be disclosed at moments of emotional crisis. Bellario in *Philaster* typifies the Beaumont and Fletcher transvestite. His/her role and to a lesser extent those of Urania and Aspatia display the lure of the androgyne (for a male spectator): in his male disguise he is almost exaggeratedly feminine, regularly described as 'pretty', 'gentle', or innocent, and so dependent that, since he does not qualify for his master's love, he wants nothing other than to die at his hand; and he is also extraordinarily beautiful. The sexual ambiguity of the figure enables it to represent a stereotype of womanliness in the way that a female impersonator, by playing womanliness as a role, discloses it as socially constructed. The most developed page figure is Bellario, whose ambivalent sexual appeal is the fulcrum of the play's love-plot; it is the only one where the disclosure of the character's true sex is denied both within the fiction and to the audience until the play's final moments. S/he has in fact made a vow of concealment, 'never to be knowne / While there was hope to hide me from mens eyes / For other then I seem'd' (V, v, 180), but the revelation is required in order to permit the union of Philaster to Arathusa, which cannot proceed while Arathusa stands accused of sexual impropriety with Bellario. In terms of the plot this is a relief all round, since the lies of those who have impugned Arathusa's chastity are now exposed and the dynastic succession is assured; but for the audience the effect must be a more complex one, especially since the revelation is effected by means of that conventionally symbolic gesture of discovery, the letting down of the woman's hair. The main plot of the play depends on the fact that Bellario, supposedly a boy, is so attractive that Philaster can become passionately jealous of Arathusa's attachment to him while at the same time conscious of a strong, if undefined, feeling for the boy himself. Bellario's allure is recognised, and discussed, by a considerable number of the characters including Megra, Pharamond, Dion and the King, as well as Philaster and Arathusa themselves.[23]

The incidence of the word 'boy' is extremely high in the play, and while it is strongly associated with qualities of pathos and dependency, 'pretty helplesse innocence', as Philaster calls it in a piece of descriptive exposition, it is also imbued with disturbingly sexual connotations. The lascivious Megra taunts Prince Pharamond by telling him that Arathusa, whom he expects to marry, has in her service 'a Hilas, an Adonis' who must 'when you are wed, / Sit by your pillow, like young Apollo, with / His hand and voyce binding your thoughts in sleepe' (II,iv,24); 'The Princess does provide him for you and for herself.' The epicene attractions of singing pages are dismissed by Pharamond and Megra in favour of a more mature sexuality: 'I find no music in these boys. / *Megra*. Nor I. / They can do little, and that small they do / They have not wit to hide.' In a central scene Philaster tries to trap Bellario into an admission of intimacy with Arathusa, pretending that he has ordered Arathusa to prove her love for him by sleeping with the page as his substitute. The emotional content of the scene is highly complex. The increasingly disturbed and passionate tone of Philaster's interrogation is created by his use of wordplay and *double-entendre*; for him this is a conscious rhetorical choice, contrasting with the innocence of Bellario's answers. But although the page attempts to purge Philaster's language of its guilty connotations, his detailed accounts of Arathusa's affectionate behaviour towards him take on such strong colouring from Philaster's jealous punning; alongside Philaster's innocent reading of Arathusa's actions that there emerges for the audience the possibility of an alternative, and more ambivalent one:

> *Philaster.*   Oh *Bellario*:
> Now I perceive she loves me; she does shew it
> In loving thee my boy, she has made thee brave.
> *Bellario.* My Lord she has attir'd me past my wish,
> Past my desert; more fit for her attendant,
> Though farre unfit for me, who doe attend.
> *Philaster.* Thou art growne courtly boy. [*Aside.*] Oh, let all women
> That love blacke deedes, learne to dissemble here,
> Here, by this paper; she does write to me,
> As if her heart were mines of Adamant
> To all the world besides, but unto me,
> A maiden snow that melted with my lookes –
> Tell me my boy, how doth the Princesse use thee?
> For I shall guesse her love to me by that.
> *Bellario.* Scarce like her servant, but as if I were
> Something allyed to her ...
>
>   (III, i, 157–72)

The labyrinthine structure of the dialogue temporarily destabilises the audience's perceptions of each of the characters, and licenses many possible permutations in their interrelationships: Philaster may be cunningly jealous or acutely perceptive; Arathusa may be innocently affectionate or consciously seductive; Bellario may be a conscious sexual substitute for Philaster in Arathusa's eyes or a harmless love-object, a self-projection for Philaster; he may be an innocent pawn, or, as Philaster believes, this may be a role he uses to dissemble. The ambiguous terms exchanged between the two speakers in this scene – duty, courtly, use, servant, kind, service – recur in other contexts where Bellario's relationship with Arathusa is in question, in III, ii, for example, where Arathusa is interrogated first by the King her father and then by Philaster about her page. The King's style is direct and crude:

> *King.* He speakes, and sings, and playes?
> *Arathusa.*   Yes sir.
> *King.* About eighteene?

Arathusa. I never ask'd his age.
King. Is he full of service?
Arathusa. By your pardon,
Why do you aske?
King. Put him away.
Arathusa. Sir?
King. Put him away I say, 'has done you that
Good service shames me to speak of.
(III, ii, 14–19)

A few lines later Philaster confronts Arathusa, whose grief at the prospect of dismissing Bellario, as her father has ordered her to do, confirms his jealousy: 'O never, never such a boy againe, / As my Bellario.' The intensity of Bellario's involvement in his role as go-between for Philaster and Arathusa is cited by Arathusa as proof of the page's loyal and devoted service:

> Who shall now bring you
> Letters, rings, bracelets? Loose his health in service?
> ... Who shall take up his Lute,
> And touch it, till he crowne a silent sleepe
> Upon my eye-lids, making me dreame, and cry,
> Oh my deere, deare Philaster?
> (III, ii, 62–3; 66–9)

The image of the singing Cupid-like figure[24] recalls Megra's earlier implication that the page might be serviceable to both sexes; the nature of Bellario's devotion to both Arathusa and Philaster, their passionate feeling for him, and his entanglement in their relationship make the true direction of his sexuality a burning issue.

The text itself provides no explicit clues as to Bellario's real identity; the nearest it comes is in Dion's brief reference in the first scene to his absent daughter away on a 'tedious pilgrimage'. Before he makes an appearance onstage, Bellario is described by Philaster to Arathusa, as 'a boy, / Sent by the gods, an orphan, the trustiest, lovingst, and the gentlest boy' who will act as go-between for them; that Bellario has a significant part to play in the outcome of the narrative is signalled in Philaster's lines to the audience after Bellario's first scene:

> The love of boyes unto their Lordes, is strange;
> I have read wonders of it, yet this boy,
> For my sake (if a man may judge by lookes,
> And speech) would out-doe story.
> (II, i, 57–60)

For readers familar with romance tradition, these references might provide strong hints as to how this text is to be read, and they would expect the mysterious page, like prototypes such as Zelmane in *Arcadia*,[25] to be revealed as a girl in disguise. Stage representation could, of course, strengthen such hints. Theatre-goers who had seen Shakespeare's romantic comedies might recognise the underlying model. To an extent, the feelings of the lovers Philaster and Arathusa for one another are displaced onto the boy. But none the less the audience is denied the full reassurance of the girl-page convention throughout almost the entire action, and at a very late point when Bellario appears 'in a Robe and Garland' playing Hymen for the scaffold wedding of Arathusa and Philaster, a confusingly epicene image could again be invoked. The disclosure is contrived with the greatest theatricality: Megra renews her accusations against Bellario and Arathusa at the eleventh hour, and the King, to settle the question once for all, orders Bellario to be stripped ready for torture. Dion is to the fore in preparing to execute the King's command on the page, punning brutally: 'Come, sir, your tender flesh / Will tire your constancy' (V, v, 83).[26] So it happens naturally that Bellario leads Dion aside to make his disclosure privately. The subdued emotion of father and daughter at this point contrasts strongly with the outbreak of joy moments later when Philaster greets the news with the repeated cry 'It is a woman.' This is a moment which offers complex possibilities for the audience. If Bellario, as in the Q1 text, 'discovers her hair', might not the conventional nature of this gesture of revelation, especially if combined with the theatrical effect of an unrealistically long female wig, function to unsettle the notion of gender stability? The sign of woman is proclaimed the truth, and the truth of Bellario's 'real' sex unravels mysteries and testifies to the further truth of Arathusa's sexual innocence. Yet will not Bellario as 'girl' look and seem much less real than the 'boy' she has so convincingly impersonated throughout the play?

The many parallels between the roles of Bellario and Viola in *Twelfth Night* serve to clarify the differences: Bellario is never revealed to the audience as female until the end, and there is no equivalent for Sebastian. The audience is allowed an ironic perspective on the nature of the relationships between Viola and Orsino and Viola and Olivia which excludes from them the possibilities of homoerotic attraction. Although Olivia has been betrothed both to a maid and man, 'nature to her bias drew in that' and Sebastian is there to provide her with all that Viola cannot. Viola's androgyny is only a role, an improvisation, a provisional expedient; it is not a vision of the ideal or a position at the midpoint of a sexual spectrum. It is part of a joke she shares with the audience: 'a little thing would make me tell them how much I lack of a man', she says in aside when called upon to use the manly qualities she does not possess. But Bellario would have preferred to hide her sex forever; and her skill in playing the part of 'boy' is faultless. The one test she would have failed, performing as lover to Arathusa, she is thought already to have passed, and no one, not even

Arathusa, can imagine that she 'lack[s] of a man' until she is forced against her will to confound the universally accepted fiction of her sexuality with the truth. Unlike *Twelfth Night*, *Philaster* does permit the stability of gender and sexual identity to be held up to question; the way in which the passionate feelings for one another of the lovers Philaster and Arathusa are displaced onto Bellario temporarily entertains the possibility of sexualities which are not gender-specific, and allows for the existence of the erotically stimulating androgyne at the boundary between maleness and femaleness. The stage representation of the page figure may be seen to play deliberately on the audience's expectations of this role, bringing to consciousness the awareness both of the conventions associated with the girl-page, and the conventions according to which an actor's true sex is or is not part of the meaning of his stage role.

In *The Honest Man's Fortune* (1613)[27] the play on the social and sexual conventions of the page role is more self-conscious, though less central to the theatricality of the drama as a whole. The page, symbolically named Veramour ('true love') initially in every action conforms to the Beaumont and Fletcher girl-page stereotype. His devotion to his master is supreme: he begs to be allowed to continue in the service of the good-hearted but prodigal Montague, who can no longer afford to pay his retainers, and like Bellario, he is prepared to shed his own blood on his master's behalf. He idealises Montague, and is in turn extravagantly praised by Montague for his fidelity:

> O what a scoff might men of women make,
> If they did know this boy!
>   (IV, i, Glover and Waller, X, 252)

He is employed by Montague as go-between, and preferred to the household of Lamira, where, in pathetic page style, he entertains the ladies with precocious talk and sings a sad song. The ethos within which these characters operate is that of the elevated heroic virtue which informs the moral scheme of *Arcadia* and has been taken by Danby and others as a prefiguration of the Cavalier mentality.[28] Within *The Honest Man's Fortune* this ethos is evaluated by comparison with another, less stoically and morally refined; and as an extension of this comparison, the page role, which, in the main plot of the play, is an integral element in the aristocratic love–honour nexus, in the subplot, is treated very differently. Juxtaposed against the noble characters in the main plot is an array of low comic and socially inferior types including a money-grubbing citizen and a dissolute upstart courtier, who try to exploit Montague the 'honest man' for their own gains. The courtier, Laverdine, who like the Country Fellow in *Philaster* cannot understand the refined moral code which determines the behaviour of the aristocracy, assumes that Montague's honourable treatment of the

Duchess of Orleans is a cover for an illicit affair, and that Montague's page is therefore a whore in disguise. The association of women's transvestite disguise with prostitution is a common one in this period,[29] though the audience is never invited to share Laverdine's moral perspective; but at the point in the play when the two characters first confront one another, and Laverdine expresses his opinion of Veramour's true sex and identity in asides to the audience, the probability of Veramour's being a disguised girl is strong. The play is half over, and up to this point the page role has been cleverly constructed as the stereotype so as to imply, in terms of the generic conventions of tragicomedy, that a disclosure of transvestism will eventually be made. Laverdine's inference seems to pre-empt this. At the same time Veramour expresses an entirely different conception of the page from that of romance. Openly solicited by Laverdine for sexual favours, he replies:

> Lie with you! I had rather lye with my Ladies Monkey: 'twas never a good world since our French Lords learned of the Neapolitans, to make their Pages their Bedfellows, it doth more hurt to the Suburb Ladies, than twenty dead vacations.
>
> (III, i, Glover and Waller, X, 250)

The androgyne of romance is translated shockingly into the ganymede of satire; Laverdine's response, which concludes the scene, extends the idea of sexual perversity in a literal-minded reading of Veramour's speech:

> I thought so, I know by that 'tis a woman, for because, peradventure she hath made trial of the Monkey, she prefers him before me, as one unknown.

In the next scene Veramour's sexual ambiguity is the subject of bawdy by-play between Veramour and the waiting woman, Charlotte. Charlotte appears to be in love with Montague (though this, of course, turns out to be a pretext, since their social inequality would be a barrier to marriage), and Veramour, observing it, advises his master to 'be a curious avoider of womens company' (IV, i, Glover and Waller, X, 253); Charlotte interprets his possessive attitude towards his master, not according to romance convention as the page's fidelity but rather in terms of comedy or satire as sexual jealousy, and assumes he is a woman in disguise. The dialogue here, with its implied accompaniment of explicit action, creates a moment when stage conventions for representing gender are openly in question:

> *Charlotte.* I do most dangerously suspect this boy to be a wench; art thou not one? come hither, let me feel thee.
> *Veramour.* With all my heart.
> *Charlotte.* Why dost thou pull off thy Glove?
> *Veramour.* Why, to feel whether you be a boy, or no.
> *Charlotte.* Fie, boy, go too. I'll not look your head, nor comb your locks any more, if you talk thus.
>
> (IV, i, Glover and Waller, X, 253)

The audience is forced into recognition of the relationship between the character's 'given' gender within the narrative (Charlotte is a female role) and the true sex of the actor, and to an acknowledgment that gender may be conventionally constructed rather than natural. Veramour continues to tease Laverdine – and the audience – with his ambiguity, even making him a riddling promise, that:

> When you bring it to the test, if there be not one Gentleman in this house will challenge more interest in me than you can, I am at your disposure.
> (IV, i, Glover and Waller, X, 258)

An audience who had seen *Philaster* might well be encouraged by this to expect that Veramour will turn out to be a girl in love with Montague, and the play fulfil the generic demands of romance. But although the long last scene enacts justice and revelation, with the Duke and Duchess of Orleans reconciled and Lamira's three upstart suitors dismissed in favour of Montague, the mood and manner are not unequivocally those of romance. Laverdine is the first of the suitors to be turned away, exposed at length as a vainglorious fool by Montague; so complete is his disgrace that when he asks for a boon and brings in Veramour dressed in women's clothes it may be that the audience will already have realised that his sexual desire for her is self-delusion. He is now alone in his belief that she is a woman, which looks like a naive misreading of theatrical convention. Veramour mockingly confesses to Montague:

> I am a poor disguis'd Lady,
> That like a Page have followed you full long for love god-wot.
> (V, i, Glover and Waller, X, 277)

He tells the Duchess of Orleans that he has adopted boys' clothes in imitation of theatrical fashion:

> I took example by two or three Plays, that methought
> concerned me madame / I took that habit.
> (V, i, Glover and Waller, X, 277)[30]

Finally he is physically searched (again!), and proven male; Laverdine's mistake is subjected to universal ridicule. Laverdine's discovery may recall Morose's in *Epicoene*, where again the revelation that someone who appeared to be female is actually male functions as a reversal of 'the romantic pattern in which the revelation of true gender serves to make marriages possible and happy endings restore social harmony'.[31] But where the transvestite device in *Epicoene*, which is revealed at the very end of the play by the only character who has been party to the deception, implies that it is impossible to tell the difference between the sexes,[32] the effect of the ending of *The Honest Man's Fortune* is not so clear.

The treatment of Veramour's transvestism and Laverdine's involvement with it in this play may be considered in connection with the satire on the theatrical and literary naivety of the Citizen and his wife in *The Knight of the Burning Pestle*;[33] they share Laverdine's unsophisticated attachment to romance and his misreading of dramatic convention. And although it is difficult to know how to interpret the page role in the earlier part of the play before the development of the Laverdine action at the end of Act III, it may be that the audience is at first also encouraged to read it in romance terms. But the text leaves open large gaps where meanings are to be produced through theatrical representation; how the role of Veramour was played by the boy-actor cannot be re-created, but the actor's true male sex must have been projected so as to produce some of these meanings. How does the deliberately created confusion about Veramour's sex work? Does it allow the view that gender may be a matter of convention and social construction? Or does the play's reductive comic ending show that it can always be biologically determined, and anyone who does not accept this is a fool?

Two further plays deal with issues of gender difference. In *The Loyal Subject* (1618) transvestite conventions are inverted through a boy dressed for most of the play as a girl; in *Love's Cure* (?1605) the respective contributions of nature and society to the creation of gender are assessed in a plot centring on transvestite siblings. In *The Loyal Subject* Young Archas, the son of the General Archas, who is the loyal subject to the tyrannical Grand Duke of Moscovia, is disguised as a woman, Alinda, for his own protection at court; his uncle Archas's brother, the author of the device, is himself disguised for the same reason as a humble military captain. The Duke's tyrannical behaviour is the central fact of the play; his irrational desire for vengeance against the General Archas puts the whole family at risk, and necessitates the disguises, which are not formally revealed until the end. The disguised Alinda is attractive not only to the Duke, whose tyranny is, typically, sexual as well as political, but also to his virtuous sister, Olimpia; the triangular pattern, as in *Philaster*, distantly recalls *Twelfth Night*. Alinda's disguise is only one of several intrigue plots in this complexly constructed play, the main focus of which is the Duke's relationship with 'her' father, Archas, but none the less it is distinctively handled. Fletcher avoids the connotations of effeminacy that usually accompany depictions of cross-dressing by men in plays and in other literature of this period,[34] despite the fact that one of Alinda's several roles is functionally equivalent to the girl-page. When she first appears as Alinda in front of Olimpia and her attendants she is characterised as a virgin, mysteriously sorrowful, extremely deferential to Olimpia in whose household she is to serve, capable of singing 'when my griefe will give me leave'. But the commentary of Olimpia's women, who discuss Alinda prior to her entry, distinguishes her as sexually anomalous: her attractiveness is offset by certain masculine characteristics including 'a right good stomach', a strong arm, a dark skin, and 'a manly body'. These hints define a performance style for the actor as well as preparing the audience for the outcome; but at the same time the Duke's mechanically lustful response to his first sight of Alinda ('What handsome wench is that there? ... Is she not wondrous handsome?') is not to be read as sexually confused; Alinda cross-dressed as woman is no equivalent to Bellario cross-dressed as a boy. Her role is neither comic nor pathetic. Her biological masculinity makes her not an inept and imperfect woman but a woman who is better than natural. She is as attractive as any woman, especially to the Duke, but stronger and braver; in the face of attack on Moscovia by the Tartars she surprises Olimpia with her courage: 'How cam'st thou by this spirit? our Sex tremble' (I, iv, 16). She also lacks such female failings as jealousy and small-mindedness, displayed by Olimpia's other waiting women, who fear that her evident superiority will get them demoted from favour. These scenes clearly imply the view that sex difference is natural, and that those qualities which define it, such as courage for men and timidity for women, can never be totally suppressed.

Predictably, Alinda's good looks and devotion endear her to Olimpia, who sighs more than once 'If thou wert a man – '; the two are strongly attracted to one another and they are allowed an emotional scene of parting, when Olimpia makes Alinda leave the court in order to escape seduction by her brother, the Duke. But the more titillating and theatrically ambiguous use of Alinda's disguise may be made in her scenes with the Duke. Here, the confrontation between a sexually aggressive tyrant and a strong-willed and articulate woman eager to preserve her virginity is re-enacted: how significant a part of its meaning is the fact that this 'woman', unlike Celia in *The Humorous Lieutenant* or Evanthe in *A Wife for a Month*, both praised as exemplary of feminine virtue for their fortitude in similar situations, is actually a man? Is Alinda, as spokesman for chastity, to be taken in the same spirit, or does her transvestism function here to undermine the apparent moral message? From the text, it appears that Alinda's real sex is hardly at all in play; she upbraids the Duke for his wanton invitation like a figure from a moral play, reminding him that he owes allegiance to another mistress:

Alinda.   Her name was Beau-desert: Doe you know her now sir?
Duke.   Beau-desert? I not remember –
Alinda.   I know you doe not.
           Yet she has a plainer name; Lord Archas service.

                                                    (III, iii, 58–60)

Perhaps her speech answering the Duke's assertion that he loves her face can be read for the riddling ambiguity with which sex-changed characters refer to their appearance or identity:

> I do not love it my selfe Sir, 'tis a lewd one,
> So truly ill Art cannot mend it; 'sod if 'twere handsome,
> At least if I thought so, you should heare me talke sir
> In a new straine.
>
> (III, iii, 82–5)

On the other hand, Alinda is also playing the role of unsophisticated country girl in a corrupt court, and the assertive modesty of these lines may belong to this role and thus lack transvestite innuendo. In a later scene she returns to the Duke a jewel he has forced her to accept, claiming he has ruined her reputation with Olimpia and denouncing him for lying; where is the focus here? Is it on Alinda as a man in woman's clothes playing – even overplaying – the role of affronted virgin? Does the context leave room for the scene to be read as parody?

A conclusion that resolves the transvestism in conventional fashion is prepared for at the beginning of the last act when Alinda appears in Olimpia's household 'as a young gentleman', in fact as 'her' own brother, and contrives to discover Olimpia's true feelings for her supposed gentlewoman, now apparently lost. The audience is now reassured of a happy outcome for the romantic subplot, so that the full disclosure of Alinda's identity in the last scene can be reserved for a *coup de théâtre* when his timely appearance prevents the destruction of his family, reunites him with his father, and forces the Duke to acknowledge the consequences of tyranny. The final emphasis is not on Archas/Alinda's transvestism, but on the function of the disguise in redeeming both his family and the Duke, and so neatly is this closure constructed that the questions raised earlier by Alinda's role-playing can be by-passed without damage to the final effect of resolution.

Love's Cure, or, The Martial Maid, however, addresses itself to issues of gender difference more directly. It has been suggested that the play was written as a direct, and conservative, response to 'the transvestite challenge',[35] although this position is complicated by difficulties over the dating of the play. The main plot concerns a brother and a sister, Lucio and Clara, who have been brought up separately and in the clothes and identity of the opposite sex; they are now mature and must resume their true identities. The action derives from their struggles to do so; in particular, from the difficulties both encounter in casting off the sexual roles to which they have become accustomed. The text leaves no doubt that gender is biologically determined and that sexuality is properly and naturally polarised. Lucio's feminine and Clara's masculine behaviour is perverse and inappropriate; in order to return to their true selves they must rid themselves of the accretions of custom, which is constantly regarded in the gender debates of this period as the opposite of nature.[36] As the witty servant Bobadilla tells mannish Clara, 'Custome hath turn'd nature topsle-turvy in you' (II, ii, 96). In I,iii the long separated family is reunited; Alvarez the father has been fighting for Spain in the Netherlands, assisted by a young man whom all assume to be his valiant son but is actually his daughter, while the real son has been brought up by his mother disguised as a girl at the household in Seville. The parents, confronted with cross-dressed offspring, a belligerent fighting daughter and a timid son who hides from the sight of a sword, recognise that they must act promptly:

> Now our mutuall care must be
> Imploy'd to help wrong'd nature, to recover
> Her right in either of them, lost by custom.
> (I, iii, 176–8)

It is assumed that the distinctive qualities proper to each sex will not need to be learnt; Lucio and Clara have only to abandon their acquired gender roles as they cast off the clothing of the opposite sex and 'wrong'd nature' will automatically reclaim them. Lucio is urged by his mother, Eugenia, 'Change those qualities thou didst learn from me / For masculine virtues, for which seek no tutor' (I, iii, 80). But Eugenia is mistaken about the ease with which Lucio and his sister can expect to return to 'normal'; and the reluctance of both to change the clothes and the behaviour that accompanies them is rendered in broadly comic terms in II,ii, where they first appear in sexually appropriate dress. But although each complains of the unfamiliar clothing in the same terms – that it is restrictive – the implication is that the differentiations of fashion are justifiable and not merely conventional. Lucio needs boots, spurs, and a sword because he must be ready to fight and act aggressively as required of 'the young Cavalier, Don Lucio, Sonne and heir to Alvarez'. Clara must be 'limited, confin'd, hoop'd in' by a farthingale to control her sex's inherent wantonness: 'women's hanches onely are most subject to display and fly out' (II, ii, 72). Equally, she does not need to carry weapons. As Bobadilla, who is the play's low-comic truth teller, says:

> What have you to doe with Armors, and Pistols, and Javelins, and swords, and such tooles? remember Mistresse: nature hath given you a sheath onely, to signifie women are to put up mens weapons, not to draw them.
> (II, ii, 87–9)

It is nature, and not just custom, that requires Clara to learn sewing and Lucio fighting, but they overcome their repugnance for these sex-stereotyped activities only when they fall in love and natural instinct at last asserts itself incontrovertibly. A process of transformation is charted in Clara, the more fully rendered of the siblings, whereby she at first admires Vitelli, her father's enemy, for his valour and swordsmanship, but then finds her feeling changing from comradeship to love, and from a sense of equality to one of submission. When he asks her for a favour she gives him her sword, a richly symbolic gesture betokening a promise of her virginity as well as of sexual conformity.

Male and female transvestism are differently treated in the play. At few points are they equally monstrous. Lucio's effeminacy is primarily comic; he is a parody of the shy young girl, obsessed with needlework and housekeeping, primly horrified by Bobadilla's lewd punning. He is hopeless as a swordsman and is humiliatingly shown up by his sister. Clara, on the other hand, belongs to the tradition of the woman-warrior[37] in terms of which her adoption of a male role can be read as positive and admirable. The play even opens with a narrative account of her heroism at the siege of Ostend, when in male disguise she rescued the general's son in battle thus winning a royal pardon for her father, who had committed a murder. At her first appearance on stage, in man's attire, she is beautiful, like a woman, but also dignified, and brave; as her mother says she is 'more then woman' whereas her cross-dressed brother 'transform'd by his soft life, is lesse then man'. Her depiction alternates to some extent between martial maid and hoydenish Hic Mulier, though the latter image is marginalised in minor scenes while the former is integrated into the play's larger narrative of the blood-feud between the house of Alvarez and that of his rival, Vitelli. Clara's achievement of womanliness is defined through her relationship with Vitelli, who has an attachment to a whore, Malroda, which he must break off. The play does not demand any sympathy for Malroda, since she is in turn deceiving Vitelli with another lover; and thus her claim that prostitutes are created and ruined by their clients ('having made me unfit / For any man, you leave me fit for all') need not be taken seriously.[38] The focus is more on Vitelli's dilemma as the helpless victim of woman at her most treacherous through the strength of sexual desire, and Clara not only remains faithful to him despite being aware of his deception of her with Malroda but also intervenes with her sword to save his life when Malroda sets him up for a surprise attack. The honourable Clara is sexually contrasted with the treacherous whore; Clara is the idealised true lover like Beatrice in *The Dutch Courtesan*, and although she has to promise Vitelli that she will 'abjure all actions of a man' before he will commit himself to marry her, yet her manliness has had an essential role to play both in winning his love and preserving his life.

Where effeminacy is weakness and deficiency, manliness is strength and surplusage. Yet the play does not confirm sexual stereotypes and traditional evaluations of gender roles unequivocally. The validity of the masculine code of honour which governs Alvarez and Vitelli's conduct of their blood-feud is questioned in several ways. The low-life characters throughout the play represent an alternative set of values, in particular preferring self-interest before honour; and their comic cowardliness in IV, iii, the scene where Lucio's dormant valour first begins to wake, helps undermine the notion of manhood taken seriously in the feud. Lucio himself, whose defective masculinity seems at first to reaffirm the value of the ideal, is used to offer a critique of it.[39] At the beginning of IV,iii Alvarez is so disgusted by his son's inability to conform to an acceptable standard of masculinity that he orders Lucio to take a test of manhood by attacking the next man that he meets and raping the next woman. Lucio does manage to carry out the first command when his father is attacked by Vitelli's followers, and his natural sense of filial duty overcomes his habit of timidity. But when in the next scene he encounters Vitelli's sister, Genevora, and is thus presented with an ideal opportunity to fulfil the rest of his father's order, he fails to do so. Genevora is surprised, but also delighted, when Lucio is too innocent to understand that a sexual encounter might go beyond a mere kiss, which is all Lucio asks. Lucio in soliloquy affirms the return of his natural male instincts:

> My womanish soul, which hitherto hath governd
> This coward flesh, I feele departing from me;
> And in me by her beauty is inspir'd
> A new, and masculine one: instructing me
> What's fit to doe or suffer.
>
> (IV, iv, 53–7)

Thus the equation Alvarez would make between manliness and violence is cancelled out; Lucio follows up his own notion of a masculine soul's instructions by defeating a rival, who is, of course, a supporter of Vitelli, and then sparing his life. In the play's final scene Alvarez and Vitelli meet in confrontation determined to settle the feud in a concluding bloodbath, but the women, by threatening to commit suicide, eventually prevail upon them to be reconciled, thus convincing the men of the reflexively destructive nature of their code of honour. The language of Genevora's threat implies the sword/phallus parallel of Bobadilla's speech, which is used throughout the play:

> The first blow given betwixt you, sheathes these swords
> In one anothers busomes.
>
> (V, iii, 177–8)

Although, as Dollimore says, *Love's Cure* represents a 'theatrical containment of the transvestite challenge'[40] in which social roles are seen as contingent on biological gender and thus inherently determined, the play does provide a critique of an influential concept of masculinity and a validation of the contribution of womanliness to the social order.

Masculine women are less sympathetically treated in two other plays, *The Sea Voyage* (*c.* 1625) and *The Double Marriage* (?1621), where there is no effeminate man to offset them.[41] In both plays, as in *Love's Cure*, the woman's masculinity is a response to anomalous circumstances in which the normal social order has been set aside; it is an aberration in need of correction. In *Love's Cure* and *The Sea Voyage*, which are comedies, a resolution whereby the women are happily restored to their 'natural' conditions of femininity is achieved, but in *The Double Marriage*, a tragedy, Martia's unnaturalness, filial as well as sexual, brings about her death. In *The Sea Voyage* the women have formed their own commonwealth on the remote island where they have been shipwrecked, and organise it on Amazonian principles. They occupy themselves in hunting, and their strict leader, Rosellia, permits them limited access to men only for procreation. Their situation, like that of the transvestite siblings, is explored in terms of the conflict between the demands of society and the promptings of natural instinct. The women's commonwealth, which constitutes their society, has not been proposed in any spirit of feminist experimentation, but as an unfortunate necessity. As soon as the women are introduced, which is not until halfway through Act II, for their plot-line is only one of several, it is made clear that Rosellia has forced them into Amazonian ways in which none of them privately believes.[42] Hippolyta, Crocale, and Juletta, who enter 'armed with bows and quivers' gloomily discuss the deprivations of a single-sex celibate life, which they think can be attractive only to the woman who is too old to 'feel the want of that which young maids long for' (Rosellia) or else, like Rosellia's daughter, Clarinda, is too young to remember men. Crocale subverts the commonplace of pastoral innocence and security from 'lustful men' by her acknowledgment of the primacy of heterosexual desire: 'We must and will have men.' Women are incomplete without men, and such desire is instinctive and universal. Crocale is wrong in believing Clarinda exempt, because as soon as she sees the shipwrecked Albert lying unconscious, his wounds bound up by a woman's hair, she acknowledges that a 'fury / For which my ignorance does not know a name, / Is crept into my bosom' (II, i, Glover and Waller, IX, 23). Crocale, who can interpret the signs, remarks:

> I see, that by instinct,
> Though a young Maid hath never seen a Man
> Touches have titillations, and inform her.
> (II, i, Glover and Waller, IX, 24)

The sexual nature is inherent, not acquired. Clarinda does not need to have seen a man or received any education or social training to display, fully developed, one of the most commonly accepted features of the female stereotype: jealousy. The knowing tone of Crocale's lines colours Rosellia's first appearance, which follows immediately. The entry is broadly comic, at the expense of women. As Clarinda in parody of the eager virgin bends to kiss Albert, her mother bursts in:

> Child of my flesh,
> And not of my fair unspotted mind,

Vn-hand this monster.
(II, i, Glover and Waller, IX, 24)

The potentially subversive aspects of Rosellia's ensuing attack on men for their sexual tyranny are largely defused by Fletcher's construction of her as comic harridan.[43] The lines in another context could articulate straight out the bitter irony of sexual power relations, but here their surface message is undermined by the politics of the representation of women in this scene:

> The Soveraignty
> Proud and imperious men usurp upon us,
> We conferr on our selves, and love those fetters
> We fasten to our freedomes.
> (II, i, Glover and Waller, IX, 24)

It transpires eventually that Sebastian, who is introduced early in the play as an ageing nobleman displanted from his home by the French, has lost his wife and daughter in a shipwreck, and has long lived miserably on the island, is in fact her husband, and the play ends with their reunion and forgiveness of their enemies.

Satire on the sort of feminism represented by the Amazons is one mode by which the play represents sexuality and gender; a further set of meanings is created by the use of *The Tempest* as a model, not only for the situation of the exiles from civilisation cast away on a primitive island, but also for the exploration of instinctive sexuality. But the effect of this subtext on *The Sea Voyage* is limiting rather than liberating: Rosellia, like Prospero, wants vengeance on those enemies who have wronged her and her child; but since they have not, as she believes, killed her husband, and the audience knows him to be already available on the island and only waiting in the wings for the comic resolution, her speeches about the nobility of revenge are empty rhetoric. Clarinda's role echoes Miranda's, though she is more of a Camilla-like virgin huntress[44] than a tremulous adolescent. But her involvement with Albert, the captain of the shipwrecked Frenchmen, and jealousy of Aminta, whom she does not know to be Albert's betrothed, eroticises her innocence and also renders it comic. The intrigue situation which arises because Albert and Aminta have to dissemble their feelings for self-protection demonstrates that, although Clarinda may have been brought up on a remote island, her attitudes and values, which are entirely defined in terms of sexuality, are just the same as every other woman's; *The Tempest*'s complex assessment of the relationship between culture and nature is entirely absent.

The exploration of sexuality is ultimately a side-issue in this play; and the subject of women's power is either mocked, in the failed Amazons, or else evaded. How is it that Rosellia and her women have taken control of the island, and cope much more capably with their inhospitable environment than the men? By contrast with the French sailors squabbling over scraps of disgusting food and contemplating cannibalism, they are obviously far more civilised, and their community, if not ideal, is at least established. But these are questions the play does not face.

In *The Double Marriage* the idea of feminine forms of power is explored through the antitheses in the two women involved in the double marriage. Juliana, the true wife of Virolet, is strong in the tradition of the virgin martyr;[45] the first scene of the play is modelled on *Julius Caesar*, and Juliana, like Portia, has to educate her husband to believe in female virtue. Virolet at first wishes to exclude his wife totally from the conspiracy he is planning against the tyrant Ferrand because it is a 'design of weight, too heavy for her knowledge'; but when she declares she would prefer him to die valiantly to free his country than continue to live under the tyrant's rule he is so impressed with her integrity that he reveals the plan:

> Oh, more than woman!
> And more to be belov'd . . .
> Such a Masculine spirit,
> With more than Woman's virtues, were a Dower
> To weigh down a King's fortune.
> (I, i, Glover and Waller, VI, 326–7)

This manliness in a woman is admirable, like the continence of Ordella or Evanthe, because although it overgoes what is naturally womanly it supports rather than challenges male prerogatives, and a male-centred concept of virtue, defined in relation to the etymology of Virolet's name. The name suggests not just virility, manliness,[46] but *virtus* in the classical sense of a public, civic virtue devoted to the well-being of the state. Though the religious ethos of the play is drawn from Christian as well as classical concepts, in the first part a classical moral scheme is suggested by numerous references to classical prototypes of vice and virtue as well as by the *Julius Caesar* parallels. Public good, and by analogy, reason, and manliness, are prioritised over private interests, passion, and the feminine. Juliana transcends her sex in her readiness to set the good of the state above domestic happiness, and in her ability to suppress 'weak Womens fear' (V, i). When she is captured and tortured by the tyrant, she endures torment on the rack, which is depicted onstage. She endures so stoically – 'more than a woman, beyond flesh and blood' – that Ferrand, honouring her 'invincible fortitude', lets her go; but the torture has permanently disabled her and deprived her of the ability to bear children. Her physical infirmity in the Christianised second half of the play turns her into an idealised female hero, where her ruined body becomes the symbol of her womanly constancy, bearing her sufferings in patience.[47] Her virtues qualify her for a place in history, as 'a new Martyr heaven has begot, to fill the times with truth' (III,

iii, Glover and Waller, VI, 367). The Griselda model, not a common image for female virtue in the Beaumont and Fletcher plays, is implicitly present, especially when Virolet announces his intention of casting her off to take a second wife; it is his father Pandulpho who gives voice to the indignation Juliana does not admit. She dutifully submits to her husband's decision:

> Farewell, Sir, like obedience, thus I leave you,
> My long farewell: I do not grudge, I grive Sir;
> And if that be offensive, I can dye,
> And then you are fairly free.
> (III, i, Glover and Waller, VI, 372)

The second wife, Martia, in contrast, is an Amazonian woman, who has spent all her life at sea with her father, the exiled Duke of Sesse, turned pirate. As in *The Sea Voyage*, *The Tempest* is a sub-text for part of the play to account for Martia's unnatural upbringing, and to motivate her father's longing for revenge on Ferrand, though the nature/culture theme is implicit rather than openly addressed. She is initially a glamorous figure, a kind of superwoman, admired by the sailors as 'the Image of the warlike Goddess' with 'manly soul' contained in 'a body made so delicate / So soft for sweet embraces' (II, i, Glover and Waller, VI, 337). But when she falls in love with Virolet, deserts her father, and in return for saving his life demands he marry her, she is revealed as evil and manipulative, the strong woman who abuses her power and has to be eliminated. Her father, stung by her treachery, vows to pursue and kill her; and she becomes an unprincipled virago whose admiration for Virolet's 'manly mind' is really only lust, which turns to hatred when he refuses to consummate their marriage. She then tries to forge a women's pact against Virolet with Juliana. In Act IV woman as wife and whore confront one another, but Juliana will not collude in revenge against Virolet, or even acknowledge that he has wronged her; Martia sees in this submissiveness an enabling condition for masculine sexual tyranny:

> This foolish dotage in soft-hearted women
> Makes proud men insolent.
> (IV, iii, Glover and Waller, VI, 371)

But Juliana's feeling for Virolet is devotion and not dotage, and while Martia is progressively demonised, so Juliana emerges more clearly as 'The best of women / Of wives the perfectest ... Sweeter in thy obedience than a Sacrifice' (III, i). As with Rosellia, it is a woman whose womanliness is compromised and inauthentic who puts forth feminist views. Sexual tyranny is exercised by Martia rather than Virolet, and the play offers an analogy between her role and Ferrand's. As Naples must be freed from the oppression of Ferrand's unjust rule, so manliness (particularly Virolet, but also Martia's father) must rid itself of the monstrousness of so unnatural a woman. At the end of the play she has become Ferrand's mistress, allying herself with his tyranny and against her father who is now the leader of a rebellion; the citizens' repeated demand for 'liberty, liberty, liberty' (V,i) requires to be met by her death as well as Ferrand's. Her father waits until he has killed Ferrand before proceeding to the completion of his revenge by killing Martia, 'a scene which I would not act alone'. But in the end he is saved from the blood-guilt of filicide by the Boatswain, who carries out the killing on his behalf.

Martia's Amazonianism is not comic like Rosellia's, but emblematic of the destructiveness of female sexuality when it usurps masculine power. In Juliana is depicted a female power which is called masculine because of its unusual strength but is always directed to the support and promotion of masculine ideals and is therefore non-threatening to the accepted hierarchy of male–female relations. It is a power achieved through moral qualities such as loyalty to the ideal of political freedom and fortitude under duress; its exclusion from sexuality is suggested by the physical disabilities including infertility resulting from torture. The distinctively female image of power which finally emerges is a negative one: that of the suffering saint and heroic martyr. Martia's beauty belies her femininity, betokening not her 'sexes softness' (Virolet, II, i, Glover and Waller, VI, 349) but ruthlessness and cruelty. Her first appearance to Virolet, when he falls in love with her, is signalled by *Tempest*-like 'strange Musick within, Hoboys' which suggests something eerie and supernatural; Virolet recognises the theatricality of the moment in his brief admiring comment on Martia: 'The face o' th' Maske is alter'd' (II, i, Glover and Waller, VI, 348). Throughout the play theatrical references suggest the meretricious and warn of the deceptions of appearance;[48] Martia's enchantment temporarily emasculates Virolet, who feels himself 'a man again' (IV, i, Glover and Waller, VI, 385) only when he is rid of her. She is an ambiguous figure, a 'glorious whore' (IV, i, Glover and Waller, VI, 387) like Vittoria Corombona, whose bold spirit continues to arouse the admiration of her father's sailors even while they realise she must be destroyed. These ambiguities result in some contradictions. Virolet sees himself in his double marriage as the victim of a genuine dilemma of honour, bound by conflicting but equally strong moral ties to both women (III, i, Glover and Waller, VI, 371); Ronvere, the tyrant's tool-villain, envies him for being 'belov'd and sought to, / By two incomparable women' (IV, i, Glover and Waller, VI, 380). But Martia's status as virago and whore cancels out the validity of this dilemma, and complicates the play's view of Virolet as an honourable man tragically ruined by conflicting loyalties. In the soliloquy in Act IV which he begins, in the conventional posture of the troubled hero, by reading from a book, he laments the unfairness of having to suffer for committing an honourable act; the marriage to Martia is to be seen as a political requirement, for the sake of his country:

Why am I touched thus,
Having perform'd the great redemption
Both of my friends and family? fairly done it?
Without base and lascivious ends.
(IV, i, Glover and Waller, VI, 381)

The earlier scene representing his and Martia's mutual sexual attraction is now discounted, and Martia's glamour forgotten. As Shepherd says, the 'real centre of interest' in this play is manliness[49] and the issues of women's power are subordinated to it. The images of the female saint and the Amazonian virago are manipulated to show that women's power for good is spiritual and not social; and 'masculine spirit' in women is allowable only if it serves to reinforce masculine dominance, not to challenge it.

Chapter 3
Misogyny and Manhood

Beaumont and Fletcher's dramatic representation of sexual relations and issues of sexual identity is concerned in various ways with the depiction of misogyny. Linda Woodbridge, in *Women and the English Renaissance*, has identified the stage misogynist as a conventional type, commonly presented as a comic figure with a bias which stands in need of correction or reform. Some versions of this type may appear sympathetic and attractive, like Benedick in *Much Ado about Nothing*, others as repulsive and unbalanced. At the end of the play the former may be reformed and socially integrated, where the latter can only be subjected to punishment or public humiliation. The misogynist was a figure with a comparatively long stage history by the time Beaumont and Fletcher began their careers, and although he appears in two early collaborations, *The Woman Hater* (*c.* 1606) and *The Captain* (*c.* 1609–12), the type as such seems to have had no particular lasting appeal for them, perhaps because by this time it had begun to appear 'clichéd and tedious'.[1] But even if the type itself had outlived its usefulness, which may be debatable in view of the interest in the Swetnam controversy,[2] this is by no means to say that misogyny as a discourse about sexual relations was in recession. Valerie Wayne[3] remarks that an effect of the tendency of Renaissance texts to identify misogyny in a specific individual is to present it as a residual ideology, which can be dismissed when this particular character is reformed or defeated; and in fact this presentation is deceptive, because there existed a variety of means, including the debate about women itself, by which 'misogyny was fully sustained in the culture ... the ideology of marriage that valorised chastity as yet another means of containing women's desire was its complement, not its opposite.' These suggestions, made in relation to *Othello*, are particularly apt for a number of Beaumont and Fletcher texts.

Misogyny features prominently in various forms in their representations of sexual relations both in terms of male characters who hold or are concerned with misogynistic attitudes, and of female characters who embody the syndrome of characteristics commonly attributed to women by misogynists; the representations of soldiers, and the evaluation of military life and values in contradistinction to the domestic allow for the exploration of misogynistic attitudes, and so too does the depiction of women as tyrannical and/or lustful. It is also possible to read as implicitly misogynistic certain plays which appear to represent sexual relations, particularly the sex-war, from a perspective sympathetic to women, but where this representation may be deconstructed so as to reveal the male-centred subjectivity from which it derives. *The Woman's Prize* (*c.* 1611?)[4] and *The Scornful Lady* (*c.* 1613?) are two such plays. Representations of manhood can be relevantly examined in this connection: not manhood in the most general sense of manliness but rather manhood as it is constituted and defined in relation to the feminine. This definition is explored in the Beaumont and Fletcher plays in two specific areas of human activity. One of these, marriage, will be examined elsewhere; the other is the relationship between military and civil, more specifically domestic, life, which has already been mentioned as an integral aspect of the subject of misogyny. The plays to be discussed include one which contains more of Beaumont's work (*The Woman Hater*), several which are regarded as being entirely the work of Fletcher (*The Captain, The Woman's Prize, Bonduca*), and others which are the products of various kinds of collaboration (*Cupid's Revenge, The Scornful Lady, Thierry and Theodoret*); this may be of interest in relation to the whole question whether there are differences in the treatment of women and sexual relations between the two playwrights.[5]

The Woman Hater, which Finkelpearl, whether or not intentionally disregarding *Love's Cure*, calls 'the earliest surviving play in the Beaumont and Fletcher canon',[6] probably written in 1606, is largely Beaumont's, though recent critics find increasing evidence of contributions from Fletcher.[7] It is a self-conscious, sophisticated, witty play with the same keen sense for the topical and the fashionable as *The Knight of the Burning Pestle*, written the next year. The misogyny of Gondarino, the title-character, is 'placed' as a humour, when he soliloquises about the revulsion that women arouse in him, and regarded as absurd and unbalanced by Oriana, who makes it her mission to restore him to nature by a kind of negative aversion therapy:

> I must not leave this fellow, I will torment him to madness,
> To teach his passions against kind to move,
> The more he hates, the more Ile seeme to love.
>
> (II, i, 396)

She will counter his excess with one of her own, displaying the triumph of female wit over male unreason. But his is a deep-seated passion, not merely a fashionable pose, originating as a reaction to his late wife's infidelity, and it drives him beyond virulent anti-feminist outbursts to malicious counterplotting in order to destroy Oriana's reputation in the eyes of the Duke who wishes to marry her. In fact the situation is so developed that it is Oriana's chastity and resolution that must stand trial rather than Gondarino's perversity, and in the second half of the play the dramatic interest is deflected from the misogynist to the woman he has slandered. But the Duke and his courtiers do not recognise Gondarino as a misogynist, believing his expressions of dislike for women to be merely a pose which will provoke women's legendary curiosity and enable him the better to get access to them:

> [he] seemes not to endure
> To see, or to be seene of any woman,
> Onely, because he knowes it is their nature
> To wish to taste that which is most forbidden:
> And with this show, he may the better compasse
> (And with farre less suspition) his base endes.
> (II, i, 111–16)

This interpretation of Gondarino's behaviour is itself based on misogynist assumptions which encourage the Duke to pay far more credence to Gondarino's slandering of Oriana than would otherwise seem reasonable. As part of her 'cure' of Gondarino Oriana pretends to attempt to seduce him; and he is able to incorporate this ploy into his own plan for discrediting her with the Duke by convincing the Duke that she really is a wanton.

But the sexual politics of this play are more complex than may initially appear. The Duke is satirically 'placed' in the opening scene as a ruler who likes to keep his entourage guessing as to why he rises at dawn.

> I think your grace
> Intendes to walke the publique streetes disguised
> To see the streetes disorders

suggests Lucio, offering the audience a hint that this is perhaps to be another 'disguised duke' play.[8] But this Duke is self-consciously rejecting conventional stage models; instead of being 'a patterne for all Princes, / That breake my softe sleepe for my subjects good' (I, i, 16–17) he has risen at dawn in order to court a woman. (This scene is one of several where *Measure for Measure* is invoked as a subtext.) Oriana's brother, Count Valore, is also a role-player; at one moment he is conventionally warning her against the corruptions of court life, the next describing in soliloquy how pleasant it is to be recognised as a courtier at the playhouse. Neither character is accorded a fixed moral identity. But Oriana's selfhood is also problematised. In the scene where she pretends to tempt Gondarino she enacts seduction as role-playing; in an opening invocation to Venus she entreats:

> Whether he will soonest bee moov'd with wantonnesse,
>   singing, daunceing, or beeing passionate, with scorne, or with
> sad and serious lookes, cunningly mingled with sighes, with

smiling, lisping, kissing the hand, and making short cursies;
or with whatsoever other nimble power, he may bee caught,
doe thou infuse into mee.

(III, i, 21–6)

The scene is short but has considerable erotic potential. Oriana blazons her own beauty and the 'Chimmick power' of women to arouse men to Petrarchan adoration; she wooes Gondarino as one who 'has all the organs that belong to a man, / And working to' to enact his manhood. At the same time, of course, she switches into satiric mode in short asides. Oriana is apparently the one in control of the action here, ridiculing her antagonist with an eloquence and flexibility he cannot counter, and directing all the comedy of the scene against him. Yet may not her success be seen to undermine itself? She represents woman as Gondarino fears her: lustful, loquacious, irrepressible; she implicitly validates masculine sexual anxiety.

Gondarino's success in causing not only the Duke but Oriana's brother himself to doubt her chastity is self-evidently due not to the skill of his plotting but to the underlying distrust of women shared by all the male characters, and perhaps endorsed by the representation of femininity as role-play, which makes such a charge plausible. So great is the anxiety Gondarino's charges have aroused in Oriana's menfolk that they are prepared to expose her to a public trial of chastity at his behest:

If you hope to trie her truly, and satisfie your selfe what
frailtie is, give her the Test: do not remember Count shee is
your Sister; nor let my Lorde the Duke beleeve shee is faire;
but put her too't without hope or pitie.

(v, ii, 49–52)

The trial is held in the final scene when, before a concealed audience of the Duke, the Count, and Gondarino, Arrigo, one of the Duke's followers, threatens Oriana with death unless she agrees to sleep with him; she refuses, and thus Gondarino's assumptions about the universal weakness and sensuality of women are publicly disproved; yet he is not converted. The Duke and the Count are greatly relieved by her display of moral strength, and congratulate her on her chastity; the Duke rewards her with an offer of marriage. But still Gondarino cannot suppress his misogynist predictions:

Duke, thou has sold away thy selfe to all perdition; thou art
this present houre becomming cuckold.

(v, iv, 96)

In the closing moments of the play, and at the point of affirmation that the heroine's chastity may co-exist with her wit, such a defiant resistance to correction is absurd but also frightening in its capacity to survive. The punishment devised by Oriana, whereby Gondarino is forced to sit still and be subjected publicly to the fondling and caressing of court ladies, demonstrates and reinforces his horror of women and sexuality, not only displaying, but also justifying misogyny. The final touch is provided by the appearance of the old deaf country gentlewoman who, impervious to his abhorrence of her, has previously begged Gondarino at length to present a petition at court on her behalf; her renewed solicitations of him provoke even Oriana to pity his misery, and he is allowed to leave for some unspecified destination where no woman will ever appear. Despite the fact that, as McLuskie says, the play may be taken as dramatising 'the theatrical triumph of witty women over misogynist men, an artistic preference for Beatrice over Griselda',[9] the extent of Oriana's triumph is a limited one; alongside this optimistically feminist account of sexual politics co-exists a more conventional and conservative one, according to which Oriana must make a public display of her virtue to an audience of male adjudicators before it can be accepted, and the importunings of a sexually unattractive woman are worse punishment than a liar and slanderer deserves.

The other play in which a misogynist is a central character is *The Captain*; this is largely Fletcher's work,[10] and has neither the self-consciousness nor the generic security of *The Woman Hater*. The writer of the Prologue draws attention to it as a generic anomaly:

> This is nor *Comody*, nor *Tragedy*,
> Nor *History*, nor any thing that may
> (Yet in a weeke) be made a perfect Play.
> (*Works*, I, 551)

This uncertainty stems in part from the play's treatment of sexuality; not only is Jacamo, the title character, less evidently signalled as a stage misogynist than Gondarino, but the main female character, Lelia, is, like Franceschina in *The Dutch Courtesan* with whom she has much in common, a successful prostitute who attempts in a notorious scene to seduce her own father. In both cases, attributes of comic characterisation are offset by others of a very different nature. Jacamo is a soldier[11] with a strong and seriously expressed sense of the irrelevance of his abilities and experiences to peacetime life; he is aware of his own status as an outsider:

> *Fabritio.*   Captain Jacamo,
>   Why should you thinke so hardly of your vertues?
> *Jacamo.*   What vertues? by this light I have no vertue,
>   But downe right buffeting: what can my face
>   That is no better then a ragged Map now
>   Of where I have marcht and traveled profit me?
>   Unlesse it be for Ladyes to abuse, and say
>   'Twas spoil'd for want of a Bongrace when I was young.
>   (II, i, 84–90)

The life of a soldier disables him for anything else. Jacamo imagines that his friend Fabritio, who is the more socially flexible of the two, might in peacetime please an 'honourable' master to the extent of becoming 'Clarke a'th Kitchen' and marrying a ladies' maid after she has lost her virginity, but cannot foresee himself rising to any profession higher than that of 'a forlorne Tapster, or some frothy fellow, / That stincks of stale beere'. His lack of civilian finesse – he presents himself as barely literate – is not a simple matter of deficiency, as opposed to the sufficiency of peacetime; rather he perceives peace itself as a 'cold dull misty' time of low energy when masculine virtue cannot shine or flourish. He wishes he had been born female to suit the time's effeminacy 'to sit still and sing, / Or be sicke when I list, or any thing / That is too idle for a man to thinke of (II, i, 12). This identification of war with the masculine and peace with the feminine consistently privileges war and maleness; according to this homology Jacomo's state of mind is commendably manly, especially by comparison with the sneering effeminacy of the gossiping gentlemen, Lodowick and Piso, who mock him for roughness and lack of sophistication. Significantly, Jacomo wishes that he had been a whore, the female type most suited to the ease and licence of peacetime, and his vision is embodied in Lelia, whose depravity legitimates Jacomo's attitude to the female. Yet this evaluation of masculinity co-exists uneasily with another, whereby Jacomo's misogyny is defined as the boorishness of a man who fears rejection by women and needs to forestall its possibility. This alternative account of misogyny lends itself much more readily to comic action than does the first; thus Jacomo appears in several scenes in which he behaves ineptly in women's company and gets rumbustiously drunk in a tavern, where, his sexual inhibitions temporarily set aside, he kisses male and female companions indiscriminately. Frank, the marriageable young gentlewoman who loves him despite the mockery of her friends at so irregular a choice, continues in her affection although he refuses to entertain it and embarrasses her in public. Eventually her persistence wins out, and his misogyny is revealed as a lack of confidence in himself for which Frank's devotion will compensate:

And I did not thinke it possible any woman
Could have lik'd this face, it's good for nothing, is't?
(V, iv, 81–2)

With such self-effacing utterances Jacomo promises to reform, to 'have my head curld, and powderd' to suit himself for his new role of lover. But the taming of Jacomo has not been easily achieved; before it can come about he must be humiliated by having a pot of piss poured on his head and being tied down in a chair so that he cannot escape listening to Frank's declaration of love. The punishment recalls Gondarino's forced exposure to women's caresses, but with the difference that it appears to achieve

Jacomo's socialisation; his marriage to Frank is one of three celebrated in the play's last scene.

The contradictions between the two accounts of misogyny, however, are not effaced, but rather exposed, by the play's conclusion. The identification of marriage with social harmony is questioned by the arbitrariness of the second wedding, between Julio, hitherto a client of Lelia, and Clora, Frank's friend; this is pointed out by Angelo, Julio's friend, in an isolated moment of Fletcher's own dramatic self-consciousness:

> If a marriage should be thus slubberd up in a play, e're almost
> any body had taken notice you were in love, the Spectators
> would take it to be but ridiculous.
>
> (V, v, 32–4)

After the weddings Frank's brother Frederick appears to announce joyfully that war will shortly break out, and Jacomo's command is to be restored. He calls at once for wine to celebrate. The conventional comic ending of the gallant's reform and marriage is subverted; the changed situation requires his unreformed self once more, and wives, notoriously, are no part of a soldier's life.[12]

The third wedding is between Lelia and Piso, one of the cowardly gentlemen who mocks Jacomo's style of manliness; the conduct of the Lelia plot, which is equal in importance to the Jacomo plot, also focuses disturbingly on some aspects of the place of sexuality in society. Lelia as prostitute is a kind of parallel to Jacomo, and she is also the kind of woman he most despises. She prosecutes her desires, which are sexual, as aggressively as he maintains his adherence to military values, and in the play's terms her aggression is not merely anti-social but also depraved and threatening. She is even more dangerous because she is not depicted, as lustful women regularly are, as physically disgusting, but on the contrary as irresistibly beautiful. Like the Bower of Bliss in *The Faerie Queene* she embodies a corruption which is genuinely tempting. To Julio she is theoretically as deadly as the plague but actually:

>   As a Rose at fairest,
> Neither a bud, nor blown, but such a one,
> Were here a *Herculaes* to get againe
> With all his glory, or one more then he,
> The god would choose out mongst a race of women
> To make a mother of; she is outwardly
> All that bewitches sense; all that entises,
> Nor is it in our vertue to uncharme it.
>
> (III, i, 23–30)

She is much more powerful than the men who desire her and so they cannot be blamed for succumbing to her almost supernatural charm; the music of her voice has Orpheus-like power to enrapture her listeners (III, i, 31-40). Yet, like Jacomo, she must be tamed, but without the ambivalence that exists in relation to Jacomo's taming. A comparison between *The Captain* and *The Dutch Courtesan* illuminates how their different emphases in the treatment of prostitution can none the less lead to a similar moral outcome.

Marston's prostitute is a foreign woman whose comically accented speech underlines her status as a social outsider; by class and profession she is excluded from serious consideration as a human subject by the gentlemen she services, although she does not recognise this and has to be subjected to humiliation and treated as a criminal when her revengeful plotting against her unfaithful lover's mistress fails. Lelia is not excluded from human subjectivity as comic, but rather because she is so depraved, as shown in the notorious scene where she attempts to seduce her own father in the face of his passionate efforts to convert her to a recognition of her wickedness.[13] Incest is clearly invoked as the acme of sexual licence, as desire that is so dangerous because it recognises no limit or social control. But Lelia refuses to acknowledge her desires as sinful, and has to be forcibly dragged away, biting and screaming, to punishment. This is both physical and spiritual; she will be kept in largely solitary confinement and 'heare of nought but death and damning' until her sins have been washed away in 'a well of living tears'. At the end she reappears, subdued, modest, sparing of speech, and vowing to be a faithful wife to the uncaring husband her father has obtained for her. Not only has Lelia been socialised, but she has experienced something in the nature of a religious conversion; the father's language in IV, iv when he comes to her in disguise is strongly religious, and the scene recalls prototypes of the sinning woman's conversion by a man[14] although it does not fully follow this pattern. But Piso's acceptance of marriage to a whore, conventionally the fate of a gull, is conditional on the fact that Lelia is rich:

> So I may have the meanes
> I doe not much care what the woman is.
> (V, v, 115)

Her transformation into the ideal of socially acceptable womanhood, the chaste and submissive wife, is not matched with any such transformation on his part. It is the woman's excessive sexual energies which require to be moderated and channelled.

The relation of women to the military world is examined directly in *Bonduca* (c. 1609-14), a tragedy written solely by Fletcher. The play endorses Jacomo's identification of the military sphere with virtue which is exclusively masculine through its depiction of Caratach, the British general, whose stratagems are more than once destroyed by the incompetent tactics of his cousin, the warrior-Queen Bonduca. In *The Faerie Queene* and other contemporary depictions of the Saxon queen she is often seen as a 'victorious Conqueresse' and a symbol of native British valour in the face of colonising Roman forces, a woman without the usual weaknesses of her sex;[15] but Fletcher rejects this image at the outset of the play. It begins with Bonduca's speech of rejoicing in her two recent victories over the Romans ('a woman / A woman beat 'em Nennius; a weak woman, / A woman beat these *Romanes*') which is immediately undercut by Caratach, who enters, unnoticed, and wryly comments at the end, 'So it seems. A man would shame to talk so'. The heroic and potentially radical image of the woman-warrior is replaced by the stereotype of the talkative woman. Bonduca has to be instructed by Caratach in the proper attitude to warfare, which strictly regulates its rhetoric; her exaltation over a British victory as a triumph of the oppressed over the oppressor, women over men, is impermissible, and defamatory to the masculinity of Rome, which he regards with a homoerotic admiration:[16]

> I love an enemy: I was born a soldier;
> And he that in the head on's Troop defies me,
> Bending my manly body with his sword,
> I make a Mistris. Yellow-tressed Hymen
> Ne'er ty'd a longing Virgin with more joy,
> Than I am married to that man that wounds me:
> And are not all these Romane?
>
> (I, i, 57–63)

The gender confusion in Caratach's images implies that the relationships of war break down normal gender boundaries and subsume the relationships of marriage; the enemy to whose sword his own body 'bends' and submits becomes not a rapist but both a mistress and a husband. Not surprisingly the sexual injuries that happen to women in war are discounted; in a world where wounds are identified as embraces the rapes of Bonduca's daughters win no sympathy from Caratach, who tells them in a memorably terse line, 'You should have kept your legs close then'. Even the goddess of war refuses to endorse any claim to justice for the 'insulting wrongs, and ravishments of women', which the First Daughter particularly stresses. Women can only usurp, and not legitimately possess, authority in war; Caratach tells Bonduca and her daughters more than once to go home and spin[17] and the British defeat in III, v, which occurs although their army apparently outnumbers the Romans by ten to one, is due to Bonduca's faulty tactics. The daughters' active involvement in the war effort is depicted as treacherous and dishonourable; when they capture and prepare to execute four Roman soldiers caught scavenging (including the despicable Judas, who is subsequently responsible for Hengo's death) Caratach upbraids them soundly and displays proper chivalry in letting the Romans go, after first feeding them.

This is one of the most subtly misogynistic of all the Beaumont and Fletcher plays; *Bonduca* resembles *King Lear* in its endorsement of patriarchal values, and here female sexuality is directly emasculating;[18] when Junius, a Roman captain, falls in love with Bonduca's younger daughter, his love for an enemy is the opposite to Caratach's, ridiculous, irrational, and degrading. Her sexually impure condition (she has been raped) is a further insult to the 'young and lustie' Junius, who has been known in better days to 'leap at sixteen like a strong Stallion'. Junius allows himself to be tricked through his desire for Bonduca's daughter into the British camp, but once again Caratach foils the women's stratagem, releasing the Romans whom he calls 'Gentlemen' and 'tall soldiers' and reviling his nieces as sluts. Junius and his commander celebrate his release from sexual slavery with singing and wine; women are disease-ridden and disgusting:

> Their bodies of so weak and wash a temper,
> A rough-pac'd bed will shake 'em all to pieces;
> A tough hen puls their teeth out, tyres their souls;
> *Plenae rimarum sunt*,[19] they are full of rynnet,
> And take the skin off where they are tasted; shun 'em,
> They live in cullisses like rotten cocks
> Stew'd to a tendernesse, that holds no tack.
>   (IV, i, 34–9)

The imagery combines softness and fluidity with corruption; the women can aspire to moral health only by dying bravely, as Bonduca and her elder daughter do. Besieged in their fortress, they refuse Roman offers of mercy and take their own lives. The second daughter is at first reluctant and appeals to Bonduca as her mother for protection, but she is persuaded by her sister's vision of an afterlife:

>   Where eternal
> Our youths are, and our beauties; where no Wars come,
> Nor lustful slaves to ravish us.
>   (IV, iv, 110)

The heroic image of the three women alone on the walls of their fortress surrounded by the Roman army is tempered but not destroyed by such recourse to conventionally feminine styles of consolation. The First Daughter compares herself proudly to the Roman models of female self-sacrifice, Portia and Lucrece, whose heroic motivation she calls into question; temporarily, the play draws on the traditional politics of Roman–British history whereby the British embody the true faith of a humble people devoutly honouring their 'blest household gods' in 'thatched houses' in contrast to the idolatrous worship of tyrannous Rome![20] But although Bonduca's death is commended by the great Suetonius – 'Give her fair funeral; / She was truely noble, and a Queen' – this tribute seems perfunctory by contrast with the extensive eulogies of Penius, the Roman commander who has killed himself in the preceding scene. Penius's funeral procession in fact takes the last-act position that might have been Bonduca's, and the pathetic death of the brave child Hengo, Caratach's nephew, which occurs in the play's closing moments, entirely relegates Bonduca's death to second-division status. At the end Caratach yields honourably to Suetonius, and the Roman and British commanders congratulate one another on their virtue. This reconciliation affirms a bond between men and includes a tribute to the dead Hengo but omits any mention of the women; Hengo, though only a child, belongs to the world of honour and glory which is closed to Bonduca; as in *The Maid's Tragedy* the elimination of the woman who claims power and enacts violence serves and reinforces values which are definitively gendered male.

Although the treatment of sexuality in *Bonduca* is extensively coloured by a misogynistic notion of women as emasculating, disease-ridden, and substanceless, Bonduca and her daughters none the less achieve some distinction from this sort of generalisation through the courage of their deaths. But the heroism of these deaths is implicitly debunked in the comic episodes when Petillius, having witnessed the suicides, finds himself infatuated with the elder daughter for her 'fiery spirit'; his comrades jeer at him for letting his 'beastly' self overcome his better self. He recognises his condition as pathological – 'the bots'; eventually he is cured of it by doing acts of military valour, and restored to full manliness.

Women's emasculating power operates not only on soldiers but also on rulers. In an early Beaumont and Fletcher collaboration, *Cupid's Revenge*[21] Bacha, the young widow, who is first lover to Leucippus, the Duke's son, and subsequently wife to the elderly Duke, is a female version of the tyrant, and like Lelia in *The Captain* an embodiment of Lust. Like a morality character, she presents the meaning of her behaviour directly to the audience; when Leucippus declines to resume his former relationship with her once she has married his father she is angered, and soliloquises:

> I will make him know
> Lust is not Love, for Lust will finde a mate
> While there are men, and so will I: and more
> Then one, or twenty.
>
> (III, ii, 226)

But Bacha's 'two-facedness' is not so much an aspect of her characterisation as a treacherous and untrustworthy woman; rather it is a reflection of her shifting between subject-positions from which to speak. In dialogue with Leucippus on her first appearance she is to him the helpless widow who repents of permitting her own seduction, while at the same time she is to the audience the wily woman who only plays this role; she is

Misogyny and manhood

a characterised speaker. In her asides and soliloquies, however, she is directly self-explanatory,

> Just as you are a Dosen I esteeme you: no more: does he thinke I would prostitute my selfe for love? It was the love of these pearles and golde that wanne mee.
>
> (II, ii, 71–3)

This alternation between voices is comic in effect; the situation of Leucippus and Bacha is also comic, with an ironic inversion of the regular power relations implicit in the seducer-and-victim situation whereby it is Bacha, apparently the victim, who is really in control. Much of Bacha's role is in fact a comic one, yet her 'discontinuity of being', to use Catherine Belsey's phrase,[22] is functional in constructing her as the villainous outsider, the infinitely destructive woman.

Bacha's readiness to sleep with her step-son represents, like Lelia's acceptance of the idea of incest, appetite that is evil in acknowledging no boundaries; but Bacha is not merely lustful, she is also tyrannous, threatening to torture and kill Leucippus if he will not serve her. Like the tyrant who is also a usurper, she schemes to consolidate her power, taking a corrupt servant as her instrument and planning to infiltrate Urania, the daughter of her first marriage, into the royal line, and marry her to a foreign prince. This latter motif is more fully developed in *Philaster*, and the comparison illuminates how the issues of usurpation and contamination of the royal blood line, though implicit in the narrative material of *Cupid's Revenge*, are inflected in a moral rather than a political way. The initial impetus for Bacha's scheming against Leucippus is his sexual rejection of her; from being merely an ambitious widow prepared to exploit the old Duke's infatuation for her despite her revulsion towards him she becomes a power-crazed villain, the more dangerous because, Iago-like, she incorporates the weakness of her victims into her own strength. The doting Duke sees merely the protective nurse-wife figure she chooses to display in his presence, and only the audience is privy to the fact that she is secretly poisoning him; Leucippus eventually realises that she has slandered him to his father and almost brought about his death, but he is too chivalrous to act against her.

The Lords Agenor, Dorialus, and Nisus represent commonsense opinion; the cynical and misogynistic tone of their commentary on the royal marriage is offered as honest truth-telling; but even they are temporarily, and crucially, disarmed by Bacha's skilful playacting in III, iv when she persuades them to urge the Duke to hand power over to Leucippus for the safety of the kingdom. This she knows will confirm the belief she has already fostered in the Duke that his son is aiming to usurp him. The anti-feminist proverbial wisdom cited by Dorialus in this scene is thus implicitly confirmed for the audience by Bacha's two-faced behaviour:

Dorialus [aside]. I was never cousend in a woman before, for commonly they are like Apples: If once they bruse they will growe rotten through, and serve for nothing but to asswage swellings.

(III, iv, 187–90)

She affirms such stereotypes of women by acting them out in her own asides:

> The fool that willingly provokes a woman,
> Has made himselfe another evil Angell,
> And a new Hell, to which all other torments
> Are but meere pastime.
>
> (III, iv, 142–5)

Only the citizens stand outside her ambit; they both recognise her wickedness and act forcefully against it, rescuing Leucippus from the scaffold and organising themselves into an army in his support. But Leucippus, to the exasperation of his cousin and loyal follower Ismenus, insists on disbanding this army and refusing to take any action against his stepmother's now open hostility. This passivity in a royal heir is in one way accounted for, in the play's terms, as Cupid's revenge through the instrument of Bacha on a royal family which has attempted to deny his power; in the end Leucippus is stabbed to death by Bacha just before she uses her knife on herself. He admits as he dies that manhood is worthless if a 'weak woman' can destroy it.[23] In the play's last lines, Ismenus, the new ruler, orders Bacha's body to lie unburied in a ditch. She is a criminal and an outcast, like Tamora in *Titus Andronicus*, whose corpse is treated in a similar way.

The figure of the monstrous woman reappears with more distinctively tragic features in *Thierry and Theodoret*, a play whose action revolves round the polarisation of woman as supremely virtuous or supremely vicious.[24] It is a more distinctly misogynistic play than any discussed so far. Its premise is that a king's power is absolute and so too are the demands of male power and values. Despite the questioning of the doctrine of royal absolutism in other plays, and the fact that the upholders of the doctrine in this play, the brothers Thierry and Theodoret, are neither strong nor particularly virtuous, the play makes the orthodox link between regal and masculine supremacy both of which are endorsed in its conclusion. Women are valued when submissive and chaste, like Memberge, Theodoret's daughter, who is preserved so as to marry Martell, a 'noble kinsman' to the brothers, and continue the royal line; the possibility of her ruling in her own right is never entertained, although she is the only direct descendant. Ordella, Thierry's wife, is outstanding both for submissiveness and chastity in ways that astound not only her husband but also his wicked mother, Brunhalt; her virtue is displayed in her willingness to subordinate herself to her husband's needs, the primacy of which neither she nor anyone else questions. The play accepts that women may be sacrificed to serve men's needs; Theodoret is willing to offer up Memberge's life to prevent war, and Thierry to kill an unknown woman in order to restore his sexual potency. The ideal of woman as chaste and submissive is further endorsed by the portrayal of Brunhalt herself. In her, the play raises the grim spectre of the monstrous woman who refuses to conform to these norms. Her lust, cruelty, and tyrannous readiness to lie and deceive in furtherance of her desires brings about the destruction and deaths of both her sons and her virtuous daughter-in-law. She is a witch, a sexual monstrosity, and a perversion of the sacred ideal of motherhood – 'mother of mischief', 'mother of these angers', 'your murdering mother, your malicious mother', 'this mad mother'. In showing the horrors wrought by such a woman, who ends by choking herself 'impatient of her constraint', the play gives vent to the misogynistic fear of woman whose appetites, if not regulated, recognise no limits of decency or morality, and affirms the need for male control and order.

Brunhalt is an unnatural mother, a tyrannous queen who abuses her power, an ageing woman abandoned to lustful desires, and even a witch who traffics in magic in order to ruin her son's marriage. Although a queen, she is not a ruler, and she does not rebel against the patriarchal system that has conferred kingdoms on her two sons yet left her apparently a royal widow without other official status. Brunhalt often uses the word 'power' which for her means the free exercise of the will. She curses her elder son, Theodoret, when he attempts to persuade her to exercise restraint, and invokes the demonic powers of women to destroy him:

> Brunhalt
> From this accursed houre, forget thou bor'st him,
> Or any part of thy blood gave him living;
> Let him be to thee, an Antipathy,
> A thing thy nature sweates at, and turnes backward:
> Throw all the mischiefes on him that thy selfe
> Or women worse than thou art, have invented,
> And kill him drunke, or doubtfull.
>
> (I, i, 133–7)

She is constructed so as to embody the antithesis of the mother, especially in her inordinate sexual desires; in the opening scene, Theodoret, having unsuccessfully urged her to reform by appealing to the exemplary aspect of her role as queen, denounces her as a lecher:

> With what face dare you see mee, or any mankind,
> That keepe a race of such unheard of relicks,
> Bawds, Letchers, Leaches, formall fornications,
> And children in their rudiments to vices,

> Old men to show examples and (lest Art
> Should loose herself in act) to call backe custome:
> Leave these, and live like *Niobe*.
>
> (I, i, 119–25)

The reference to Niobe as the model for the chaste and grieving widow highlights Brunhalt's behaviour as doubly inappropriate, for a widow and for a queen; she is not prepared to accept any constraint on her freedom and is tyrannously absolute in imposing her power on others, threatening disobedient male followers with sexual subjugation in the form of gelding. Her second son, Thierry, to whom she flees, Lear-like, when displeased with Theodoret, is himself an absolutist who regards his subjects as 'poore dust' in the face of 'the whirlwind of my absolute command' (II, i, 39–40); but although he claims to be capable of the sexual extravagance that conventionally characterises a tyrannical ruler, he is proud to be 'the maister of a continence' that spares the wives and daughters of his subjects. For Brunhalt and her sons the political aspects of the ruler's power are largely disregarded; authority and social control are defined only in terms of the expression and/or limitation of sexuality. As in the military context of *Bonduca*, an equation is made between valour and abstinence. Devitry, 'an honest Souldier of fortune' notices that Brunhalt's house is out of bounds to soldiers. When Protaldye, Brunhalt's proletarian lover, is given charge of Thierry's army he is cowardly and inept. He scorns to train the soldiers by 'worme eaten presidents of the *Roman* wars' and instead indulges them in drinking and wenching. Martell, the honest Ismenus figure of this play, describes his cowardice as a sexual disease, which requires the severity of militarism to cure it:

> An armor like a frost will search your bones,
> And make you rore you rogue.
>
> (II, iii, 85)

But Protaldye's corruption is not suppressed until too late; a surrogate for his vicious mistress, he stabs Theodoret in the back at Thierry's wedding feast. The play has no example of manliness; Brunhalt has Theodoret, the more independent of her sons, killed off, and renders Thierry impotent before torturing him to death; her lover is weak and cowardly. Manhood cannot exist in such conditions. The only power, for good or ill, is female, though Ordella's virtue is not, like Evanthe's, redemptive, and Brunhalt's power is in the end self-defeating.

Brunhalt destroys not only manliness as such, but also productive sexuality. When the princess Ordella, a beautiful young virgin, comes from another kingdom to marry Thierry she is outraged. The arrival of another queen signifies loss of power to Brunhalt, and it seems important that she defines the nature of this loss very specifically; it is not of political

Misogyny and manhood

power or authority, but of a personal form of recognition due to her as a woman and of influence over the King. She cannot bear:

> to have my sleepes
> Lesse inquirde after, or my rising up
> Saluted with less reverence, or my gates
> Empty of suitors.
> (II, i, 281–4)

There is a gap between the surprising modesty of Brunhalt's expressed needs and the violence of her rage at the prospect of being thwarted. Here she speaks as a selfish and demanding mother who craves the exclusive attention and concern of her children; but when she speaks her own epitaph it is in much larger terms; she calls herself:

> A woman in her liberall will defeated
> In all her greatnesse crost, in pleasure blasted.
> (V, ii, 116)

The hatred of Thierry's future bride is constructed as petty female jealousy; this is the mother-in-law whose unwanted presence blights the happiness of the younger generation. She plots to destroy the marriage by rendering Thierry impotent, and then by causing him to kill Ordella in order to restore his manhood, but her plots are thwarted by Ordella's extraordinary virtue. As Brunhalt is excessive in her female sexuality, so Ordella is deficient, but this deficiency rather than being a lack is the quality that makes her better than woman.

When Brunhalt questions Thierry after his wedding night she is expecting to hear that his prospect of marital happiness has been disrupted by his failure to consummate; she asks, 'Are you a man?' The play offers contradictory accounts of Thierry's own sexual condition; when Brunhalt and Lecure are discussing the potion which will temporarily render him impotent and thus make Ordella hate him, Lecure refers to him as one 'that to all else did never faile / Of as much as could be performde by man' implying that he is sexually experienced, but here Thierry seems to regard himself as sexually on equal terms with the virginal Ordella. His responses assert a Pauline view of sexuality as weakness. He rejects the identification of adulthood with sexual experience; that he and Ordella are still 'no man' and 'no woman', but this is preferable to the poor and 'ridiculous' satisfaction afforded by sexual consummation. Yet by a characteristically Fletcherian volte-face, Thierry is quickly persuaded by Brunhalt that even better than this elevated mutual chastity would be an heir born of the uniquely virtuous Ordella, even though it transpires that the price for restoring his potency will be the sacrifice of a woman's life. Thierry, supported by Martell, welcomes this pronouncement without any remorse for the idea of a human sacrifice, since he believes it to have been made by a magician. The chosen woman, who is to be the first seen leaving the Temple of Diana at dawn, will be by extension 'mother of Princes, whose grave shall be more fruitfull / Than other marriage beds' (III, iii, 63–4), and therefore need not be married. It turns out, of course, that, as Brunhalt arranges, this woman is Ordella herself, veiled so that Thierry does not at first recognise her. But not only is she perfectly prepared to die so that her husband may beget children on another woman, she even takes upon herself responsibility for his impotence, condemning her own womb as fatal 'like a grave, [that] buries those loyall hopes, / And to a grave it covets' (IV, i, 181). Ordella's behaviour is another example of how in this play natural sexual functions and relationships are displaced. The mother destroys one son's manhood and kills the other, afterwards denying that she was actually his mother; the wife can only become a mother vicariously, by dying to make way for a successor. Her love for her husband is demonstrated first by her willingness to accept that he cannot make love to her, and second by her readiness to die so that he can make love to someone else. The only acceptable woman is one who regulates her sexuality to the point of suppression.[25]

Brunhalt acknowledges no constraints of any kind in the pursuit of her desires, and this is her strength; her sons, and particularly Thierry, are inhibited by a sense of filial duty from recognising what she really is, and even when he is dying and finally forced to see her as the cause of all his suffering, Thierry still tries to appeal to her maternal sensibility:

> O mother, do not lose your name, forget not
> The touch of nature in you, tenderness,
> 'Tis all the soule of woman, all the sweetness.
> (V, ii, 102–4)

The son's inability to throw off the claims of the mother disables him from fighting back at her wickedness, and Brunhalt cynically manipulates such instinctive loyalties, while utterly discounting their validity. She dismisses Thierry scornfully: 'Holy foole, / Whose patience to prevent my wrongs has kill'd thee.' The relationship of Brunhalt to Ordella, 'saint of thy sexe', who makes a final appearance to Thierry in the play's last moments before they both die, reproduces the polarisation of Goneril and Regan with Cordelia.[26] But the refiguring of *King Lear*'s plot is more radical than this parallel implies, because Brunhalt is really Lear, not Goneril and Regan, and a wicked queen with good sons instead of a good king with bad daughters. *King Lear* may certainly be read as misogynistic, even without any effort to appropriate the play for feminism, but *Thierry and Theodoret* openly confirms the assumptions of misogyny in Brunhalt; the unnatural mother is a more disturbing figure than the unnatural daughter, one who is more powerful and less easy to disown. Her sons can in no way be held responsible for her vicious nature, which is troublingly mysterious in origin, but they can eradicate it only at the cost of behaving unnaturally themselves.

The fear of women behind the construction of such a stereotype in tragedy may emerge also in comic characterisation which is not entirely dissimilar. *The Scornful Lady*, a Beaumont and Fletcher collaboration,[27] is a play in which most of the characters are known only by type-names: Elder and Younger Loveless, the two gallants, Moorecraft, a usurer, Savill, a steward, and so on. The woman referred to in the original speech-prefixes as either 'Abigail' or – ironically as it turns out – 'Younglove' is the comically lustful waiting gentlewoman to the Scornful Lady. Her reduced social status and her age – she is 'towards fiftie' – enable the men to be sarcastic and insulting at her expense without fear of reprisal. The ribald account of her that Young Loveless gives his elder brother in the play's opening moments, which locates the play at a very specific historical moment, establishes the nature of the brothers' camaraderie as anti-feminist:

> *Young Loveless.* O this is a sweete Brache.
> *Elder Loveless.* Why she knows not you.
> *Young Loveless.* No, but she offered me once to know her: to this day she loves youth of eighteene ... she lov'd all the Players in the last Queenes house once over: She was strook when they acted lovers, and forsook some when they plaid murtherers.
>
> (I, i, 40–8)

Younglove's sexual preferences and her theatrical naivety recall the Grocer's Wife in *The Knight of the Burning Pestle*, a similar version of this stereotype. Younglove, however, is unmarried, and naturally her one aim is to find herself a man. Her frank and undiscriminating efforts in this direction highlight the more mannered and complex sexuality of the Lady who loves Elder Loveless but will not show her feeling. She is dominated, like Brunhalt, by will, yet allowed the awareness that her will to power and freedom is also self-destructive:

> Is it not strange that every womans will
> Should tracke out new waies to disturbe her selfe?
> If I should call my reason to accompt,
> It cannot answere why I stoppe my selfe
> From mine owne wish; and stoppe the man I love
> From his; and every houre repent againe,
> Yet still goe on.
>
> (V, ii, 1–7)

The Lady speaks here and elsewhere (see, for example, V, ii, 63–72) as 'every woman' and articulates that aspect of female otherness that is often defined as frowardness, perversity, wilfulness. The female desire for power and self-determination is construed as unnatural and self-defeating. A woman's internal impulses are self-contradictory. Younglove's 'will' also seeks a fulfilment which is unnatural, since she pursues every man she meets, irrespective of the slights she will incur. The comedy of the soliloquy in which she gives an account of herself is broad and unforgiving; it invites the audience to accept that middle-aged women's sexual desires are repulsive and ludicrous, and to recognise women's unstable status in the commodity market. The Lady can afford to indulge her 'will' because she is rich and young, but a woman who finds herself in Younglove's position deserves only ridicule:

> Alasse poore Gentlewoman, to what a misery hath age brought thee? To what scurvy Fortune? thou that hast been a companion for Noble men, and at the worst of those times for Gentlemen: now like a broken Servingman, must begge for a favour to those that would have crawl'd like Pilgrims to my chamber, but for an apperition of me ... Old men i'th house, of fiftie, call me Granam; and when they are drunke, e'ene then, when Jone and my Lady are all one, not one will doe me reason.
>
> (IV, i, 1–6, 12–14)

Her ridiculous efforts to attract Welford, an unwanted suitor of the Lady's culminate in open insults directed at her physical appearance: 'Avoide old Satanus: Goe daube your ruines, your face looks fowler then a storm' (III, i, 340). Both Young Loveless, who is a disreputable prodigal, and Elder Loveless, the play's romantic hero, insult Younglove too. When Elder Loveless has been humiliated publicly by the Lady he turns his rage against women on Younglove:

> Thou with a face as olde as Erra Pater,
> Such a prognosticating nose: thou thing
> That ten yeares since has left to be a woman,
> Outworne the expectation of a Bawde.
>
> (IV, i, 315)

Though Younglove herself is offended by his language, the Lady says merely, 'Let him alone, 'is crackt'. She recognises that her own behaviour towards her suitor in pretending to faint in order to get him to declare his feelings for her has been capricious and wilful. In the play's terms Elder Loveless's anger is therefore justifiable. That the gratuitous insults to which he gives vent are seen as the regular currency of sexual discourse indicates the anti-feminist premises the play takes for granted. Younglove is available for sexual insult to the last. She is eventually paired off with the foolish but good-natured curate, Sir Roger, a humble suitor she had once rejected and who is now her last resort, and when they join the other couples for a communal wedding feast at the play's close Young Loveless sneeringly reminds Sir Roger that his bride is 'horse flesh'.

Finkelpearl[28] contrasts attitudes to women in *The Scornful Lady* and *The Woman's Prize*; in the former he finds evidence of a 'mixture of traditional antifeminine material and pure perversity in the character of ladies' which is characteristic of Beaumont, whereas the latter play, written only by Fletcher, 'employs the same kind of material but handles it with far greater sympathy for women'. It does not require a discussion of attribution[29] to see that this distinction is a simplification. Though the prologue of *The Woman's Prize*, possibly written for a revival in 1633,[30] presents this as a pro-feminist play, addressing itself to women as if the play is defending them, it can also be read as a play which exploits the conventions of the sex-war in order to depict women as the demons and viragos men believe them to be. The situations built on female trickery and anti-male stratagems expose men's helplessness in the face of women's cunning, and allow for the open expression of misogynistic fears. By inverting the situation of *The Taming of the Shrew*, and depicting Maria, Petruchio's second wife, as turning the tables on him, the play may be seen to reveal anxiety about women's uses of their sexual power. At the end this anxiety is assuaged; Maria presents herself to Petruchio in just the roles he would desire, as a virgin and his 'servant'.

In some senses *The Woman's Prize* has it both ways; for instance, its relation to *The Taming of the Shrew* invites a pro-feminist perspective on Petruchio's continued violence and his fear of losing his reputation as a woman-tamer, but at the same time it is evident that the amount of dramatic space allowed to his articulation of grievance at Maria's usage, in contrast with the limited opportunity for self-expression afforded to Kate in Shakespeare's play, skews the play round to his viewpoint. In a variety of ways the play's dramaturgy constructs its viewpoint as masculine.[31] Petruchio is its central figure; he has more scenes and more lines than Maria, including two long misogynistic soliloquies of about thirty lines apiece in Act III. Although it is initially the women who devise the stratagems, the focus is always on Petruchio and his responses; and latterly he begins to create counter-stratagems of his own. Much of the women's activity is presented through the men's narration, in particular by Petruchio's two servants, Pedro and Jacques. These, like the various male servants in *The Taming of the Shrew*, support their master's interests but also take on the function of commentators, thereby ensuring that, in the absence of any female equivalent, the choric voice of the play is distinctly gendered male. At some length Pedro and Jacques describe the army of women marshalled to Maria's assistance in a virtuoso comic passage of bawdy grotesque which was censored in both Folios (II, iv); they also discuss the drunken behaviour of some of Maria's supporters (III, ii), and comment disapprovingly on her shrewish treatment of Petruchio (V, ii). These passages create a perspective from which the audience is invited to interpret the women's behaviour as disorderly, justifying the clichés of misogyny. The power of Maria's tongue is particularly stressed:

> Pedro.   Oh her tongue, her tongue.
> Jacques.   Rather her many tongues.
> Pedro.   Or rather strange tongues.
> Jacques. Her lying tongue.
> Pedro.   Her lisping tongue.
> Jacques.   Her long tongue.
> Pedro. Her lawlesse tongue.
> Jacques.   Her loud tongue.
> Pedro.   And her lickrish –
> Jacques. Many other tongues, and many stranger tongues
> Then ever Babel had to tell his ruines,
> Were women rais'd withall; but never a true one.
> (v, ii, 35–41)[32]

Of course, the servants' fear of their new mistress and her power to scold is comic in its excess; and these lines appear in a scene perhaps ten minutes away from the end of the play so that the audience will be alert to the play's preparations for closure. But the cumulative effect of these devices of representation cannot be ignored. Elsewhere, scenes of female activity are enclosed within passages of male commentary. In IV, ii the faithful Pedro and Jacques appear with their master, concluding their account of the way in which the women's disorderly behaviour has wrecked the house, taking down 'all the hangings / Brasse, Pewter, Plate, ev'n to the very pispots'. Petruchio sends them away to tidy up, and left alone on stage soliloquises briefly about the confusion into which Maria's capricious behaviour has thrown him:

> I shall finde time for all this: could I finde her
> But constant, any way, I had done my business.
> (IV, ii, 12–13)

She enters during his musing, not noticing him, and he stands aside to listen to her speech, commenting on it in asides to the audience for a passage of fifty lines or so, before he comes forward to confront her. After their angry exchanges she storms out, vowing to cuckold him, and the scene ends with a few lines from Petruchio, again alone, wishing for a spell to cure him of his love for her. Thus, although the audience may enjoy the spectacle of a witty woman outdoing her husband in verbal as well as physical trickery, the construction of the scene presents the woman from the man's viewpoint; he reveals to the audience his real 'self', the self which despite being hurt and bemused is still loving, whereas the woman has no 'self' other than that manifested in display.

The sympathy for Maria's position as second wife to the termagant Petruchio, which is evoked by the commentary of Petruchio's friends Tranio

Misogyny and manhood

and Sophocles in the play's opening scene, is soon forgotten. Not only is she well able to stand up for herself, especially with the support of a women's army, but Petruchio's dilemma as victim is dramatically more powerfully represented than Maria's need to abuse him. In his two long soliloquies he addresses himself directly to a male audience, which is invited to share his sense of humiliation at Maria's ill-treatment:

> If I were unmarried,
> I would do any thing below repentance,
> Any base dunhill slavery; be a hang-man
> Ere I would be a husband: O the thousand,
> Thousand, ten thousand waies they have to kil us!
> (III, v, 126–30)

His predicament is that of all husbands exploited by demanding and uncontrollable wives. At the climax of his second speech he lists the ways in which women destroy men through their sexual appetites, either excessively demanding or totally denying, or 'like Scorpions' transferring 'poyson with their tailes', none of which has any specific relevance to his own situation with Maria. This is part of the play's general discourse of misogyny, which emphasises the monstrousness of female sexuality. In lines cut from the Folio texts[33] Jacques describes the tanner's wife who leads the women's army:

> her plackett
> Lookes like the straights of Gibralter, stil wider
> Downe to the gulphe, all sun-burnt Barbary
> Lyes in her breech.
> (II, iv, 45–8)

There are a variety of references to the size of the female appetite, and to its incontinence; and the love of the women's army for strong drink embodies the image of woman as the leaky vessel whose unstopped orifices will let out all her husband's honour.

That women are also victims is acknowledged in the representation of Maria's sister, Livia, who has to find ways of escaping from marriage to the rich but repulsive old man, Moroso, whom her father has chosen for her. But the subplot does not seriously offer any kind of balancing feminist perspective to offset the main plot. Moroso's inadequacy as a husband and, by extension, Petronius's tyranny in forcing him on his daughter are acknowledged by male and female characters alike; Petronius's espousement of Moroso's cause is rather a conspiracy of the old against the young, in keeping with the Plautine antecedents of *The Taming of the Shrew* as well as of this play, than a depiction of patriarchal tyranny. Moroso's physical repulsiveness is comic rather than fearsome or even disgusting and never poses any real threat to Livia. The ploy she adopts in V, ii, pretending to be on her death-bed, which enables her to trick her father and Moroso into ratifying her marriage-contract with her true lover, Rowland, is typical of the quick-witted stratagems in Plautine-derived comedy by which the young get the better of the old and acquire their money.

The comic conclusion reinstates the institution of marriage on terms which appear to accept the women's strategies but none the less indicate that the familiar conventions governing male–female relationships are back in place. Maria, who has never carried out her threats to cuckold Petruchio, hands over to him the total responsibility for her being: 'All my life . . . I dedicate in service to your pleasure.' Petruchio acknowledges her gift by pronouncing her a model for all wives. Rowland has confirmed the validity of his stolen marriage to Livia by bedding her; Petronius is content with this evidence of his second son-in-law's control of his wife's sexuality and wants only to become a grandfather within a year. Petruchio once again recruits the men in the audience to his side in the play's final couplet:

> And Gentlemen, whoever marries next,
> Let him be sure he keep him to his Text.

Chapter 4

Sex and Tyranny

Beaumont and Fletcher's tyrant plays have been, since Coleridge, the one area of the canon generally agreed to have some direct political content, although the bias of it has been disputed.[1] From his readings of *The Maid's Tragedy*, *Valentinian*, *The Loyal Subject* and *Rollo, Duke of Normandy* in particular, Coleridge formed his influential view of Beaumont and Fletcher as 'the most servile *jure divino* royalists', which he repeatedly expressed. But recent critics, writing in the light of new views of the operations of power in the early modern period, particularly in its relation to theatre, have re-evaluated the politics of the tyrant plays. Rebecca Bushnell, for example, in *Tragedies of Tyrants* uses the traditional opposition between the true king and the vicious ranting tyrant as a basis for exploring the changing representations of tyranny in the Elizabethan theatre, especially in the light of Tudor and Stuart doctrines of absolutism. In her discussion of the interaction between effeminacy, illicit desire and illegitimate rule in stage representations of the tyrant, she draws on several Beaumont and Fletcher plays, dismissing the view of them as apolitical, and claiming instead that in their depictions of lustful rulers they 'intricately developed the tradition of a sexualised politics in which desire defines sovereignty and tyranny'.[2]

The exercise of uncontrolled appetite had, of course, been an attribute of the tyrant since Plato.[3] In the Beaumont and Fletcher plays it is largely, but not entirely, depicted in sexual terms. This fact together with the large number of lustful rulers in their plays has usually been ascribed purely to their interest in sexually titillating material. But as Bushnell shows, the plays in which these characters appear can also be read politically in relation to the discourse of tyranny available in Jacobean times. R. Y. Turner also argues for the plays as a direct response to the contemporary political climate, seeing them not in Coleridgean terms as supportive of absolutist doctrine but rather as attempts to negotiate 'the difficulties of living under a ruler who claims absolute power'.[4] It is not necessary here to recapitulate Bushnell's excellent account of the changing representations of the tyrant in the contexts of humanist and then of absolutist conceptions of sovereign

101

power; but it is important to recognise that the absolutism promulgated by James I created new challenges for the dramatists to face when depicting relationships between subjects and rulers, and to consider how new models for such relationships might interact with traditional accounts of tyranny.

The doctrines of hereditary kingship and the divine right conferred on the hereditary successor to a throne were an important aspect of Tudor policy for creating dynastic nationalism; it was Anglican orthodoxy, as defined in the *Homily against Disobedience* (1571), that the deposition or killing of a legitimate monarch who happened to be evil was totally proscribed.[5] Elizabeth herself strongly supported these views of sovereignty,[6] but she did not give expression to them in ways which provoked debate and challenge like her successor, who set out an uncompromisingly absolutist view of the royal prerogative in *The Trew Law of Free Monarchies* (1598) and *Basilikon Doron* (1599), both reprinted in the year of his succession to the English throne. Plays about tyrants and bad rulers were not lacking on the stage during Elizabeth's reign, but they did not consistently engage with problems created for the subject by the monarch's enforcement of his rights. The stage images of tyrant and of true king were separate and distinct: the tyrant was treacherous, irrational, disordered and excessive in his appetites and his rhetoric, like Herod, Cambises, or Richard III. Often he was also a usurper. But under James there was increased interest in the limits of the ruler's power; the antithesis between king and tyrant was challenged by the hypothesis of the legitimate monarch who none the less exhibited characteristics traditional to the tyrant. James himself did not evade such hypotheses, but always countered them with absolutist reasoning, as that 'the wickednesse ... of the King can never make them that are ordained to be judged by him, to become his judges' or 'a wicked King is sent by God for a curse to this people, and a plague for their sinnes'.[7] But in the theatre it is impossible to construct such unequivocal positions, even if the dramatists had wanted to, especially in a theatre with a cultural tradition in which ideas of tyranny, theatricality and rhetoric were intertwined. Even in *Macbeth*, a tragedy which dramatises the killing of a monarch who is both virtuous and legitimate and which represents moral and spiritual chaos created in a realm by the rise of a tyrant, the absolutist position is compromised by the implicit recognition in the scene between Macduff and Malcolm (IV, 3) that there is no final distinction between the moral character of the king and the tyrant.[8]

Tyrannous behaviour was an appropriate subject of stage spectacle in two ways: it allowed for a display of passion and excess since the tyrant himself was characterised by tendencies to exhibitionism and theatricality; and it lent itself to moralising. Like Elyot and Puttenham, Sidney justified tragedy as a morally improving spectacle for rulers,[9] although he undermined his own argument with the account of Alexander Pheraeus who wept at the theatre yet did not cease 'to make matter for Tragedies' by his own tyrannical practices. Shakespeare's tyrant plays, *Richard III* and *Macbeth*, allow audiences to witness exhibitions of criminal behaviour, but these are ultimately significant as purgative preparations for the founding of the truly royal and legitimate line of kings. Human resistance to such tyrants is less important than the mystical power which reinforces it: Richard III and Macbeth are destined to die so that the throne can pass to its rightful inheritor, and therefore the roles of Richmond and Macduff as adversaries are limited. In the Beaumont and Fletcher plays, however, the form and nature of the subject's resistance to tyrannous oppression is central; and it is commonly offered by a woman. This is the most obvious and most frequently used connection between tyranny and sex in these plays, but it is not the only one. Beaumont and Fletcher also draw on traditional aspects of the tyrant's nature which call into question notions of gender: in Greek classical culture, excessive displays of feeling, and the inability to subject the passions to the control of reason, were regarded as effeminate. Issues about the nature and scope of the ruler's desire readily arise and can be explored within the context of the tragedy of blood or of the tragicomic romance, shielded from overt political application by generic convention. Such issues were of course close to the heart of the theory of absolutism; the frequency with which they appear might suggest, on the one hand, that the playwrights were preoccupied with ways of representing the conditions of living in an absolute monarchy and, on another, that they recognised the dramatic potential here for creating certain kinds of theatrically exciting situation. They wrote for a theatre where tragedy was typically, and tragicomic romance commonly, set in a corrupt court that was either foreign or historically remote or both, and involved the overthrow of a ruler.

Given the existing fund of generic conventions, and the interest in and flair for developing theatrical situations of a certain kind which Beaumont and Fletcher consistently demonstrate, it is not surprising that so many of their plays are concerned, in one way or another, with rulers whose behaviour and style could be classified as absolutist: in approximate order of performance, *Cupid's Revenge*, *Philaster*, *The Maid's Tragedy*, *A King and No King*, *Valentinian*, *Rollo, Duke of Normandy*, *The Loyal Subject*, *The Custom of the Country*, *The Double Marriage*, *A Wife for a Month*. Some of these plays are discussed elsewhere; I intend in this chapter to deal only with those where the problems posed for the subject by the ruler's attempts to enforce absolutist principles are expressed in sexual terms. In one group, *The Maid's Tragedy*, *Valentinian* and *Rollo, Duke of Normandy*, the ruler is legitimate but behaves like a tyrant, and the focus is on the right-thinking subject's dilemma; in another, *A King and No King* and *The Loyal Subject*, the ruler's moral character itself is central, and the plays explore the problem of how his power for evil can be limited or controlled. Finally, there are two late plays, *A Wife for a Month* and *The Double Marriage*, which show the ruler's will challenged by the opposed desires of his subjects. By choosing these plays to examine I am concerned with the relations of authority not only within the state but also between the sexes. If there is a critique of absolutism, however indirectly offered, does it extend, in plays where the object of the ruler's oppression is a woman, to a critique of patriarchal control?

The idea that *The Maid's Tragedy* is a political play in any sense has been challenged recently,[10] especially by Walter Cohen who says it is 'out of touch' with moral and political issues but 'plays with them', that is, trivialises them in such a way as to prevent their acquiring any significance. But Bowers[11] and Finkelpearl relate it very convincingly to the questions of the subject's duty to the monarch and the ethics of tyrannicide which were highly current issues in the opening years of James's reign. The assassination of Henry IV of France in 1610 had had a strong effect on the timorous James, causing him to increase his own personal protection,[12] and this is a likely year for the play's composition.[13] Parliamentary debates on the subject of the King's prerogative took place in 1610,[14] the year in which James had been obliged to ban Cowell's *Interpreter*, because of the tremendous hostility it aroused by championing the King's prerogative over the common law.[15] *Valentinian*, probably only a year or two later,[16] is often linked with *The Maid's Tragedy* in its handling of the divine right issue, both by those who see the plays as absolutist and those who do not.[17] The plays have much in common, though there are obvious dissimilarities. *Valentinian* deals with historical material from the decadence of the Roman empire in the fifth century, while the plot of *The Maid's Tragedy* is entirely invented and its pseudo-classical setting on Rhodes merely a conveniently remote and transparent fiction. Predictably, *Valentinian* has a larger political context and the life of the emperor's corrupt and idle court is set off against a background of military unrest in the collapsing Roman empire. The soldiers long for an aggressive expansionist policy as pursued by Julius Caesar or Germanicus, while the Emperor himself follows in the decadent line of Nero, Tiberius, and Caligula. *The Maid's Tragedy* by contrast is almost deliberately dehistoricised; the King has no personal name, and the wars from which Melantius has been summoned home are not specified. The corruption of the court is represented as well as described in *Valentinian*, by depictions of the Emperor's retinue of bawds, pandars, and flatterers, while the King in *The Maid's Tragedy* has no favourites or intimates, and there is no depiction of general sexual decadence. The major difference is in the women characters; Lucina is a wife of outstanding virtue whom the Emperor, unable to possess by any other means, rapes, while Evadne has willingly colluded in her own corruption by the King, readily becoming his mistress in order to further her own ambition, and agreeing to a marriage

Sex and tyranny

which will dishonour an innocent man in order to protect her position. Although Lucina is not shown as a timorous victim, she is not given an important scene in which to challenge Valentinian before the rape, and afterwards, when Maximus and Aecius debate the ethics of the rape-victim's behaviour, she takes the conservative position that suicide is the only honourable course. Maximus, her husband, supports this view which rests on patriarchal values; if she lives, his descendants will be dishonoured by this taint in the family history, and any plea of innocence she might make would have no weight balanced against the fact of rape:

> When they read, she liv'd,
> Must they not aske how often she was ravish'd,
> And make a doubt she lov'd that more than Wedlock?
> Therefore she must not live.
> (III, i, 242–5)

Lucina too accepts that only her death can speak her innocence; she has no other voice. In *The Maid's Tragedy* Evadne does speak for herself. She challenges female stereotypes by refusing to regard herself as a victim; she is strong and aggressive, forcing Amintor into the victim's role in their wedding night confrontation. He is so horrified by her revelation that she is not a virgin that he foresees a total breakdown in the conventional structure of sexual relationships if it should be known:

> Hymen keepe
> This story (that will make succeeding youth
> Neglect thy ceremonies) from all eares.
> Let it not rise up for thy shame and mine
> To after ages, we will scorne thy lawes,
> If thou no better blesse them; touch the heart
> Of her that thou hast sent me, or the world
> Shall know: there's not an altar that will smoake
> In praise of thee: we will adopt us sonnes,
> Then vertue shall inherit and not blood;
> If we doe lust, we'le take the next we meet,
> Serving our selves as other creatures doe,
> And never take note of the female more,
> Nor of her issue.
> (II, i, 214–27)

McLuskie suggests that this speech acknowledges 'the political connection between the sexual control of women and the maintenance of social order' and this connection might be seen as evidence for the presence in the play of 'a subversive and radical sexual politics'.[18] But allowing for the expression of challenging ideas at specific points in a play need not mean that the challenge is taken up in the dynamic of the play as a whole. I hope to show that in their representation of the relationship of sex and tyranny *The Maid's Tragedy* and *Valentinian* are significantly similar.

The starting point for this representation is the conception of the ruler who in each case is legitimate but corrupt. The ruler forces the issue of the subject's duty of obedience to his ruler by invading his subjects' privacy. The invasion takes a sexual form. The ruler's desire for a woman is enforced in a way which bears directly on her family and its honour, as well as on her own personal integrity. This act of oppression is intended in both plays to epitomise the ruler's failure to embody the right relationship to his subjects; in *The Maid's Tragedy* it also symbolises a larger corruption which is not fully represented, but in *Valentinian* this corruption is extensively detailed, particularly through accounts given by Aecius, Pontius and others of the Emperor's neglect and dishonourable treatment of his army and mismanagement of colonial territories. He is politically inept and personally tyrannous; his subjects perceive him as lacking in responsibility:

> They say moreover ... that of late time, like *Nero*,
> And with the same forgetfullness of glory,
> You have got a vaine of fidling, so they terme it.
> (I, iii, 144–9)

In *The Maid's Tragedy* the court is not in itself decadent and the King's corruption is apparently limited in effect, though Evadne's denunciations of her seducer magnify the significance of his intemperate desire. She calls him 'such a tyrant, / That for his lust would sell away his subjects, / I, all his heaven hereafter' (V, i, 93–5). Intemperance, the inability to control the appetite by the exercise of reason, is central to the humanist view of tyranny; by centring their plays on an act of lust through which a ruler violates the rights of his subjects, Beaumont and Fletcher draw on a concept of tyranny different from that which is now more common. As Bushnell puts it: 'In contrast to the modern view that the tyrant is marked by his will to absolute power, for these writers [Renaissance humanists] tyranny lies not so much in power itself but in desire as a form of power.'[19]

The meaning of such expressions of desire is in part generically conditioned in both these plays, where the action is shaped by the conventions of revenge tragedy. When a crime is committed which dishonours a member of a family, then the kindred of the victim are obliged to retrieve this honour by proceeding against the perpetrator. That the perpetrator's status or position constitutes an obstacle to the achievement of the revenge is conventional; that he is a legitimate ruler operating by a code according to which his person is inviolable constitutes an extension of the revenge formula especially devised to create debate around Jacobean absolutism. The effect of this extension is particularly apparent in *The Maid's Tragedy*, which is closely modelled on *Hamlet*;[20] as in Shakespeare's play, an innocent man discovers that he has been wronged by a King, but in Hamlet's case the issues are different because the King is a usurper. Amintor and Maximus, the husbands who have been dishonoured by their rulers, are confronted with a conflict between two sets of ethics. Amintor has no doubt which has priority; the name of his wife's lover renders him powerless:

> in that sacred name,
> The King, there lies a terror, what fraile man
> Dares lift his head against it? let the Gods
> Speake to him when they please, till then let us
> Suffer and waite.
> (II, i, 307–11)

Maximus, who is not an absolutist, is faced by a dilemma of a different kind; the divine right issue is here decentralised in that it is the friend, Aecius, not the husband who speaks for it, and Maximus recognises that he cannot be revenged on Valentinian without first killing Aecius, whose principles will oblige him to protect his ruler's life at all costs. Resistance to tyranny is conflated with the duty to revenge. But this does not emerge as a way of legitimising the resister's behaviour; in *The Maid's Tragedy* the resisters contrive a way to achieve the revenge without themselves carrying it out, and in *Valentinian* Maximus, although not directly responsible for Valentinian's death, becomes in the end corrupt and tyrannous and is himself murdered.

To look at the plays from the perspective of revenge drama tends to suppress a central fact: the direct victim of the tyrant's lust is the woman and not her male kinsfolk. The tyrant's invasion of the woman's body may emblematically stand for his pollution of the state,[21] an equivalence more clearly defined in *Valentinian* where the outstanding chastity and incorruptibility of Lucina make her a figurehead for the ideal of 'Empire', even to those who do not respect virtue as such; Ardelia, one of Valentinian's bawds, says:

> She has the Empire's cause in hand, not loves;
> There lies the maine consideration,
> For which she is chiefly borne.
> (I, ii, 72–4)

But it is both more, and in some ways less, than that. Since each of the women is married, the tyrant's act is a violation of the family as well as of the individual, and it creates a problem which can be solved only by death.[22] Since both accept that they have been irretrievably polluted by intercourse with the tyrant – Lucina immediately and Evadne eventually – they take responsibility for their own deaths, although, of course, the handling of these suicides is entirely different. But neither situation is presented so as to endorse the hard-line patriarchalist view of rape as put forward in traditional versions of the Lucrece story, whereby the woman's chastity is her total identity, and once it is lost she becomes a tainted and worthless vessel. In Evadne's case, the issue is deflected, since her status as virgin seduced by the tyrant is constructed only retrospectively, in the scene where she kills the king; here she accuses him in traditional terms:

> I was once faire,
> Once I was lovely, not a blowing rose
> More chastly sweet, till thou, thou, thou foule canker,
> (Stirre not) didst poison me: I was a world of vertue.
> (V, i, 75–8)

The accusation fleshes out the cause for grievance her family has against the King, but is very much secondary to the issue of the defamation of honour.

In *Valentinian* the conventional view is strongly put when, in the aftermath of the rape, Lucina confronts the Emperor and begs him to kill her as the logical conclusion to his act, 'the sacrilegious razing of this Temple'. But in the lengthy debate on the ethics of suicide which ensues between Lucina, Maximus, and Aecius, alternative views are aired; Aecius takes the line, supported in early accounts of the Lucrece story,[23] that Lucina, having been 'compeld and forcd with violence' is not responsible for the deed and, in fact, has a duty to survive in order to demystify the mythology surrounding rape-victim suicide, 'to teach the world such deaths are superstitious'. In making Lucina kill herself, Fletcher has changed his immediate source story, D'Urfé's *L'Astrée* Part II (1610), where the Lucina-figure, Isidore, makes her husband vow to be revenged on Valentinian, and survives long enough to wash her hands in the dead Emperor's blood.[24] He has chosen to remodel his plot on the Lucrece story, and thus to emphasise Lucina's role as victim, and also to foreground the divine right issue. This constitutes something of a dilemma for Lucina as well as for her menfolk, and considerably intensifies the effect of the rape in defeating the will of the victim to live. Before the rape, Lucina, although averse to courtly values, respects the concept of imperial authority; she calls Valentinian 'God-like' (I, ii, 145) and 'sacred' (II, vi, 12), and appeals to him as 'Father of the Empire's honour ... too neere the nature of the Gods, / To wrong the weakest of all creatures: Women' (II, vi, 31–3). But in the passionate scene between them after the rape her initial determination to force him to a recognition of its meaning is worn down by his cold assertion of absolutist principle:

> Know I am far above the faults I doe,
> And those I doe I am able to forgive too.
> (III, i, 119–20)[25]

He justifies his unlimited expression of appetite by the belief that legitimacy in a ruler confers god-like power; his crimes are beyond the reach of state authority:

> Justice shall never heare ye, I am justice.
> (III, i, 34)

There is no way out for Lucina and she acknowledges this:

> Why then I see there is no God but power,
> No vertue now alive that cares for us.
> (III, i, 145–6)

Fletcher has resisted making Lucina a Christian, and the Christian rhetoric consistently present in the text makes the denial of this option more evident; thus he has avoided the triumphant overthrow of the tyrant by the virgin martyr that occurs in plays like Massinger's *The Virgin Martyr* or Webster's *Appius and Virginia*, and forced the question of the limits of royal power to seek more directly secular and political answers. In Shepherd's view this renders Lucina's suicide 'a little ineffectual' and draws the 'political teeth' of the virgin martyr tradition.[26] More to the point, it creates theatrical space for the remainder of the play to assume the shape of a revenge tragedy by which the dangers of openly challenging absolutism can be delicately negotiated. Valentinian is killed by a loyal follower of Aecius in a manner which constructs military honour as as equally demanding an ethic as divine right; and Maximus himself becomes corrupted by the chance to achieve supreme power and is eventually murdered.

In *The Maid's Tragedy* the issues arising from the victimisation of a woman by the tyrant are very differently handled, though once again the controversial nature of the play's politics is seen to demand a delicate approach. Just as Lucina can challenge the Emperor's claim to the right to act outside the law only by taking her own life, thus deflecting the problems of justice and revenge onto her husband, so it seems as if in *The Maid's Tragedy* again a man must take responsibility for responding to a crime done against a woman. Yet starting from the characterisation of Evadne, there are elements of the controversial and the subversive in this play's treatment of power. Initially, Evadne's relations with her husband and her lover reverse the accepted structure of power relations between the sexes. Not only has Evadne willingly become the King's mistress, but rather than submitting to the implications of the conventional equation between loss of virginity and loss of honour she is able to deploy her sexuality as a potent weapon. In the wedding-night scene with Amintor she is not ashamed to reveal herself as other than the blushing virgin he expects; in fact, it is Amintor who is the virgin, and Evadne who possesses the sexual authority with which to disrupt the progress of the scene. She rechannels it from the direction which both the audience and Amintor expect it to take, and redirects the action according to her own requirements. In a subsequent scene, similarly structured to subvert expectation, it is the King who is filled with apprehension that his plan to marry off his mistress to an ineffectual groom has not worked and Evadne who must reassure him that their liaison is still intact. But the manner of her reassurance throws a perverse new light on the meaning of divine right. When he accuses her of violating an oath never to love another man she corrects him:

> I swore indeede that I would never love
> A man of lower place, but if your fortune
> Should throw you from this height, I bad you trust
> I would forsake you, and would bend to him
> That won your throne, I love with my ambition,
> Not with my eies.
> (III, i, 171–6)

She counters his threat to punish her with a more effective threat of her own, which reveals the tyrant vulnerable rather than strong through his appetite:

> It is in me then,
> Not to love you, which will more afflict
> Your bodie, then your punishment can mine.
> (III, i, 181–3)

The absolutist belief that the King's mystical status confers on him an authority independent either of his legal or his natural powers operates in the play in two ways: it empowers Evadne to threaten the withdrawal of her love should he lose his status, but it disablingly fragments her husband, who is torn between the requirements of two incompatible codes which simultaneously demand and reject revenge. As the King is 'meere man' he has wronged his subject, trespassing on his rights and invading his private territory; but as he is King he has simply exercised his prerogative. 'The King may doe this and he may not doe it', as Calianax says. Thus the orthodoxy of divine right can, from the subject's viewpoint, be expressed only as a paradox; that Evadne does not take the orthodox view either of male–female relationships or of kingship shows her subverting both sexual and political stereotypes. In the course of the play her disorderliness is corrected, but not by her husband's converting her to share his absolutism. The agent of her reformation is Melantius, her brother, who forces her to re-evaluate her behaviour on conventional lines. Guided by him she now sees herself as the powerless victim, disabled by her sex from effective performance in the real world of male-dominated action; repentant, she promises Amintor to atone as best she can for her shameful behaviour:

> Yet perceive I will
> Since I can do no good because a woman
> Reach constantly at something that is neere it.
> (IV, i, 252–4)

Paradoxically, then, although, unlike Lucina, she is enabled to take revenge on her own behalf, she can do this only when she has rejected the image of herself as strong and active, and conformed to the conventional patriarchal stereotype of the repentant whore. Accordingly she represents herself to the King just before she kills him as 'a world of vertue' ruined by a debauched tyrant, a distinct re-evaluation of the politics of their relationship from the one she provided earlier in the play.

This reassessment of Evadne's role functions to suppress the fact that she has been made a scapegoat by her brother; the appropriateness by which she becomes the revenger for her own dishonour enables Amintor to evade the problematic choice between incompatible codes, and Melantius to survive with honour, his friend redeemed from disgrace and his own hands clean of blood. She exonerates the men from the guilt they would have incurred as tyrannicides and allows the notion of murdering a king, however wicked, to retain its mystical horror. The play's final lines offer a somewhat ambiguous consolation: transgressing monarchs should not feel too secure since there may be subjects prepared to risk divine wrath in order to eradicate them.

Whether the critique of absolutism offered in *The Maid's Tragedy* and *Valentinian* amounts to risky unorthodoxy[27] or emerges ultimately as compromised[28] depends for a reader on critical perspective; theatrically, the texts are open to a range of interpretation. Three further elements could condition and shape an audience's response: the representation of militarism, and of court ritual and ceremony, and the staging of the ruler's deaths. The plays share a strong military background and the generals, Melantius and Aecius, in different ways bring military values to bear on their roles as resisters of tyranny. The demands of court and of army directly conflict; Melantius has returned unwillingly from foreign wars in response to the King's command to attend Amintor's wedding and is repelled by the 'soft and silken wars' of the celebrations. In *Valentinian* Captain Pontius must be silenced for voicing criticism of the Emperor's effeminacy. Danby defines the competing codes in *The Maid's Tragedy* as '*jure divino* royalism' and 'the simplifying madness of war',[29] but the texts can better be read as uncritically approving of military values, represented as loyalty, integrity, and masculinity.[30] The ruler and his army are bound in a relationship of mutual dependence and responsibility; Melantius's immediate response to hearing from his sister's own lips the name of her lover is to recognise the King's failure of duty to the soldiers who uphold his power:

> My worthy fathers and my services
> Are liberally rewarded, King I thanke thee:
> For all my dangers and my wounds thou hast paid me
> In my owne metall, these are soldiers thankes.
>
> (IV, i, 125–8)

The representation of militarism in these plays operates as a critique both of the rulers themselves and of the theory of absolutism; not only does it reveal the rulers as effeminate, but it also proposes a theory of power whereby the king derives his right to rule not from divine prerogative but from an acknowledgment of the obligations he has to the welfare of his subjects. The prominence of court ceremonial contributes to the same end. The masquing which celebrates Amintor's wedding and the ceremonies for Maximus's coronation are treated ironically.[31] Strato's blunt account of the function of the masques, which is spoken in the opening moments of *The Maid's Tragedy*, implies the inhibiting effect of court control: 'They're tied to rules of flattery.' In *Valentinian* the numerous scenes of court ceremonial identify this kind of spectacle with decadence and corruption: Lucina is welcomed to Valentinian's court by music, a display of jewels, and specially commissioned songs, and the Emperor has music playing while he attempts to seduce her; music and song accompany his dying pangs; and Maximus's coronation ceremony is preceded by a comic scene between the master of ceremonies and the court poet whose invention is running dry. The all-purpose quality of courtly iconography is amusingly suggested in this behind-the-scenes dialogue:

> *Paulus* [the poet].   A Grace must doe it.
> *Lysippus* Why let a Grace then.
> *Paulus*   Yes it must be so;
>   And in a robe of blew too, as I take it.
> *Lysippus* [*aside*].   This poet is a little kin to'th Painter
>   That could paint nothing but a ramping Lion,
>   So all his learned fancies are blew Graces.
> *Paulus*   What think ye of a Sea-nymph, and a heaven?
> *Lysippus* Why what shold she do there man? Ther's no water.
>
> (V, v, 12–19)

Just as the mystique by which the Jacobean court authorised its own power basis is exposed in these representations of ceremony, so the mystique of kingship is exposed in the stagings of the rulers' deaths. Both are managed with a high degree of theatricality. In *Valentinian* the Emperor's death is turned into a public spectacle. Poisoned by Aretus, he is brought onstage in a chair, visibly degenerating while courtiers, physicians, and the Empress attempt consolation and the astonishingly beautiful lyric 'Care-charming sleep' is sung. In an extraordinary *coup de théâtre*, his physical agonies are duplicated by Aretus, who is a stage ahead of him, dying from a self-administered dose of the same poison; Aretus takes a pleasure at once masochistic and sadistic in exhibiting his torments as he recalls Valentinian's crimes:

> See me Cesar,
> And see to what thou must come for thy murder;
> Millions of women's labours, all diseases –
> ... womens feares, horrors,
> Despaires, and all the plagues the hot Sunne breeds –
> ...
> Are but my torments shadowes.
>
> (v, ii, 88–94)

The exhibition of the ruler's punishment is less spectacular in *The Maid's Tragedy*, but the body on stage functions similarly to signify mortality and the corruptibility of power, and to demystify the idea of the sacredness of the king. Evadne's killing of the King in the bed they have shared mingles eroticism and sadism. In her opening soliloquy, which draws on *Hamlet* for a subtext, she insists on rousing him from sleep in order to 'shape his sins like furies till I waken / His evil angel, his sick conscience', and the interview between them is concluded by a ritualistic (and perhaps orgasmic) wounding sequence:

> This for my lord Amintor.
> This for my noble brother, and this stroke
> For the most wrongd of women.
>
> (v, i, 109–11)

The body of the King lying centre stage tied to the blood-stained bed, is discovered by his gentlemen of the bed-chamber, and then by his brother. The private horror becomes public when Strato enters to announce that Melantius has seized the fort and is already on its walls 'delivering the innocence of this act'. Thus Evadne's vengeance is acknowledged as more than personal vindication; it is a political *coup* which dethrones a tyrant. The body in the bed is an image for the private truth of tyranny suppressed by the public mystique of kingship. Here I take issue with Janet Clare who in '*Art made tongue-tied by authority*' argues that 'the King's murder becomes a crime of passion rather than, as in *The Second Maiden's Tragedy*, a political act against a tyrannical and dissolute ruler.'[32] Of the two plays it could be argued that *The Maid's Tragedy* is the more politically conscious in its representation of tyranny. In the latter, the significance of the tyrant's desire for a woman who is committed to another man can be read both in terms of the emotional dynamics of a love-triangle (echoed in the subplot) and in terms of various specific topical allegories, both political and religious, but it does not comment on the public operations of tyrannical power.[33] The Tyrant is a usurper who has deposed the true king, Govianus, solely to obtain the Lady's love; his inability to deal effectively with Govianus, whom the Lady loves, is determined by emotional rather than political factors – his fear of alienating the Lady whose love he wishes to win rather than command. The problem of tyranny is simplified; usurping tyrant and true king are schematically separated, and the latter survives in order to contrive the death of the former, and the restoration of a legitimate monarchy. The spectacle of the death scene is organised around a moral victory of virtue over vice rather than the notion of a political *coup*. There is only the most perfunctory of allusions to the public consequences for the state of the Tyrant's death, in Govianus's remark, 'Well, he's gone, / And all the kingdom's evils perish with him' (V, ii, 193–4). In contrast with *The Maid's Tragedy*, this play narrows and delimits the meaning of a tyrant's murder.

Rollo, Duke of Normandy, known by its alternative title *The Bloody Brother*,[34] has much in common with *The Maid's Tragedy* and *Valentinian*, with which it was associated in the seventeenth century – by Rymer, for instance, who analyses it with *The Maid's Tragedy* as one of 'The choicest and most applauded English Tragedies of this last age'. Like *Valentinian*, it has a historical source, Herodian, *Roman History*, Book 4; the popularity of the play in the 1630s and the fact that it was chosen for a surreptitious performance in 1648 suggest that the chronicle of civil war and national disunity in medieval Normandy spoke to audiences conscious of national divisions in the mid-seventeenth century. The current critical neglect of it, even with the reawakened interest in politicising the Beaumont and Fletcher canon, contrasts strongly with its early popularity and high reputation[35] and also with possible indications that it then was seen as having political connotations or content.[36] Once again the behaviour of a legitimate but tyrannical ruler creates a dilemma for his subjects, particularly for a principled kinsman who holds orthodox views on divine right. The ruler is challenged by women; first by his mother Sophia and then by Edith the woman he lusts for. Edith plans to stage a seduction scene for Rollo in which she will disarm and then kill him, but she is prevented from doing so by a soldier, who sacrifices himself (as the soldier Aretus does in *Valentinian*) in killing Rollo for her. The woman's implication in the dilemma of tyranny is less than in *The Maid's Tragedy*, since although the tyrant lusts after her, he neither violates her body nor corrupts her, and the issues surrounding absolutism are less problematic. In fact, the elements of compromise and evasion which create the complexity of *The Maid's Tragedy* have been ironed out so that the play makes a more direct, and more orthodox, statement about political order, albeit one which suppresses the problem of absolutism. Aubrey, who succeeds to the throne after Rollo's assassination, is doubly authorised to rule, being both a divine rightist whose principles are never compromised like Amintor's or marginalised like Aecius's, and the

Sex and tyranny

natural successor by blood. Rollo's tyranny combines elements of Senecan superhuman villainy with Marlovian ambition. One of the play's models is *Richard III*, and Rollo like Richard, but unlike the King in *The Maid's Tragedy* or Valentinian, has to gain his power by plots and stratagems. He is not an established ruler. He is advised in his schemes by an Iago-like follower, Latorch, who stifles the promptings of Rollo's conscience with Machiavellian counsels.

The influential presence of the evil counsellor, clear obverse to Aubrey, and the Machiavellian aspects of Rollo's behaviour generalise the concept of tyranny from the image created in *The Maid's Tragedy* and *Valentinian* where tyrannical desire was largely identified with predatory sexuality.[37] As in *Richard III*, the women characters challenge tyranny, but their moral stance is not compromised as in the cases of Queen Margaret or Anne; Sophia and Edith are idealised images of 'strong' women, of a type with which Fletcherian dramaturgy is sometimes especially associated.[38] The powerful oratory of Sophia in the play's first scene, where she urges her warring sons to put the country's good before their own ambition and make their country strong by uniting their factions, moves all bystanders:

> May never Womans tongue
> Hereafter be accus'd, for this ones Goodness
> (I, i, Glover and Waller, IV, 257)

comments Aubrey, admitting the effectiveness of the woman's voice. But Rollo is soon persuaded by Latorch to replace his acceptance of 'your mother's triumph' with a more conventional evaluation of woman's speech:

> My Mothers tears and womanish cold prayers,
> Farewel, I have forgot you.
> (II, ii, Glover and Waller, IV, 260)

Sophia discovers the limitations of her power literally in the scene where the brothers again confront one another, and she tries to shield Otto with her body from Rollo's attack; this does not deter Rollo, who uses the doctrine of absolute power to justify his disregard for moral ties, and slays his brother. Sophia now withdraws from any attempt to control her son, acknowledging her inability to operate in the political arena; her role as challenger of tyranny is taken over by the other women, Matilda her daughter, and Edith, who devise alternative means to solve the problem.

Male opposition to Rollo is ruthlessly suppressed by execution; Aubrey's absolutist compromise, arguing that since Rollo is legitimate heir it is for the country's good that he is kept on the throne, reads like political defeatism. The women opt out of politics and band together to devise an unorthodox solution utilising their sexual advantages. Edith, whose father, Baldwin, has fallen victim to Rollo's excesses, plans to revenge herself and her country by disarming Rollo through seduction and then killing him. Sexual authority will substitute for political power. The power of Rollo's tyrannous desire will be turned against him. Borrowing jewels from Matilda to enhance her beauty, Edith sets up a seduction scene for Rollo, with a banquet and amorous music. In her opening soliloquy she prays for her feminine attributes to be strengthened and divinely endorsed so that she can take on the role of revenger:

> give me flattery,
> (For yet my constant soul ne'er knew dissembling.)
> Flattery the food of Fools, that I may rock him
> And lull him in the Down of his desires;
> That in the height of all his hopes and wishes,
> His Heaven forgot, and all his lusts upon him,
> My hand, like thunder from a cloud, may seize him.
> (V, ii, Glover and Waller, IV, 306–7)

But the play with role-reversal initiated in the idea of woman as both seducer and murderer is not kept up, and the shape of the scene is re-modelled to the *Richard III* pattern. Sexual power is transferred to Rollo, who pretends to be moved to repentance by Edith's beauty; and Edith, who has not Evadne's perverse strengths, begins to succumb to his flattery, and has to be rescued. Hamond, a soldier, whose brother Rollo has murdered, breaks in and the tyrant dies only after attempting to use Edith's body as a shield, in an inversion of the earlier scene when Sophia tries to interpose herself between the brothers. Thus Edith's chastity is preserved and her courage vindicated, for she has urged Hamond to disregard her safety to ensure Rollo's death.

The play's ending is conventionally shaped by revenge-play formulae which implicitly endorse the principle of legitimate succession. For all Rollo's tyrannous excesses his murderers are not exonerated; Hamond has been wounded in the fight and dies, while Edith, though praised by Matilda, is despatched by Aubrey to spend her life in a cloister. Aubrey succeeds to the throne, his claim made 'surer than blood or mischief dare infringe again' by marriage to Matilda. The similarity to the ending of *The Maid's Tragedy* by contrast shows up the greater potential for subversion in the earlier play. The device of woman as king-killer is less daringly handled, since sympathy for the virginal Edith, who acts to revenge her father as well as to save her country, is completely unequivocal, and in any case she is prevented from committing the act herself. Rollo's Senecan monstrousness – he is called an 'abhorred and impious . . . monster' by his sister – removes from the discourse of politics the issue of the honest subject's dilemma in the face of the ruler's unreasonable behaviour. The political aspect of the play's resolution in the investment of a virtuous new and also legitimate ruler is subordinated to the finality of revenge-style closure.

A King and No King constitutes a more inventive and unconventional contribution to the debate on the politics of absolutism. Although R. Y.

Turner does not discuss it in his article 'Responses to tyranny in John Fletcher's plays', and does not include it in the long list of plays he mentions which deal with life under a tyrant, there can be no doubt that its account of kingship is deeply concerned with questions of tyranny and absolutism; and this may well be one of the reasons for its considerable popularity in the seventeenth century, along with *The Maid's Tragedy* and *Valentinian*.[39] The sensational theme of incest and the potential titillation in the tragicomic aspects of its aversion have been the focus of much twentieth-century criticism of the play, which has often censured it for granting audiences the chance to see 'licentious fantasies symbolically projected'.[40] It is usually featured in that tradition of Beaumont and Fletcher criticism, mentioned by Bushnell, which has 'indiscriminately mixed political, moral, and aesthetic categories in a way that recalls Humanist rhetoric against tyranny'; thus the moral weaknesses in the characters, their tendencies to excess and instability are imputed to the plays, and even the playwrights themselves.[41] But *A King and No King* can alternatively be read as a text which uses the notion of incest – the ultimate taboo act – as a test by which to discover the limits of the permissible. Although it makes play with the generic conventions of tragicomedy which enable the reversal and retraction of what appear initially to be established situations and accepted principles, this is not to say that its only significance is as 'a kind of philosophical pipedream';[42] the King's desire for his sister is not identified with the tyrant's conventional lust (she reciprocates his feelings), but instead provides a kind of worst-case scenario for testing that logical corollary of absolutist theory which proposes that for a ruler, desire is its own legitimating principle. Thus power creates legality and exonerates from blame. This idea is an extension of Valentinian's:

> Know I am far above the faults I doe
> And those I do I am able to forgive too.
> (III, i, 119–20)

By various means the play presents Arbaces as an absolutist whose rhetoric is constantly held up to scrutiny. His opening speech returning victorious from foreign wars begins with an expression of his own worth, shaped by hyperbole:

> They that plac't me here,
> Intend it an honour large enough
> For the most valiant living, but to dare
> Oppose me single, though he lost the day.
> (I, i, 90–3)

His style is 'placed' by comments from his interlocutors; Tigranes, also a king, who is being addressed, calls it forthrightly bragging, and Mardonius, the good counsellor figure, defines Arbaces' manner as excessive in his asides: 'Its pitty that valour should be thus drunke' (I, i, 141), and does not flinch from direct confrontation with the King:

> You told Tigranes, you had won his Land
> With that sole arm propt by Divinity:
> Was not that bragging, and a wrong to us
> That daily venturde lives?
>
> (I, i, 275–8)

As in *The Maid's Tragedy*, the challenge to absolutism's insistence on its independence from the ruler–subject bond comes from a soldier, who asserts the King's need for an army to support his power. The comedy of the posturing braggart Bessus also functions to mirror and satirise Arbaces' claims to power, and especially to dominion over truth. He is the only one to express no horror at the contemplation of incest. The paradox whereby his fearful attempt to escape from battle results in a mistaken attack on the enemy which actually procures the victory (I, i, 68–71) prefigures the paradox whereby Arbaces achieves kingship through finding himself 'no king'.

If hyperbole is one of Arbaces' modes, paradox is the other. His selfhood is ultimately unstable, fragmented by 'sudden extremities' (I, i, 506):

> He is vain-glorious, and humble, and angrie, and patient, and merrie, and dull, and joyfull, and sorrowfull, in extremities in an houre.
>
> (I, i, 81–3)

And the dilemma in which he finds himself when he falls in love with his sister is explored through the paradox in the situation of the ruler who had previously believed his desire could sanction every act. Of all the Beaumont and Fletcher rulers, Arbaces both enacts and expresses absolutism most fully. In addition, there is what Jean-Pierre Teissedou calls 'le presence massive du paradigme royal' in the play;[43] and it is important that this is one of the few tyrant plays where the situation of tyranny is explored from the tyrant's perspective rather than that of his subjects.

Arbaces' interpretation of the meaning of royal prerogative is extensively defined in the first two acts, and it is suggestively articulated through many of the conventional attributes of tyranny, particularly the refusal to hear himself criticised, and the domination of passion over reason. His meeting with Panthea, though long-projected, is delayed until Act III, with accompanying build-up of tension. Then, when he first sees her, he cannot bring himself to speak to her; his next reaction is to deny their sibling relationship, and condemn to death anyone who asserts it. His rhetoric implies that the fulfilment of his desire as king now requires the overthrow of order, and of natural law:

> Shee is no kinne to me, nor shall shee be;
> If shee were any, I create her none,
> And which of you can question this?
>
> (III, i, 161–3)

He then acknowledges explicitly the horrifying implications of such an application of power:

> Such an ungodly sicknesse I have got,
> That he that undertakes my cure, must first
> Orethrow Divinity, all morall Lawes,
> And leave mankinde as unconfinde as beasts,
> Allowing them to doe all actions
> As freely as they drinke, when they desire.
> (III, i, 192–7)

His passion releases a variety of responses. Bessus, whose name and nickname ('Captain Stockfish') suggest bestiality, offers to act as procurer for the King; Mardonius believes it is a divine punishment for his tyranny. Arbaces himself is unmanned by his surrender to desire; Mardonius describes his changed behaviour:

> Hee has followed mee through twenty roomes, and ever when I stayed to await his command, he blushes like a girle, and lookes upon me, as if modestie kept in his businesse.
> (III, iii, 3–6)

It is Mardonius who describes the complete transformation of order that will ensue if Arbaces commits the act of incest:

> If you doe this crime, you ought to have no lawes; For after this it will bee great injustice in you to punish any offender for any crime.
> (III, iii, 97–8)

Arbaces' acknowledgment of Mardonius's virtue and his horrified rejection of Bessus's offer has both ethical and political meanings. In terms of the vestigial morality-play framework that surfaces most evidently in this part of the play it functions as a moral test which the King, after a struggle, passes; politically it constitutes a redefinition of sovereignty. The basis both of the King's power and the prohibition against incest is rational law, and even if man is accursed for having bought his reason 'at too deare a rate' (IV, iv, 132) the divinity which Arbaces so often cites does not sanction its contravention.

Yet the denouement of the play does not give an unequivocal endorsement to this position, although it cannot be said to subvert it. The plot contrivance by which Arbaces turns out neither to be Panthea's brother nor the true king enables the couple to legitimise their passion and prepare for marriage. Michael Neill finds in it a 'libertine scepticism' by which words are, after all, mere sounds: 'titles are jests' (I, i, 226), and 'language proves to be not the projection of a divinely inspired reason, but a mere decoration on the surface of reality.'[44] The handling of the revelation, especially in comparison with other romance plays which conclude with tragicomic revelation scenes such as *Cymbeline*, has a kind of perfunctoriness; although

Gobrias, Arbaces' real father, and Arane, his supposed mother, unravel the hidden history of Arbaces' parentage in conventional romance style in the play's last scene, there is no reunion of severed kinsfolk nor even any lines in which Panthea herself can be told the truth and acknowledge Arbaces as a legitimate lover. The play is quickly concluded with Arbaces eliciting 'loud thankes for me, that I am prov'd no King'. At the last moment his dilemma has been resolved by a dramatic trick and since his bride-to-be is actually the legitimate monarch he will continue to enjoy royal power. Nevertheless Neill's reading of the play, which insists on its fundamental unseriousness, neglects to account for the critique of absolutism effected in the central scenes. Arbaces' dilemma turns out to have been unreal because he was neither a king nor Panthea's brother in the first place but the problems posed for the ruler who finds himself testing the limits of his prerogative are real. The play makes serious examination of the King's relation to law through his relation to desire; and its narrative of romance does not undermine the conclusion that power and desire must be limited: to realise desire totally is to cease to be a king.

The Loyal Subject is another 'test-case' play which examines the problem of how a ruler's power can be controlled when it is exercised in such a way as to infringe the interests of his subjects and to create political disorder in his country. The ruler is legitimate but morally unstable, and he is poised between antithetical counsellors, the wise and loyal Archas, a general, and the scheming and hypocritical Boroskie. The morality-play structure echoes *A King and No King* but the focus here is rather on the general, and the testing of his loyalty to a ruler who is young and misguided. If Heywood's *The Royall King* (1602) is to be regarded as the text standing behind *The Loyal Subject* (as *Hamlet* stands behind *The Maid's Tragedy*), then Fletcher's shifts of emphasis are extremely striking.[45] In Heywood the King (Edward I, returned from the crusades) is an authoritative figure who is persuaded to test the apparently total devotion of his subject, Lord Martial, by courtiers who are jealous of his high favour. Martial's loyalty is subjected to a number of trials and ordeals: being made to hand over his offices to enemies, to bring his fairest daughter from the country up to court, and at one point being sentenced to death for appearing to rival the king in wealth and munificence. But the king's virtue is never compromised, and he never acts in ways which can be construed as weak or ineffectual. In conclusion, when he brands Martial's enemies as traitors and acknowledges Martial as the truly loyal subject, he emerges as wise and all-knowing, and Martial's obsequious devotion as totally justified. A subplot in which the rival claims of virtue and wealth are debated, and true loyalty of a captain humbled by circumstance acknowledged by the love of a good woman affirms the conventional morality of the play. Beside it, Fletcher's text appears as a sceptical re-evaluation of the claims of absolutism.

Sex and tyranny

In a variety of ways the absolutist issue is diluted in *The Loyal Subject*, and the Duke of Moscovia represents a comic vision of misapplied power, his potential for tyranny undermined.[46] He is defective as a guardian of his people and a leader of his country, but he is not a monster of appetite. In fact, the motif of the ruler's lust is comically treated through a reversal of some of the regular conventions, chiefly that the woman he most desires turns out to be a boy in disguise (actually Archas's son), and that far from exercising an active sexual threat to her he is intimidated in her presence and outmatched in the wit-combats they play. His sexual ineptitude is mirrored in his military incompetence. The appetite for power displayed in the tyrannous desires of Valentinian and Arbaces is displaced onto the unprincipled favourite, Boroskie, whose evil influence is responsible for the Duke's political mistakes. Like Bessus, he is a cowardly soldier who deserts his place in time of war. The Duke appoints him to Archas's position as commander of the army, but the soldiers have no respect for him; and at moments of crisis, when the Tartar army threatens Moscow, and later, when civil dissent led by Archas's elder son, Theodore, in revenge for his father's mistreatment breaks out, Archas has to be called in again to restore order. This mistreatment has taken the form of the physical torture of the elderly Archas, ordered by Boroskie who wishes to destroy his charismatic rival and has exceeded the warrant given him by the Duke in doing so. In a climactic scene (IV, vi) the tortured Archas appears onstage, presenting his injured body as a spectacle to the horrified gaze of the spectators. His supporters urge the immediate prosecution of civil war against the Duke and Boroskie, but Archas forbids it in the one speech of the play which explicitly alludes to, and defends, the principle of absolutism:

> Is not this our Soveraigne,
> The head of mercie, and of Law? who dares then,
> But Rebels scorning Law, appear thus violent?
> Is this a place for Swords? for threatening fits?
> The reverence of this house dares any touch,
> But with obedient knees, and pious duties.
> Are we not all his Subjects? all sworn to him?
> Has he not power to punish our offences?
> . . .
> You are offenders too, daily offenders,
> Proud insolencies dwell in your heart, and ye do 'em,
> Do 'em against his peace, his Law, his Person;
> Ye see he only sorrowes for your sins,
> And where his power might persecute, forgives ye.
> (IV, vi, 67–86)

The significance of this scene is complex. Part of it derives from the visual configuration. Angry soldiers, armed with torches ready to burn the royal house, have broken in, led by Archas's son and brother, and throng the stage; a group of women enters, including Archas's daughters whose virtue the Duke has attempted to corrupt, representing another voice of opposition; the Duke appears 'above' and begs to be heard; finally Archas enters, fresh from torture. The scene stages tyranny: the old man's violated body is an emblem of cruelty and injustice, and the threatening force of armed soldiers enhances the isolation and undermines the power of the lone figure above. Yet this reading of the scene in terms of the iconography of tyranny needs to be corrected; the truth must be supplied by the addition of the absent Boroskie, real author of the cruelty and misrule represented onstage. The tortured body of Archas stands for the bodies of the raped and corrupted women who more regularly symbolise the tyrant's power. In another context, Archas's speech in defence of the ruler's divine right, which draws frequently on the religious rhetoric of absolutism, might emerge as ironic and potently subversive of royalist orthodoxy; but the dramatic situation functions to defuse this effect. After Archas's big speech the Duke is filled with penitence and the soldiers withdraw.

The Loyal Subject appears to offer a much more cautious handling of the problem of tyranny than *The Maid's Tragedy*, *Valentinian*, or *A King and No King*, even though in comparison with *The Royal King and the Loyal Subject* it is far less an affirmatively royalist text. Critics have often found it unsatisfactory because it seems to neglect the opportunities offered.[47] But there may be factors to suggest that the apparent evasions of the text were in part a defensive measure. The play was licensed for performance in November 1618 only a few weeks after the execution of Sir Walter Ralegh, a spectacle witnessed by many observers, a number of whom recorded impressions of it.[48] There was widespread sympathy for Ralegh, even from Queen Anne herself, but he had long been a thorn in the flesh of James, who had suppressed his *History of the World* in 1614, because, in the view of John Chamberlain, it was 'too saucy in censoring princes'.[49] Certain references in the play could have been read as topical allusions, particularly in the aftermath of an event widely regarded as an act of royal injustice. Appleton mentions particularly the mocking offer for sale of potatoes (a commodity associated with Ralegh) by a neglected soldier in III, v, the reference to Virginia, and the Duke's seizure of Archas's treasure (as James had seized Ralegh's estate at Sherborne while he was in prison, and assigned it to his favourite Robert Carr[50]). Archas's outburst against his betrayal when invited to a banquet by the Duke and Boroskie in order to be arrested, which he calls 'the Judas way, to kisse me, bid me welcome, / And cut my throat' (IV, v, 95–6), might have recalled the treacherous action of Sir Lewis Stukeley in allowing Ralegh to think him his friend, and embracing him before betraying Ralegh's inept attempt to escape from England by boat. Stukeley, who had been paid a large sum for his help in trapping Ralegh, was afterwards known as Judas.[51] The Russian setting of the play in itself might hint at the presence of a topical meaning. It is a comparatively unusual location for a play in this period, and sharply distinct from Heywood's play, which is set in the England of Edward I. Fletcher's uncle Giles had published *Of the Rus Commonwealth* in 1591, after his return from a period as ambassador to the court of Tsar Fedor, and this work, which showed to Elizabeth I 'a true and strange face of a tyrannical state' and presented the Russian royal family as barbaric and oppressive, was suppressed by Lord Burghley.[52] The play contains no obvious verbal echoes of the prose text or other kind of direct allusion to it, but *Of the Rus Commonwealth* and its connection with Fletcher may have thickened the already dense texture of topicality around *The Loyal Subject* in such a way as to necessitate a corresponding indirectness in the handling of potentially sensitive political themes. Its ending is particularly consolatory (and follows Heywood): Archas, though offered the chance to punish Boroskie, chooses to forgive him; and the Duke, amazed to discover Alinda's true gender, instead marries Archas's elder daughter, Honora, and his lustful urges are thus safely rechannelled into a union with the family of his loyal subject.

In several later plays Fletcher returns to the motif of the tyrant's invasive lust and embodies resistance to it in a female subject whose assertion of her will calls into question the totality of the ruler's power. In attempting to satisfy his lust the ruler also trespasses on the rights of a male subject; in *The Humorous Lieutenant* he desires the woman to whom his son is betrothed, and in *The Custom of the Country* and *A Wife for a Month* he schemes to violate a marriage-bond, even attempting literally to invade the marital bedroom. In *The Custom of the Country* Count Clodio's desire to enjoy his traditional *droit du seigneur*, by taking Zenocia's virginity before she consummates her marriage to Arnoldo, is thwarted when the couple trick him during the performance of a marriage-masque and then flee the country. The situation is a first act preliminary to a series of exciting adventures in Portugal where both male and female characters find themselves involved in various kinds of sexual enslavement, of which Clodio's compulsion to follow 'this custom, which this unrefined country / Hath wrought into a law' is only the first. The play offers various contrasts between male and female sexuality; and while Zenocia's father and husband both seek to dilute the seriousness of her dilemma she entertains no compromise: with the words 'I must have all or none' she rejects as compromise Arnoldo's suggestion that a forced rape may leave the woman morally untainted. In Clodio's claim to Zenocia's virginity may be read the notion that a subject's rights and property are his only in a subsidiary sense, held as it were in trust for the ruler, but otherwise the political implications of Clodio's belief are not developed; what this play really offers is an account of sexual tyranny.[53]

In *A Wife for a Month* the lust of the usurper, King Frederick of Naples, for Evanthe, who like Zenocia is a virgin about to be married, is more fully politicised. Evanthe counters Frederick's lust with unremitting and protracted resistance; so persistent is she that Frederick is, as Bushnell puts it, obliged to 'legislate her sexuality in order to express his own',[54] first of all sentencing her husband to death after one month of marriage, then forbidding the consummation entirely. He attempts also to destroy the bond between the couple by encouraging Evanthe to believe that Valerio's claim to be impotent is a selfish lie when in fact he is attempting to preserve her. In discovering the truth Evanthe rises to such heights of heroic defiance that Valerio sees her in the image of a saint:

> You appear the Vision of a Heaven unto me,
> Stuck with all stars of honour shining cleerly,
> And all the motions of your mind celestial.
> (IV, v, 68–70)

The result of tyrannical oppression is, perversely, the ennoblement of the subject, and the fulfilment of his/her humanity. When the full extent of Frederick's scheming is revealed, the couple decide to consummate their marriage and die together. The political solution which has been reserved for the sexual crisis is now disclosed, and the usurper's brother, the true King Alphonso, recovers from his sickness and resumes his authority. The dilemma of the right-thinking subject oppressed by demands which are both royal and dishonourable is thus revealed: Frederick was never a true king, so his desire was always, unequivocally, illegitimate. Through the situation of beleaguered chastity, the play glorifies a subject's heroic resistance to tyranny. The decorum of gender, according to which the outcome of such a situation is normally the virgin's rape or suicide, is violated, leading critics to object to Evanthe's stance as unwomanly;[55] but the play is also concerned to test and modify stereotypes of female virtue[56] as well as to offer a new model for resistance.

The Humorous Lieutenant (*c.* 1619) again stages the confrontation between the lustful monarch and the woman who resists him, though questions of tyranny are not raised here. The King here is an old man, but his age does nothing to qualify the structure of power represented in his court and his sovereignty. The expression of his sexuality is licensed and catered for by the operations of the court bawd, Leucippe, a professional madam who controls a minor business empire with a nationwide network of contacts. When commanded by the King's agent to procure Celia for him she recognises that she must draw on all her expertise to trick Celia into coming to court. The situation is a comic parallel to that in *Valentinian*, but the confrontations between Celia and the King take a different direction on account of Celia's refusal to acknowledge the absolute force of the sovereign will. In the first of these the King initially conceals his identity, only revealing it when he expects the revelation to halt Celia's resistance: 'Why then I am a King, and mine own speaker' (IV, i, 143); but her answer asserts a will to challenge his: 'And I as free as you, mine own disposer.' In the second scene she reads him a deflating lecture on the vanity of lust, and at the end denigrates his image of power. The enforcement of his will by rape, should he attempt it, would demonstrate his ineffectuality; by denying him her body, she has thwarted his sovereignty:[57]

> *Antigonus.* Can nothing in the power of Kings perswade ye?
> *Celia.* No, nor that power command me.
> *Antigonus.* Say I should force ye?
> I have it in my will.
> *Celia.* Your will's a poore one;
> And though it be a Kings will, a despised one,
> Weaker then Infants leggs, your will's in swadling clouts:
> A thousand waies my will has found to check ye;
> A thousand doores to scape ye: I dare die sir;
> As suddenly I dare die, as you can offer.
> (IV, v, 58–65)

The King then accepts this limitation on his will and withdraws from the sexual arena in favour of his son, who he knows to be Celia's real lover. The political potential of the situation is defused, and the theme of father–son sexual rivalry submerged, as the remainder of the action is directed towards a comic conclusion in which Celia finds her lost father as Antigonus emerges in the right relationship to his son.

In the last play to be discussed the subject's challenge to the ruler is played out in different terms. In *The Double Marriage* Ferrand, Duke of Naples, is both a usurper and a tyrant, so that any confrontation between ruler and subject would not of necessity involve the question of the royal prerogative. He is opposed on several fronts and eventually unseated and killed by the Duke of Sesse, whom he had forced into exile. Although one of his major opponents is a woman, his tyranny is political rather than sexual; it is specifically contrasted with the traditional sexual monstrousness of such figures as Caligula and Nero, who are said by Virolet, his enemy, at least to have abused their power 'as Kings' while Ferrand has behaved like a merchant, engrossing the country's wealth to his private uses (I, i, Glover and Waller, VI, 324).[58] When Virolet's plot against Ferrand fails, he manages to escape, but his wife, Juliana, is captured and tortured by the tyrant. The motivation for the torture is purely political; Ferrand has no sexual interest in Juliana, but wants her to reveal her husband's whereabouts. The intellectual resistance offered by Evanthe is replaced by Juliana's physical courage; she withstands the torture, administered onstage, so courageously that Ferrand in the end abandons it:

> Unloose her, I am conquer'd, I must take
> Some other way; reach her my chair, in honor
> Of her invincible fortitude.
>   (I, i, Glover and Waller, VI, 335)

Juliana's status as heroic resister of oppression is enhanced by the physical disablement which results from her torture. Her body is exhibited, like that of Archas, as a spectacle of tyranny. The motif of the tyrant's lust is displayed in another part of the play, where Ferrand further dishonours the Duke of Sesse by taking his daughter for a mistress; but the significance of this action is not related to ideas of the corruption or abuse of the female body.[59]

In this play, perhaps through the influence of Massinger, the meaning of tyranny is amplified through references to theatricality which relate the self-displaying behaviour of Ferrand both to the mimicry of tyrannical power by the foolish courtier, Castruccio, who in two important scenes dresses up and plays the part of king, and also to the meretricious allure of the Amazonian Martia. Theatrical metaphor regularly suggests the connection between power and public spectacle. Juliana, captured by Ferrand and waiting for torture, sees herself as an actor on 'a glorious stage of murder' over which the tyrant presides; as 'master of the company' he takes up her metaphor: 'Begin the scene' (I, i, Glover and Waller, VI, 334). Ronvere sees Virolet's conspiracy against Ferrand is as 'a masque, done for the King's pleasure', though to Virolet it is 'a pageant to usher our ruin'. Terms like 'scene', 'masque', 'play' and 'perform' occur regularly. Martia's appearance to Virolet on her father's pirate-ship is heralded by strange music; when Virolet sees her he comments, 'The face o' the masque is alter'd', and 'masque' is used elsewhere to refer to her beauty. At the climax the Duke of Sesse wants his killing of her to be his own 'scene', though he allows it must be completed by the presence of 'spectators'.

The scenes in which Ferrand licenses Castruccio to play at being king compare the ridiculous decrees of the mock-king in his revels with the tyrannous laws of Ferrand's police-state where ''tis death here, above two to talk together', and concludes that there is no difference between them. In the second of these scenes Ferrand and his intimates act as hidden audience while Castruccio in royal robes entertains them with a display of tyrannous appetite, calling for 'women in abundance' and rich foods. While this is going on the Duke of Sesse seizes the chance for a takeover, and occupies Ferrand's castle, crying 'Liberty and freedom'. Castruccio, interrupted in the midst of his play-acting, is glad to be relieved of his role and vows to abjure allegiance to a king ever after. Tyrannous power is identified with spectacle and with appetite; but the will of the subject to resist, represented both in Juliana and the Duke of Sesse, demystifies the spectacle and discloses the limits of that power.

Though McLuskie identifies the presence of 'a subversive and radical sexual politics' in *The Maid's Tragedy*[60] it is difficult to see it informing the tyrant plays generally, despite the presence of many strong female characters who challenge the tyrant's power. And, as I have shown, although Evadne eventually becomes the King's murderer and revenger of her own (and the realm's) corruption, her role has been redefined from that of the strong woman who can control and deploy her own sexuality to that of the stereotyped victim of tyrannical lust. Zenocia, Celia, and Evanthe courageously resist the imposition of tyrannical will, but they do so without radically challenging the social structures of patriarchy. The tyrant's conventional attribute of lust is constantly politicised to stand for the more general notions of the assertion of sovereign power against the rights of the subject; and in *A King and No King* it is redefined as the totality of absolute desire which can never be socially legitimated but requires transformation into a legally recognised form. The plays function within the Jacobean discourse of absolutism but, necessarily, they negotiate the challenges created for any dramatic representation of ruler–subject relationships with delicacy. But the deployment of strategies of indirection need not lay them open to the charges of political compromise levelled by Coleridge and later critics.

Chapter 5

Courtship and Marriage in the Comedies

This chapter focuses on a group of comedies in which the process of courtship and/or adjustment to marriage provides the major narrative impetus. In probable order of composition they are *The Woman's Prize* (?1604),[1] *The Coxcomb* (*c.* 1609), *The Scornful Lady* (*c.* 1609), *Wit Without Money* (*c.* 1614), *The Wild-Goose Chase* (1621), and *Rule a Wife and Have a Wife* (1624).[2] I have also included *The Two Noble Kinsmen* (1613) which, though generically a tragicomedy, is concerned with courtship and marriage in all areas of the plot, utilises marriage as a means of dramatic closure like the comedies, and, as I hope to show, handles these subjects in similar terms to the comedies. Although marriage is explored in tragedies and tragicomedies (in, for example, *Valentinian, Thierry and Theodoret, The Double Marriage,* and *A Wife for a Month*) to such an extent as to indicate that Fletcher and his collaborators constantly found it dramatically fruitful in many ways, its centrality to the plot designs of these comedies sets them apart from marriage plays in other genres.

The most obvious Shakespearian models for these plays are *The Taming of the Shrew* and to a lesser extent *Much Ado About Nothing* in which courtship is treated by means of the battle of the sexes; the action consists of a series of stratagems and counter-stratagems in which the man and the woman each strive to evade the other's terms. The Beaumont and Fletcher plays modify the sexual balance of *The Taming of the Shrew*, whereby the act of imposition is largely Petruchio's, and they take much further the questions raised in Shakespeare's text about the function of courtship: in plays such as *The Scornful Lady* and *The Wild-Goose Chase* the taming metaphor is applied to men as well as women, and they explore the degrees of success with which the 'wild' impulses that characterise pre-marital sexual behaviour can be socialised. It is often the 'wooing' scenes which energise these plays as a whole, in the aggression with which potential partners confront one another as well as in the displays of dominance. The variety of roles which the characters try out in order to deceive one another into disclosures of feeling create theatrical excitement, and render courtship as experimentation with a range of sexual identities. The ways in which roles can be assumed and discarded at will questions both the stability of identity, and also the nature of sexual difference: if a woman can choose the guises in which she presents herself to a man, does the recognition that there are stereotypes and that some are sexually more appealing than others mean that there can never be any final standard of 'truth' by which to categorise and evaluate behaviour? The questions posed are rarely to do with love, which is often a given that Beaumont and Fletcher are not concerned to explore; Maria and Petruchio in *The Woman's Prize* never doubt that they love one another, but the point is to negotiate terms for their relationship, not to test emotions and feelings. In *The Two Noble Kinsmen* Arcite and Palamon quarrel not over who really loves Emilia, or loves her best, but over who has the most right to love her.

By way of contrasting these plays with Shakespearian romantic comedy, Kathleen McLuskie says that in them 'the humanised patriarchy of Shakespearean comedy is transferred to a world of competitive individualism'.[3] The plays involve many forms of competition, between individuals for a partner, or more commonly between prospective partners for domination, but also between different interests. One of the important issues raised in several of the plays is the extent to which marriage serves the competing interests of individual and of society. Society is not usually represented through the claims of family and inheritance, as so often in Shakespeare; there is a marked absence of parents and guardians, and where they do appear, as in *The Woman's Prize* and *The Wild-Goose Chase*, for example, their influence is minimal. More often social pressures are defined in vaguer terms of order, regulation, and constraint, constraint particularly upon the exercise of appetite. The metaphors of travelling and exploration in foreign countries function to suggest that sexual experimentation (usually, but not invariably by men – Margarita in *Rule a Wife* is an exception) must be a preliminary to the directing of the appetite into a single, socially sanctioned, channel by which it flows home. Unregulated desire in either sex may be dangerous, and requires social control; the questioning of the adequacy of the institution of marriage to impose this control may be implied (in *The Two Noble Kinsmen*, for example) though the plays do not attempt to answer it. None the less they do recognise the reality of strong emotional drives, towards homosocial bonding as well as the expression of sexual desire, for which marriage may not easily cater.

The two plays in which Beaumont and Fletcher (and, in the case of *The Two Noble Kinsmen*, Shakespeare) explore the relationship of homosocial bonding to marriage most fully, *The Coxcomb* and *The Two Noble Kinsmen*, stand apart from the rest in that they do not take the form of wit comedy. *The Two Noble Kinsmen* is generically separate, and *The Coxcomb* owes more to Shakespearian romantic comedy, particularly in its subplot, than to the witty comedy of Jonson and Middleton, Fletcher's more characteristic mode.

But *The Coxcomb*'s relation to romantic comedy is indirect, and inclined to be parodic in its treatment of romantic themes such as innocence, pastoral, and, most to the point here, heroic friendship. Its main plot concerns male friendship as a problem in relation to marriage, and although the situation has tragic potential the play treats it in a consciously paradoxical manner. Here, the situation of the husband's friend who falls in love with the wife creates a moral dilemma for the friend who is an honest man, but when Antonio learns that Mercury loves his wife, Maria, he responds at once by offering Maria to Mercury as a mistress. Not content with merely making the offer, he goes to ridiculous lengths in the stratagems he employs to bring the reluctant couple together, including disguises as a comic Irish footman, and as a postman, which are easily penetrated by his wife. When in the latter disguise he brings Maria a letter purporting to tell of his own death she decides to call his bluff and permits the adultery to take place. Mercury's revulsion at the act, once committed, fulfils Maria's intention, for she has enabled a paradox to be proved: a wife and a friend have betrayed a husband and yet remained 'honest'. This paradox is a means by which Beaumont and Fletcher deflate idealism and reveal it as posturing. The motivation for Antonio's generosity to Mercury is a Quixotic desire for 'everlasting glory' (II, i, 192) as a paragon of the faithful friend:

> We two will be – you would little thinke it; as famous for our friendship ... if God please, as ever *Damon* was and *Pytheas*, or *Pylades* and *Orestes*, or any two that were.
>
> (II, i, 151–7)

The absurdity of this is reflected in Mercury's reaction; despite his desire for Maria he sees Antonio's act in social and not romantic terms, as self-inflicted cuckoldom, not as heroic friendship: 'Well go thy wayes, thou art the tydiest wittall this day above ground, and yet thy end for all this must bee mottly' (II, i, 194–5). He exposes the contradictions in Antonio's wish, though a married man, to perpetuate the solidarity of male community. Whether or not the play relates directly to a Quixotic source, the story of 'The Curious Impertinent' from *Don Quixote*,[4] the revelation of the folly of romantic illusion, which also shapes the subplot, relates it to *The Knight of the Burning Pestle* which has undoubted origins in Spanish romance.[5] Beaumont and Fletcher's distinctive handling of this situation is evident from a comparison with two other city comedies in which husbands' testing of their wives' chastity rebounds, in different ways, in their faces: Marston's *Jack Drum's Entertainment* (1601) and Field's *Amends for Ladies* (1611). In *Jack Drum's Entertainment* the attempt of Brabant Senior, a complacent and pretentious would-be wit, to use his wife's chastity as a means of playing a joke on a comically lustful Frenchman exposes a rich man's over-valuation of his assets and his power. He thinks it will be 'immortal for a Jest' to make the Frenchman, Sir John fo de King, believe that Mistress Brabant, whom he describes as 'exceeding wittie, but admirable chaste' to be a 'loose lascivious Curtesan', expecting Sir John to emerge ridiculed. But to the delight of the rest of the company, and particularly Brabant Senior's resentful younger brother, the Frenchman enters in the play's closing moments extolling the pleasures he has enjoyed with Mistress Brabant 'de most delicat plumpe vench dat ever mee tuche', and Brabant Senior's exposure as a cuckold is the final moment in the play's comic deflation of arrogance and lust. Like Antonio in *The Coxcomb* he is an 'honest selfe made Cuckold' (Wood, Vol. 3, V), but one whose excesses are satirically rather than comically viewed.

The wife-testing plot in *Amends for Ladies* is closer in its details to *The Coxcomb*, as well as to the 'Curious Impertinent' story,[6] but where all three characters in *The Coxcomb*, as well as in Cervantes, are virtuous, here the husband, Sir John Loveall, is an ambivalent figure, and the friend, Subtle, only too delighted to have his desire for the wife, Lady Perfect, condoned:

> All's as I wished;
> This was my aim, although I have seemed strange.
> (I, i, 431)

Field complicates his plot with a number of motifs, creating effects of uncertainty rather than richness. Sir John's feeling for Subtle is more homoerotic than homosocial; the pact with Subtle to test Lady Perfect's chastity is sealed 'by this, love's masculine kiss',

> By all our mutual engagement passed,
> By all the hopes of amity to come
> (I, i, 430)

and in the final scene Sir John claims that he would prefer to have his view of women's weakness vindicated by Subtle's successful seduction than to see his wife retain her virtue:

> O friend, it would do me good at the heart
> To have her overcome: she does so brag,
> And stand upon her chastity, forsooth.
> (V, i, 476)

But Lady Perfect lives up to her name; she is also a patient Griselda who will not complain when her husband insults her verbally, beats her, and gives away her clothes to a whore. Field's design of his plot to reflect the interests and allay the sexual anxieties of a male audience is evident; it allows not only for the titillation of scenes such as those where Sir John instructs Subtle on techniques for seduction and Subtle then reports, falsely, in detail on his success but also for the comforting certainty of Lady Perfect's proof of her innocence, at which each man in turn falls on his knees to beg her pardon. Sir John, overcome with penitence, urges her to punish him, but Lady Perfect is Cordelia-like in her forgiveness:

> Rise, rise, sir, pray,
> You have done no wrong to me.
> (v, i, 480)

By contrast, Beaumont and Fletcher's plot, in allowing honourable motives to all of the characters without foregrounding the wife's chastity, focuses on the irreconcilable nature of the husband's desires – to retain the perfect friendship alongside the perfect marriage; and it does not offer the consolatory fantasy of *Amends for Ladies* whereby the husband can be assured of the wife's virtue when she refuses the near-perfect conditions for adultery which he himself creates and controls. The conclusion of *The Coxcomb* affirms the priority of marriage bonds over the claims of friendship, which has never been in any doubt, when Maria speaks a eulogy of her husband as a man 'so sweetly temper'd',

> That he would make himselfe a naturall foole,
> To do a noble kindnesse for a friend
> (v, iii, 165–7)

and moves the bystanders to tears. The farcical quality of this plot has in any case deproblematised the issue. But in *The Two Noble Kinsmen* the clash of interests between different kinds of desire not only is not resolved but is presented as being inherently incapable of resolution. This clash is dramatised in several ways.

In the main plot the potential for conflict between the private (and specifically sexual) demands of marriage and the male commitment to action in a public sphere is the focus of the first act. When Theseus is called upon by three Queens to postpone his marriage to Hippolyta and its consummation in order to avenge the dishonourable deaths of their husbands at the hands of his old enemy, Creon, king of Thebes, he is at first reluctant:

> Why good Ladies,
> This is a service, whereto I am going,
> Greater than any war.
> (I, i, 169–71)

Marriage is a dignified, even heroic enterprise: This grand act of our life, this daring deede / Of Fate in wedlocke' (I, i, 163–4). But within this conception of marriage the power of sexual passion is acknowledged: Theseus does not dispute the assertion of the first Queen that if he once sleeps with Hippolyta he will forget the claims of duty and honour, and he therefore agrees, urged by both wife and sister, to go directly to war. He congratulates himself on his decision at the end of the play's first scene:

> As we are men
> Thus should we doe, being sensually subdude
> We loose our humane tytle.
>
> (I, i, 231–3)

The implied contradiction for a man between marital passion as sensual subjection and as heroic endeavour[7] is not explored directly, but it informs the play's treatment of the conflict between friendship and love which is adumbrated in the relationship of Theseus and Pirithous and developed at length in the situation of the kinsmen themselves.

Homosocial bonding is associated nostalgically with shared experiences and pre-sexual innocence. Hippolyta herself describes the feeling between Theseus and Pirithous as a 'knot of love' incapable of being disentangled, introducing, but not resolving, the issue of whether it is greater than Theseus's love for her. Emilia's answer is cryptic:

> Doubtlesse
> There is a best, and reason has no manners
> To say it is not you.
>
> (I, iii, 47–8)

She goes on to describe the intensity of her own affection for a girl friend, Flavina, who died, significantly before reaching puberty, and to reflect 'that the true love tweene Mayde, and mayde, may be / More than in sex dividuall'.[8] At this point she asserts that she never expects to love 'any that's calld man'. This dialogue between Hippolyta and Emilia clearly draws on the traditional debate about the best status for a woman, as maid, wife, or widow,[9] but it relates more significantly to Emilia's dilemma as unwilling victim of a sexual desire which she does not share, and to the ultimately fatal dilemma of the kinsmen.

The scene in which Palamon and Arcite catch their first sight of Emilia is so designed as to exhibit, almost schematically, the mutual incompatibility of male friendship and heterosexual love, and to contrast them, from a male viewpoint, in terms of co-operation and competition. Together in prison the kinsmen can regard themselves as a complete and perfect unit, sexually and even socially fulfilled:

> And heere being thus together,
> We are an endles mine to one another;
> We are one anothers wife, ever begetting
> New birthes of love; we are father, friends, acquaintance,
> We are in one another, Families,
> I am your heire, and you are mine: This place
> Is our Inheritance.
>
> (II, ii, 78–84)

The sense of Stoic commonplace in this language renders it as more than paradoxical phrasemaking; the kinsmen's blood relationship, as well as their total mutuality of feeling, is used to make them represent an ideal of male friendship, self-enclosed and eternally protected from the incursive corruption of the outside world, including female sexuality. Immediately after this passage[10] they see Emilia picking flowers in the garden, and though they do not hear her disparaging comment on the self-absorption of Narcissus, or the rest of her sexually charged dialogue with her woman,[11] everything is at once and forever changed for them. The childish terms in which their rivalry is expressed–

> *Palamon.* I saw her first.
> *Arcite.* That's nothing.
> *Palamon.* But it shall be.
> *Arcite.* I saw her too. –
>
> (II, ii, 160–1)

–partially restate the new currency of their relationship. While they quarrel over the right to love Emilia they show no interest in her feelings; they are not depicted wooing her. Although the context for their relationship for the remainder of their play is courtship, and they are rival lovers, the situation itself objectifies Emilia; but her attempts to avoid involvement and choice further stress how the important relationship remains that between the two men, a relationship which cannot continue to exist in its present form. When Emilia, rather than have Palamon and Arcite put to death for fighting over her, begs that they be allowed to live, provided they go separately into exile, both refuse, preferring that their relationship terminate in the death of one rather than life apart. The transition for the kinsmen from male friendship to heterosexual love is violent, and nearly fatal for them both; Emilia's response to Arcite's victory in the final tournament is not joy or relief but horror: 'Is this wynning?' (V, iii, 138).

In the end the sexual competition is absurdly concluded by an event which emphatically overthrows all the efforts of wise Theseus at rational control: Arcite is killed when his horse, Emilia's gift, goes out of control and throws him, so that Palamon, who has been doomed to death for losing in the tournament, is redeemed to marry Emilia after all. Good horsemanship is an ancient symbol of self-control;[12] this arbitrary outcome of all the attempts to regulate sexual desire seems to imply their futility. But in the subplot, on the other hand, the dilemma created by the hopeless preference of the Jailor's daughter for Palamon rather than her more suitable wooer does turn out to be capable of human resolution. Despite the generic differences between the romance mode of the main plot, with its legendary characters and aristocratic value system, centring on chivalry and heroic duty, and the comic subplot concerning humble and nameless rustics,[13] there are strong similarities between the effects of desire on the kinsmen and on the Jailor's daughter, for whom love also involves the abandonment of reason, law, and kinship ties. Yet the Doctor, whom her perplexed father consults, is more effective as a legislator than is Theseus; and his device of substituting the Wooer for Palamon both in the Daughter's fantasies and in her bed seems to work.[14] But in this situation, where the Daughter's unsuitable passion evolves into madness requiring a cure, considerations of social custom and morality can be sidestepped; the Doctor easily dismisses the scruples of both Wooer and Jailor about the ethics of sex before marriage:

> That's but a nicenesse,
> Nev'r cast your child away for honestie;
> Cure her first this way, then if shee will be honest,
> She has the path before her.
>
> (v, ii, 20–3)

This sort of resolution is unavailable within the rigorous codes of conduct by which the behaviour of the main plot characters is regulated; and moreover, Emilia's attachment to her virginity – even on her wedding day she is 'bride habited, / But mayden harted' – makes Theseus's role as legislator more complex than the Doctor's.

The play posits not only that the unruliness of sexual desire creates many problems both for society and for the individual, but also that marriage may be neither an easy nor a natural solution to them. Its focus on female desire is unusually prominent, and the number and length of the self-reflective speeches and soliloquies allotted to Emilia and to the Jailor's Daughter renders them as important to the play's design as are the kinsmen. But this in no way signifies that the play adopts a position sympathetic to women or that it is concerned to explore their problems from their viewpoint. The misdirected desire of the Jailor's Daughter and the lack of desire of Emilia are problems for patriarchal society – represented by their male kinsfolk – to solve.

In the two city comedies of courtship and marriage produced during this period, *The Scornful Lady* and *Wit Without Money*, female desire and the contention between instinct and social control are also central, but the nature of this control is differently represented: the main female characters, the Scornful Lady herself and the widowed Lady Heartwell in *Wit Without Money* are significantly without male kindred. The absence in these plays of fathers or other authority-figures who embody the structures and principles of patriarchy is important.[15] Parent–child relationships are displaced in favour of sibling relationships: each play features two brothers and two sisters and their retainers and companions. The Scornful Lady and Lady Heartwell each head their own households. The prodigals, Young Loveless and Vallentine, command alternative styles of household with their entourages of companions and hangers-on. Older male characters such as the steward, Savill, in *The Scornful Lady* and Lovegood, the Uncle, and his friend, the Merchant, in *Wit Without Money* either have no authority or are subservient to the gallants and prodigals. Though the forming of marriage partnerships between the young and eligible is at the centre of the plays, marriage is not treated as an institution to be controlled by families representing the interests of patriarchal society, but as the prize at the end of an elaborately competitive game. It is generally male needs and desires which give the action its impetus, but the women are socially and economically in a position to make their own choices, so that the narrative movement of the plot is determined by a process of negotiation between the sexes, courtship in a more obvious sense than in *The Two Noble Kinsmen*. This negotiation is usually credited in terms of a combat of wits; and wit itself is not merely a comic mode and a currency for exchange, but also an asset in its own right, and one which enhances the value of the combatants as prospective marriage partners. These comedies stand in something of an oblique relationship to city comedy proper, refusing many of its potentially relevant narrative resources in terms of plots about city wives and adultery; but they do very decidedly participate in its market-place ethos and its representation of sex as a commodity.

In the main plot of *The Scornful Lady* Elder Loveless has devalued himself as a suitor in the eyes of the Scornful Lady by making too public a show of his feelings; she therefore orders him to go abroad for a year as punishment but he refuses, and stays behind in the city in disguise. She penetrates the disguise, and also the several other stratagems he adopts to get her to accept him, and although she acknowledges his love for her, and her own for him, she will not accept him until she thinks she is about to lose him to somebody else. His trick at this point – disguising another man (in fact, a former rival) in woman's clothes as his bride – operates not only as a daringly witty stratagem but also, at least in the Scornful Lady's eyes, as an enhancement of his market value. She is most attracted by a man who seems to belong to somebody else. The relationship between Elder Loveless and the Lady is explored emotionally, through the psychology of power-play, rather than socially, as would be the norm in conventional city comedy; neither partner looks to the other for financial support, the absence of which constraint is pointed up by the subplot where Young Loveless, a prodigal, repairs his fortunes by marrying a rich widow. But in the subplot the chief currency is wit, here realised by the assertion of freedom from the constraints of economic or emotional dependency. Elder Loveless runs the risk of losing the Lady when he allows her to see that he really cares for her: in IV, i she tricks him into an admission of love by pretending to swoon, only to recover immediately and revile him in public for being so foolish as to think her capable of losing control. Young Loveless needs the Widow's money but he will not agree to reform or cast off his shiftless companions to get it; he wins her on his own terms with a witty speech in which he proves that 'the maintenance of / But Corne and water', in the form of ale, will be sufficient to provide his followers with all they need:

> In this short sentence Ale, is all included:
> Meate, Drinke, and Cloth.
>
> (IV, ii, 62)

This Widow is decidedly a wish-fulfilment figure of male fantasy like Dame Pliant in *The Alchemist*: young, rich, available, and without any desire to take charge of the power her money confers on her. Elder Loveless, who has to work much harder than his brother to get what he wants, ensnares the Lady by claiming that he has decided to marry a woman who is the opposite to her in everything: submissive, humble, and modest. She is so piqued that she insists on marrying him instantly, even kissing him in public to ensure the compact. When he reveals that this 'woman' was in fact a man in disguise the Lady acknowledges that she has been won by trickery superior to her own. Elder Loveless's device is more than merely the culminating stratagem in an escalating series; in its wit it offers a strong challenge to conventional ideas of marriage and morality. The exchange between the Lady and Young Loveless, her new brother-in-law, suggests that Elder Loveless's trick is a moral equivalent to the inversion of accepted values that Young Loveless himself embodies:

> *Young Loveless.* Now my pretty Lady Sister,
> How doe you finde my brother?
> *Lady.* Almost as wilde as you are.
> *Young Loveless.* A will make the better husband.
>
> (V, iv, 119–22)

And if 'wildness' is offered as a quality to be valued in a husband, the scene in which Elder Loveless presents the Lady with the cross-dressed Welford as his bride-to-be makes it clear that traditional qualities of a wife, both in moral terms of chastity and virtue and social terms of housekeeping skills, are not those valued by either partner in this union. City comedy is often seen as a conservative genre, typically concerned, in one critic's words, with 'the preservation of chastity and the right use of wealth – and beneath it all the stability of society'.[16] Another views as central to its ethos the property-based marriage.[17] In these terms, *The Scornful Lady* is out to shock and challenge city values. Its gaily subversive account of the place of marriage in society is completed by Welford, who, in his woman's disguise, is taken into the bed of the Lady's sister, Martha, whom he seduces and obliges to marry him. He too wins an heiress merely by taking part in a trick.

This is a fantasy world in which young people are free to choose their marriage partners without regard to family obligations, where rich widows are glad to marry spendthrift prodigals, and even usurers turn gallants and give away their money. The fantasy, however, is clearly gendered. That the Lady needs to taunt and humiliate her lover is a perversity requiring correction. When, in IV, i, after she has mocked him in front of her waiting-woman and her sister for displaying feeling and he storms out in misogynistic rage, she acknowledges the danger of her behaviour:

> I would be loth to anger him too much:
> What fine foolery is this in a woman,
> To use those men most frowardly they love most?
> If I should loose him thus, I were rightly served.
> (IV, i, 369–72)

Her generalising of her position, both in these lines and in the truism with which she ends the scene ('Women are most fooles, when they thinke th'are wisest'), reflects the stereotype of the curst, frowardly woman who needs a man to govern her perverse appetites. She is given a soliloquy at the beginning of V, ii in which to acknowledge the unnaturalness of her behaviour, and her inability to control it; it begins with two lines which illustrate that her attitude is to be seen as representative:

> Is it not strange that every womans will
> Should tracke out new waies to disturbe her selfe?

Finkelpearl admires the speech as a 'fascinating attempt at a psychological explanation of her conduct',[18] but the reversion from the particular to the general at the end of it reinforces the view that this is a variation on a stereotype, albeit a subtle one with a slant that would be topical in the decade of 'Hic mulier':

> O what are wee!
> Men, you must answer this, that dare obey
> Such thinges as wee command.
> (V, ii, 19–21)

The Lady's conclusion ascribes feminine perversity to a lack of proper control, which can only be imposed from outside, by men. Elder Loveless's parallel soliloquy, at the beginning of the previous scene, reveals his sexual insecurity; he can explain her perverse rejection of him only through the attraction of a more aggressive and lower-class rival,

> Some hinde,
> That she hath seen beare (like another *Milo*)

Quarters of Malte upon his backe, and sing with 't.
(v, i, 12–14)

Both speeches call for men to impose control over women in order to restore normal relations. For all its apparent challenge to the social and economic ethos of city comedy the gender politics of this play are not at heart subversive. In the three gentry marriages which conclude the play it is overwhelmingly male interests which are served.

Wit Without Money shares the ethos and value-system of *The Scornful Lady*, and the relationship of its central character in many ways reworks that of the Scornful Lady and Elder Loveless. Here, the woman is more powerful and the man apparently less; Lady Heartwell is a rich and desirable widow, witty, socially accomplished, well able to control her household and her band of suitors, and Vallentine a prodigal gentleman who has squandered all his wealth. But their relationship is not polarised in these obvious terms of power and dependency. Its structure is complicated by Vallentine's challenges to sexual and social convention; unlike Elder Loveless he is not in love with or even interested in the lady, nor, more importantly, is he at all concerned to restore his fortune. To the bafflement and despair of his uncle, creditors, and tenants, he has opted for the freedom of living by his wits rather than acknowledging his economic obligations as a member of the landed gentry. He has abandoned the duties and constraints, as well as the rewards, of his hereditary status as a rural landlord for the easy freemasonry of a society of urban wits:

> All good men's my meanes, my wits my plow,
> The Townes my stock, Tavernes my standing house,
> And all the world knowes theres no want; all Gentlemen
> That love society love me; all purses
> That wit and pleasure opens, are my Tennants.
> (I, i, 156–60)

His rejection of social constraint extends to women, and the eagerness of his companions – the usual trio of city wits, Fountaine, Bellamore, and Harebrain – in pursuit of the widow contrasts with his own indifference. The sexual and financial rewards of marrying someone so desirable in every way are as nothing to him in comparison with the loss of freedom. Vallentine prefers what Bristol calls, in his discussion of the politics of marriage in the context of early modern society, 'the solidarity of the male community'[19] to marriage on any terms:

> Why tis a monstrous thing to marry at all,
> Especially as now tis made; me thinkes a man,
> An understanding man, is more wife to me,
> And of a nobler tie, than all these trinkets.
> (II, ii, 45–8)

He is even at times a misogynist. From Vallentine's stance of male solidarity Fletcher creates a narrative of his relationship with Lady Hartwell in the form of a test: as a service to his three friends, who supply him with the means to live like a gentleman, he will 'try' her to see if she is worth their efforts, guaranteeing not to woo her for himself. The main plot, then, develops towards the crucial encounter of the play's central couple, each strong-minded, forceful, and with a position to uphold. Lady Hartwell's position is, of course, constructed as the antithesis to Vallentine's. Where he has squandered his money, she has a great fortune and, as his uncle admiringly says, 'well she knowes to use it'; where wit is the currency on which he lives, she, for all her material wealth, guards money carefully and will not give hand-outs to charity. In economic terms, he is the romantic, she the realist; and her attractions are identified with her material assets: according to her sister Isabella she is 'a goodly portly Lady, / A woman of presence, she spreads satten, / As the Kings ships doe canvas' (I, ii, 10–12). When she discovers her sister secretly supplying resources to Vallentine's younger brother, Francisco, in pity of his poverty, Lady Hartwell rounds on her for wasting money on a man who can make her no return; she has no sympathy for the poor-but-honest lover:

> Say the man had vertue,
> Is vertue in this age a full inheritance:
> What Joynture can he make you, *Plutarchs Moralls?*
> (III, i, 68–70)

Her anxiety to prevent Isabella from making an unwise marriage is so great that she decides to uproot her whole household, much to the annoyance of her citified servants, and move to the country, thus confirming the identification of town with the freedom of wit and country with the security of money. But before she can set off Vallentine intervenes, claiming to have come to disprove popular gossip about her. The meeting is a turning point for both: afterwards she reverses her desire to leave the town, and he revises his view of women. This scene is a variation on the theme of courtship-as-sparring-match; the couple begin as antagonists but eventually find the way to reconciliation. Vallentine attempts to goad Lady Hartwell into exhibiting the vices which he believes she, as a woman and a widow, must possess; she counters, by exposing the hidden assumptions that support misogyny. She is eloquent in her denunciation of sexual double standards by which behaviour is differentially evaluated according to gender, and convincing in the demonstration of how stereotypes of women as proud, vain, fond of gossip, obsessed with trivia are constructed to serve men's interests. She illustrates how the norms of society appear to circumscribe women and privilege men. Vallentine is deeply impressed, as the audience must also be:

Widdow. Are we not gaily blest then,

	And much beholding to you for your substance?

                    And much beholding to you for your substance?
                    You may doe what you list, we what beseemes us,
                    And narrowly doe that too, and precisely,
                    Our names are served in else at Ordinaries
                    And belcht abroad in Tavernes.
Vallentine.   O most brave Wench,
                    And able to redeeme an age of women.
                                          (III, ii, 129–34)

This display of eloquence in defence of women is in many ways similar to that of Moll Cutpurse in *The Roaring Girl*, but less compromised; Moll speaks as a social outsider, a cross-dressed woman who is not at the mercy of a sexist society to the same extent as Lady Hartwell. Lady Hartwell vindicates women from a position itself deeply vulnerable to sexist attack: that of the widow. Vallentine has earlier given voice to some of the conventionally hostile views of this figure:

    It is to wed a widdow, to be doubted mainely
    Whether the shirte you have be yours or no,
    Or those old bootes you ride in.
                            (II, ii, 26–8)

The image of the 'old bootes' operates in two ways, suggesting not only the dubiously second-hand quality of the riches with which the widow will endow her second husband, but also the well-used condition of her body. These implications Fletcher is concerned to reject in Lady Hartwell, whom Nancy Rigaud sees as a new and influential comic type, 'la veuve aussi rationelle que riche'.[20]

Thus she passes Vallentine's test with flying colours; her questioning of her own values is more perfunctory, but required to complete the pattern. She is won over by his bluntness and full of admiration for his witty strategies:

    How prettily he fooled me into vices
    To stirre my jealousie and finde my nature.
                        (III, ii, 197–8)

And in no time she finds herself turning charitable and paying her sister's bills. Vallentine for his part cannot keep the bargain made with his friends to act as disinterested appraiser, and they accordingly cast him off; the free-wit economy collapses when they refuse to bankroll him any longer. A symbolic conversion of values takes place when, having given back to his friends the clothes they had supplied him, he finds a rich new suit with money in the pockets left outside his door by Lady Hartwell's woman.

The politics of gender relations are intertwined with those of the economics of wit. Vallentine's re-evaluation of his ideas about women and marriage involves a reassessment of his relationship with the free world of unmarried men. He dispels the three suitors from Lady Hartwell's house with a satirical account of the social reality of living off one's wits: the life of tavern camaraderie is a fantasy, the reality humiliating indigence, a world of making do with what others have discarded:

> Wine that the Bell hath gone for twice, and glasses
> That look like broken promises . . .
> . . . English Tobacco
> With half pipes, not in halfe a yeare once burnt, and Bisket
> That Bawdes have rubb'd their gummes upon.
> (IV, v, 67–71)

But Vallentine still fears the humiliating loss of freedom involved in marriage and in the end must be cajoled into it by a witty stratagem of his uncle and the Merchant.[21] Despite Vallentine's compromise over his original position, the play sets a high valuation on wit; it is the means by which Vallentine not only wins the widow but also proves himself worthy of her. And she, for all her advantages of wealth and independence, must recognise, acknowledge, and reward wit. Together, the witty prodigal and the independent woman challenge patriarchal society and its money-based values.

Their courtship and marriage also constitutes a revisionist re-telling of a recent scandal involving the forced remarriage of a widow to a scoundrel. This scandal, recounted in a salacious pamphlet of 1595 by 'Oliver Oatmeale', *A Quest of Enquirie by women to know, whether the Tripe-wife were trimmed by Doll yea or no* involved a young tobacco-seller who, with accomplices, tricked and humiliated an elderly widow into marrying him; he was subsequently imprisoned in Newgate for deception. Charles Forker regards *Wit Without Money* as a conscious comment on this story, and envisages Fletcher constructing Vallentine's part 'so as to encourage the actor to wink at the audience from time to time – to enjoy, as it were, the gay self-deception',[22] but this is to assume that Lady Hartwell is to be seen as tricked, albeit in a non-offensive, 'gay' way. That the play ultimately shows the marriages serving the interests of the men, both Vallentine and Francisco, as well as Vallentine's uncle and creditors, more than those of the women is clear, but not to the extent or in the way assumed in Forker's reading. Vallentine is not a trickster but a wit motivated by desires for freedom and escape from constraints of money and social status. But like Lady Hartwell he too must revise his attitudes to the right use of money; and the partnership they evolve is offered as a new social model as well as, more conventionally, a solution to Vallentine's financial problems.

A similar system of social values is explored in *Wit at Severall Weapons* (?1613), the extent of Fletcher's contribution to which is still uncertain.[23] Once again, women and wits collude against the establishment to get what they want in a world of subversive fantasy where wit is seen as potentially capable of undermining the principles of patriarchal society. But the play's characteristically Middletonian ethical structure, whereby youth fools age and authority, modifies the stronger stress on female power in the Beaumont and Fletcher texts. The wealthy Sir Perfidious Oldcraft, the instigator of the action, is a self-made man, and like Sir Andrew Undershaft in *Major Barbara* not prepared to endorse the patrilineal system over the alternative value of wit:

> I'de rather
> Make a wise stranger my Executor, then a foolish
> Sonne my Heire, and to have my Lands call'd after
> My wit, then after my name.
> (I, i, 79–82)

His son, Witty-pate Oldcraft, will not inherit any of his father's goods unless he can demonstrate a right to them by living off his wits, which, by making a fool of his father, he easily does. But Sir Perfidious's commitment to an economy of wit is sexually compromised: in the case of the disposal of his niece's fortunes, wit is not a factor, since he plans for her to marry a rich but foolish lord, Sir Gregory Fop, so that he can retain two-thirds of her portion for himself. However, he reckons without the fact that the niece is a woman of considerable wit herself, by means of which she contrives to use the inept Sir Gregory as a cover for her own marital plans. She wants Cuningame, a man who is poor but lives up to the implications of his name. At one point she fears he is deceiving her with another woman, and upbraids herself for attempting to flout the normal rules for marital transactions:

> Who would put confidence in wit againe?
> I'me plagu'd for my ambition, to desire
> A wise man for a husband.
> (IV, iii, 7–9)

Then she discovers that Cuningame is actually testing her love, and is as impressed by his trick as he is by her frank display of jealous rage. She rejoices to marry a poor man, not from a wish to exploit her economic advantage over him, but because of the high valuation she sets on wit:

> Now blessings still maintaine this wit of thine,
> And I've an excellent fortune comming in thee,
> Bring nothing else I charge thee.
> (IV, iii, 37–9)

In the end, all the women in this play get what they want. If they are rich and witty, their choice is unrestricted; if they are poor and witty, like Lady Ruinous Gentry, resourceful wife to a decayed knight, or Mirabel, niece to the original niece's guardian, they use their wit to rechannel the money of the rich in their direction. Ultimately the play is structured to subordinate issues of gender politics and the tensions between the expression of appetite and the social requirement for its regulation to the narrative needs of an intrigue plot. By comparison, it highlights the greater concern of the Beaumont and Fletcher plays with the interests served in marriage.

The question of why and how marriages come to be arranged when there are compelling reasons in favour of the single life is explored in *The Wild-Goose Chase*, a play that was very popular in its time.[24] One of the reasons for this may be the way in which the deftly handled battle-of-the-sexes action is organised to allow for a frank account of sexual appetite in women as well as in men, although, in effect, the play is more male-dominated than *The Scornful Lady* and *Wit Without Money*. It is also more cynical in that wit, rather than functioning as an alternative currency to wealth, becomes instead a species of trickery. The social conditions are not those of city comedy, and although the setting is Paris, to which Mirabel and his companions, Pinac and Belleur, have recently returned after travelling abroad in a sophisticated foreign country – that is, Italy – it is not given any specificity; it is the backdrop to a romantic comedy of courtship amongst urban gentry where considerations of money and property are less central to the concept of marriage than the sexual dynamic between partners. The marriage-market ethos is operative to an extent; young men as well as women have male relatives with some investment in ensuring socially suitable partnerships. Nantolet, father to Rosalura and Lillia-Bianca, meets Mirabel's father, La-Castre, in the hopes of arranging an alliance between their families. He dissociates himself from the language of financial dealing ('To say more, is to sell 'em') and dwells instead on the social assets, including a tutor, which he has provided to equip his daughters for an advantageous marriage. Despite the fact that the efforts of the older guardians on behalf of their charges are sometimes inept, the male establishment is still necessary to create favourable conditions for the couples, and in particular to guide and regulate the expression of appetite in the young.

The male guardians recognise that the instinctive drive of the young men is for freedom and the postponement of marital responsibility:

> They are now for Travel,
> All for that Game again: they have forgot wooing.
> (v, i, 7–8)

'Travel' is identified with that sexual experimentation which is a recognised part of a young gallant's education. In an extension of the metaphor, men are ships, women countries to be visited; the polarities of foreign countries and home, wandering and stability, are traditional. Mirabel is reluctant to change his style:

> I will not lose the freedom of a Traveller;
> A new strong lusty Bark cannot ride at one anchor;
> ...
> Tie me to one smock? make my travels fruitless?
> I'll none of that.
>
> (I, ii, 71–2, 76–7)

All the young people are at a liminal moment in their lives, but the women's appetites cannot be allowed the diversity of satisfaction available to the men. The tutor Lugier defines their limited options:

> Husbands they must, and will have,
> Or Nunneries, and thin Collations
> To cool their bloods.
>
> (V, i, 21–3)

The safe passage from courtship into marriage for the young can be ensured only by the intervention of their elders, representing society whose interests are served by regulated and sanctioned sexuality rather than the free expression of appetite. In this, society appears to be colluding with the desires of women rather than men – at least, as these are differentiated in the main plot of the play where Oriana's own efforts to pin down the desirable but elusive Mirabel ('a loose and strong defier of all order') must be reinforced by the assistance of the united establishment of older men, including Mirabel's own father, before she is successful. Oriana is rich, young, beautiful, a virgin, all the necessary attributes of a marriage partner, and in addition she is witty and single-minded: 'my thing is marriage', she says firmly in the play's first scene, and she regards the taming of the wild Mirabel as her project: 'I, and onely I, must make him perfect'. Mirabel has all the complementary qualities: he is an heir, young, handsome and sexually experienced, and even – as he is tricked into admitting when Oriana play-acts madness – in love with her; but he is also intent on retaining his freedom. The stratagem that wins him is her disguise as a wealthy Italian; the appeal of what is exotic, foreign, and unknown seems to be the crucial point. In this guise she pretends to resist his advances:

> How can you like me, without I have Testimony,
> A stranger to ye –

He responds without hesitation,

> I'll marry ye immediately.
> A fair State, I dare promise ye.
>
> (V, vi, 71–4)

When the trick is revealed, she claims, 'I have out Travell'd ye.' His attitude is one of total capitulation, 'I'll burn my book and turn a new leaf over.' The reference is to a book of sexual conquests which Mirabel, Don Juan-like, has shown Oriana to taunt her, but the line hints also at conversion.

The conventionally conceived courtship dynamics of the main plot are in some ways undercut by the subplot which represents in the sirens Rosalura and Lillia-Bianca women disconcertingly capable of varying the appearances they present in public and who are as strongly motivated by appetite as men. In contrast with Mirabel, Bellure and Pinac, who court them, are incompetent wooers easily thrown off guard, and the discomfiture endured particularly by Bellure, who has manly attributes like the ability to fight but no skill in courtship, reveals the sexual anxieties of the would-be man about town. Oriana's resolve to catch the wild-goose Mirabel is feminised because she cannot fulfil it without male help, and because Mirabel seems to have so little personal investment in the desire for marriage that his composure is rarely troubled by her invasive ploys. The sisters' determination to be married as expeditiously as possible and to transform the raw material of husbands available in Pinac and Bellure into what they want is less acceptable. The operation of the broader comedy of this strand of the play is ambiguous; it may counteract and diffuse, but equally it may point up the threat presented to male authority by women who can manipulate the categories by which their sex is defined. Rosalura's account of how she plans to handle Bellure is suggestive:

> Peace: he's modest:
> A bashfulness, which is a point of grace, Wench:
> But when these Fellows come to moulding, Sister,
> To heat, and handling: as I live, I like him;
> And methinks I could form him.
> (III, i, 131–5)

The usual identification of man with form, woman with matter, is inverted here;[25] and further intimidating aspects of female behaviour are demonstrated in the sisters' skill with roles. They enact the range of 'Behaviours ... subtile, and new' taught them by their tutor Lugier so well as to deceive and baffle Pinac and Bellure, who naively take them at face value; particularly effective is Lillia-Bianca's playing of the woman repentant of her youthful follies who longs for nothing more than to be a submissive wife:

> Being yoak'd, and govern'd,
> Married, and those light vanities purg'd from us;
> How fair we grow, how gentle, and how tender
> We twine about those loves that shoot-up with us?
> (IV, i, 80–3)

Pinac and Mirabel too are so disarmed by this desirably womanly speech that they are left without resources of wit when Lillia-Bianca reveals it as another of her roles. These scenes represent womanliness as a code, learnt and socially constructed, and the process of courtship a lesson in how to read and operate it. That it is a male instructor who teaches the women their role-playing stresses this point. Mistakes can be costly, especially to masculine self-esteem and can afford glimpses of that 'vulnerable male ego' which Cyrus Hoy has discovered in Fletcherian romantic comedy.[26] Bellure takes his instruction from Mirabel, who promises close monitoring of his progress, to 'take thee off, and set thee on again, Boy; / And cherish thee, and stroak thee' (I, i, 59–60), but Mirabel is not infallible at deciphering women's behaviour, and in any case is quite prepared to exploit Bellure's gullibility for his own amusement. In the scene where Bellure thinks he has got the better of Rosalura by asserting male authority and bringing her to the verge of tears, only to find that her submissive behaviour is yet another facade which she can discard in an instant, such traditional 'manliness' becomes itself a role which is absurd and inappropriate. Rosalura's tears are, of course, faked, and at her command her sister and four women appear to jeer at Bellure and demolish his authority:

> 2 Woman.   Come hither to fright Maids, with thy Bul-faces?
> To threaten Gentlewomen? Thou a man? A May-pole.
> A great dry Pudding.
>
> (IV, ii, 81–3)

Manliness itself may be a fake, and worse, a cover for sexual inadequacy; Bellure is particularly stung by the women's taunts that he is 'some mighty Dairy-maid in mans clothes' or 'some Tinkers Trull with a beard glew'd on'. The man-baiting aspect of this scene recalls *The Woman Hater* (*c.* 1606) where Oriana and her women gang up to intimidate the misogynistic Gondarino with fondling and caresses, but the earlier play lacks the questioning of gender roles and the nature of sexuality posed in *The Wild-Goose Chase*. Yet the answer the play seems to offer to the question of why marriages ever take place at all – that they regulate female desire – is a crude one. The representatives of society, all male and without female partners, fathers, a brother, and a tutor, are not concerned with property or inheritance, but they must ensure that the women behave with propriety. Men can satisfy their sexual appetites 'abroad' but women are denied this option, and unlike the Scornful Lady or Lady Hartwell, cannot re-write society's rules for themselves.

As in *The Two Noble Kinsmen*, marriage is something of a compromise solution to the problems created by sexual desire, and the glimpse of it offered at the end of the play is disquietingly ambiguous. Oriana's winning trick is to show herself to Mirabel in a role he particularly enjoys, that of an exotic stranger; when the deceit is revealed he claims both to have been pleased by it, and to have recognised her anyway. But he asks for her to retain her fine clothes. Is it the point that the chief requirement of marriage is an apt choice of roles, and that the best kind of wife is a desirable stranger? Farley-Hills sums up the play comfortably as representing 'the triumph of romantic over libertine values',[27] but a production in which the relation of role-play to the arousal of sexual desire was strongly asserted would undermine this notion. The satirical force of the play's exploration of the mechanisms of sexual desire should not be underestimated.[28]

Rule a Wife and Have a Wife, Fletcher's last marital comedy, is a less open-ended play which explores gender roles through marriage rather than courtship and commits itself to some decisive statements about gender and power. It consists of two contrasted and interlocking plots in which a witty serving-woman tames her fortune-seeking husband by pretending that she is rich and owns the house actually belonging to her mistress, while the mistress for her part is tamed by an apparently timid and tractable husband. The comedy of the main plot derives from a straightforward account of gender relations in the correction of a disorderly woman by a man whom she expects to master. Donna Margarita is 'faire, and young, and wealthy, / Infinite wealthy'; she has control of her own wealth and she has decided to marry, but makes no connection between the disposal of her body and of her property. The qualities she requires in a husband are limited and specific:

> An husband of an easy faith, a foole,
> Made by her wealth, and moulded to her pleasure,
> One though he see himself become a monster,
> Shall hold the doore, and entertaine the maker.
> (II, i, 25–8)

She wants him to be 'lusty', though his main function is not to satisfy her appetites himself but to be the means by which she may do so with another man and still preserve her credit. In the source for this part of the play, the Spanish novella *El sagaz Estacio marido examinado*,[29] the heroine is, in fact, a courtesan who requires a husband in order to avoid arrest for promiscuity. Fletcher has elevated the social status of Donna Margarita, but he has retained the motif of the woman's dangerously free sexuality. Thus she has the potential to combine what Coppelia Kahn calls 'the opposing terms of female sexuality',[30] often polarised in separate characters like Franceschina and Beatrice in *The Dutch Courtesan*, but the alarming combination is forestalled by Margarita's redemptive marriage.

Margarita chooses as her husband a humble soldier, Leon, whose qualities seem to be the opposite of what is conventionally manly, except for his 'lusty body'; he is shy, slow-witted, sexually inexperienced, servile, and complaisant. She intends to dominate him completely. But once married Leon gradually reveals another self, and does it in such a way as to satirise the aggressive behaviour of wives like Margarita as sexually and socially aberrant. His role is corrective; his public exposure and humiliation of Margarita not only teaches her the folly of her disorderly appetites for sex and power but reasserts a proper balance in their marital relationship. When on their wedding day Margarita weeps with frustrated rage because Leon will not obey her orders, the Duke, who expects to become her lover, draws his sword to defend her. Leon, in turn, draws to assert his rights as husband and to teach Margarita the meaning of marriage:

> He that dares strike against the husbands freedome,
> The husbands curse stick to him, a tam'd cuckold,
> My wife be faire and young, but most dishonest,
> Most impudent, and have no feeling of it,
> No conscience to reclaime her from a Monster.
> (III, v, 182–6)

She took him for a token husband, 'the meere signe of man', but now he has realised the meaning of this sign, a meaning which he can define with the support of established structures of power. Thus he challenges the Duke's defence of Margarita:

> Put up my Lord, this is oppression,
> And calls the sword of Justice to releeve mee
> The law to lend her hand, the King to right me.
> (III, v, 122–4)

In place of Margarita's token marriage, he proposes the real thing, of which 'the husbands freedome' is the cornerstone.

Margarita is considerably disconcerted by her husband's behaviour but not yet prepared to abandon her bid for dominance. That the Duke continues to encourage her disorderliness lends a political significance to the unbalanced marriage as symbolic of social disorder. In the last act, he even infiltrates the couple's household, having himself carried in as if seriously wounded in a duel so as to get access to Margarita. This is the last straw for Leon, who draws on the extremest sanctions to assert his authority over his wife, threatening a total take-over of her mind as well as her body to procure the necessary condition of humility:

> Ile have thee let blood in all the veines about thee,
> Ile have thy thoughts found too, and have them open'd,
> Thy spirits purg'd, for those are they that fire ye.
> (V, iii, 78–80)

She now submits to him finally in the language of conversion, kneeling, and claiming to have 'lost my selfe ... / And all that was my base selfe, disobedience'. The denouement extends the religious rhetoric but within a context of staged farce. While the Duke casts off the trappings of his feigned sickness and prepares to make love to Margarita, the usurer Cacafogo, another of her suitors, lured to wait for her in the cellar, cavorts drunkenly below the stage; Margarita persuades the Duke that the mysterious sounds he hears emanate from the devil come to punish him, and confronts him with a sermon on the evils of violating wedlock:

> You rob two Temples, make yourselfe twice guilty,
> You ruin hirs, and spot her noble husbands.
> (V, v, 87–8)

He too is converted, and vows thereafter only to attend her virtuously, as a true servant. The solemn terms in which this position on marriage is put may to an extent be undercut by the staging of the scene, but undeniably the play is proposing an orthodox morality of marriage through a correction of the imbalance in the power relations between Leon and Margarita. By implication, it also endorses the egalitarianism of virtue; Leon, though of mean social rank, justifies his claim to Margarita's wealth and status by his qualities as a husband. The seal of moral approval on the marriage is conferred in the final moments of the play when Leon and the other soldiers prepare to go off to war, leaving the women at home; in this apportioning of responsibilities, social order and correct gender relations are reinstated.

The subplot inverts the terms in which relations of gender and power in marriage are examined, in that it is the wife, Estifania, Margarita's maid, who must tame her husband, Michael Perez. But for all that Perez is a cynical fortune-hunter, Estifania has no moral ascendancy over him, like Leon, for she is an untrustworthy maid-servant of 'but a scant fame' who needs to find a roof over her head. Her weapon is wit; she wins Perez by appearing to be the mistress of a comfortable and prosperous household, and when he catches her out in this trick, she plays another, this time on the usurer Cacafogo. Perez has matched Estifania's lie about her wealth with one of his own, claiming to be the owner of a casket of valuables, which of course are worthless. Estifania, however, manages to fool Cacafogo into parting with money for this casket, and Perez not only accepts her as his wife but even allows that her wit makes her superior in their partnership:

> I see I am an asse when thou art neere me
> (V, iv, 42)

Estifania represents a threat to male supremacy which is never neutralised. She wins her husband by trickery and retains him by the same means; Perez, who regards himself as sexually sophisticated and entertains cynically stereotyped views about women, has allowed himself through greed to be trapped by the type he most fears, 'a whore and theefe, two excellent morrall learnings / In one she Saint'. They are evenly matched as liars and cheats, and the play in no way idealises them. In IV, i when they describe the places each has visited in search of the other they reflect the unappealing images each sex has of the other: Perez has visited bawdy houses, plays, puppet shows, and 'goshippings', Estifania taverns, dicing houses, and surgeons. The form of their competition in abuse acknowledges their equality:

> *Perez.* Thou most vild, base, abominable –
> *Estifania.* Captaine.
> *Perez.* Thou stinking, overstewd, poore, pocky –
> *Estifania.* Captaine.
> (IV, i, 52–4)

But even so, the play's perspective is that of Perez rather than his wife. His desire for a rich wife is the motive that initiates the action and it is he who is given the asides and soliloquies that interpret it. Estifania has just enough commentary to inform the audience that her behaviour is willed and intentional, but Perez more expansively expresses the anguish of a man who sees his relationships with women as a fight for survival in which the odds are stacked against him. In the misogynistic soliloquy that opens V, ii Perez wishes that it might be declared treason for a gentleman to marry in order to save the rest of his sex from women's terrifying strength and vitality:

> Cut her apeeces, every peece will live still,
> And every morsell of her will doe mischiefe.
> (V, ii, 10–11)

He concludes by vowing, 'I must destroy her'. Estifania's resourcefulness and wit do not disguise the fact that she is capable of extinguishing her husband. Perez, though a soldier, quails when his wife confronts him with a pistol and a dagger, before she shows him the thousand ducats of which she has cheated Cacafogo. She is an image of the 'monster' Leon has fantasised in his own marriage, the man–woman, armed and triumphant, who challenges her husband at all his own games.

The effect of Estifania's triumph over Perez is perhaps diffused by the fact that she is a servant, and is clearly represented as claiming a social power she can never rightfully possess, and also by Perez himself being a type of the braggadocio whose destiny it is to be exposed and humiliated. The threat posed by Estifania is also counteracted by the more conventional sexual politics of the main plot, which, as affirmed in the play's closing moments, may be the ones to leave the dominant impression. The representation of the politics of marriage in *Rule a Wife* is significantly comparable to that in *The Woman's Prize*,[31] which Fletcher wrote perhaps twenty years earlier. Though the power relations are differently balanced between subplot and main plot in the earlier play, the play's dramaturgy again constructs a male perspective on the action, and the anxieties created in men by women's sexual appetites find expression in misogyny. From a feminist stance *The Woman's Prize* is perhaps marginally the more optimistic and less sexually conservative play, since in the relationship between Maria and Petruchio it allows for a measure of negotiation as to terms;[32] in *Rule a Wife* Margarita's kneeling to Leon in V, iii denotes her complete capitulation to him, and Estifania's resources of intelligence and cunning must be deployed to compensate the husband she needs rather than loves for her failings elsewhere.

The centrality of women to these comedies of courtship and marriage goes some way to modify the view that the plays are, as Hoy puts it, 'dominated by masculine energies and wills';[33] Leinwand[34] credits city comedy with the invention of a 'new woman', who is 'able, witty and self-sufficient', like the Scornful Lady, Lady Hartwell, Oriana and the other women in *The Wild-Goose Chase*, and Estifania (none of whom he, in fact, mentions); several of these characters appear in what turned out to be some of the most popular of the Beaumont and Fletcher plays.[35] A degree of moral fence-sitting co-exists in the plays with a challenging examination of the interests, both social and personal, served by courtship and marriage. Marriage is no longer an unproblematical symbol of social harmony and integration, but a condition arrived at after bargaining and negotiation, and achieved with a recognition of losses as well as gains. The Beaumont and Fletcher plays discard the Shakespearian emphasis on the social and dynastic functions of marriage for a closer look at the personal and emotional ones, in keeping with the trend identified in Puritan marriage manuals.[36] In doing so, they identify a number of contradictions within contemporary sexual ideology, and brilliantly adapt the familiar sex-war conventions within which to explore them.

Conclusion

In concluding this examination of sexual themes in the plays of the Beaumont and Fletcher canon I am happy to acknowledge that one of the purposes of the exercise has been a rescue attempt. For reasons I have considered at some length, twentieth-century criticism has all but ignored a huge corpus of dramatic work which was in its own time, and for a considerable part of the seventeenth century, more popular than Shakespeare's. Now that new approaches to literature and culture generally, and to the drama of this period particularly, are throwing light on a range of texts hitherto underprivileged by the standards of traditional liberal humanism, even to the extent of creating alternative 'canons',[1] it seems essential to review the Beaumont and Fletcher plays. In relation to many of the issues currently of concern to critics of Renaissance drama – dramatic representation, gender definitions, the interrelations of sexuality in the theatre with society – these plays have much to offer. In view of the long tradition of strong critical reaction to Beaumont and Fletcher's handling of sexual themes, from the queasiness of Rhymer, through the high-minded distaste of Coleridge, extending to accusations of prurience and ethical frivolity from critics writing in the 1960s, it is surprising that the re-examination of early modern sexuality now taking place in so many areas of thought has not already extended to their work.

Regarded as a corpus, the texts foreground the question of collaborative dramaturgy. This has its own interest in the wake of structuralist and poststructuralist demolitions of the notions of authorial property and individuality, but more to the point here is the connection between the polyvocal construction of meaning in such texts and the nature of the dramaturgy that results. While it would be misleading to ascribe all those dramaturgical features of Beaumont and Fletcher plays which are distinctive to this corpus to the conditions of collaboration, none the less this is true of some features, and, I would argue, of some which are particularly relevant to the articulation of sexual themes. I have in mind here the use of 'theatregrams' or repeated compositional units such as the 'pretend wanton' device, and the discontinuous style of theatrical narrative whereby plays are constructed around strong scenes, within which characters may assume a number of separate roles in relation to one another. It is possible also that what might be characterised as the moral flexibility of these plays is a function of their status as part of a collaborative corpus. 'Moral flexibility' is only one way of describing a distinctive feature somewhat resistant to definition yet capable of being rendered pejoratively, as when, for example, Donohue talks of 'moral posturing' in the plays, or Waith of 'renunciation of meaning' as a strategy to create a 'calculated succession of dramatic moments'.[2] This flexibility or open-endedness creates problems not only for liberal humanist critics: those of different persuasions, such as Dollimore and Shepherd, looking for texts to co-opt into new kinds of orthodoxies, are often unconvincing in their attempts to locate these plays ideologically in relation to issues of sexual politics.

To a certain extent this is a question of dramatic representation; in plays where there is no living tradition of performance the gaps where meanings are to be supplied in the theatre can never be truly filled. This is especially significant in a drama where the original conditions of staging and the whole sociology of theatre can be hypothesised but not recuperated. In particular, it must be recognised that the meanings of those explorations of gender roles in plays featuring transvestite characters must remain open, but also that accepted contemporary theatrical conventions would almost certainly have closed some of them off. To acknowledge this is to historicise the preference for open-ended over closed texts (or vice versa), and to recognise that the wish to discover challenges to current orthodoxies, demystifications of the workings of ideology, experimentation with accepted definitions of social and sexual roles, is often self-fulfilling. With this in mind, it can still be said that the plays raise a number of questions about sexuality, and expose certain contradictions within contemporary ideology, even if they offer no firm answers.

One of the questions that arises most persistently is to do with role-playing and its implications for the stability and fixity of identities. In the chastity plays the 'pretend wanton' role briefly adopted by so many female characters – Oriana, Clorin, Cellide, Florimel, to name but a few – seems primarily to function to resolve the sexual anxieties of men, both about their interests and preferences where women's desires are concerned and about the nature of women's sexuality itself. Apparently, women are capable of controlling their desires and regulating their own sexuality, and role-play of this kind serves to stress the distinction between the role and the actor: the representation of woman as sexually available and promiscuous becomes a fantasy-role which women assume to teach men the truth. In the theatre, this enables an audience, presumably gendered male, to enjoy erotically titillating scenes, and retrospectively to justify their experience as therapeutic. But in some instances the very success of the enactment calls its status as fantasy into question; if Celia in *The Humorous Lieutenant* or Cellide in *Monsieur Thomas* can play 'woman, perfect woman' so convincingly, the implication arises that womanliness may exist only as a series of roles prescribed by patriarchal ideology. This uncertainty co-exists with a tendency to idealise female continence as behaviour so admirable that it reverses the hierarchical relationship of the sexes and makes women better than men. But does the success of the women's role-playing stratagem undermine the very virtue it is devised to demonstrate? Is the dramaturgy riven by internal contradictions? Clearly these are not questions which a study of the texts alone can answer; but the very fact that they arise at all suggests, significantly, that the exploration of women's sexuality in these plays often serves to demystify the notion of chastity in acknowledging some of the anxieties to which it gives rise. Only in *The Faithful Shepherdess* is chastity as virginity allowed a mystical role, and here the political meanings of the play, in particular its relation to the cult of Queen Elizabeth, render it anomalous. Elsewhere, chastity, especially in the form of a temporary continence, is an enabling condition for a subsequent relationship of happily fulfilled sexuality, the guarantor of which is the woman's ability to control and where necessary suppress her sexual desires. That this relationship is achieved in tragicomedy but not in tragedy (for example, in *Thierry and Theodoret*) does not alter the meaning of female continence.

The handling of virginal chastity in transvestite roles, at least in *Philaster* and *The Honest Man's Fortune*, operates in tragicomedy or romance to destabilise rather than to endorse fixed notions of gender-identity, but in tragedy the main relevance of this role is more restricted, as a kind of double disguise. In *Philaster* the complex figuration of the erotic triangular relationship between the three principals – Philaster, Arathusa and Bellario – is distinctly more experimental in its implications than the model of Orsino/Olivia/Viola in *Twelfth Night*, and allows for the possibility of 'a flexibility of erotic attraction'[3] outside the boundaries of gender-specific sexuality. At the same time it should be stressed that this possibility is taken up only at certain moments in the play, and only before Bellario's identity is fully revealed. The closure of the play in the dynastic marriage of Philaster and Arathusa, which resolves both the romance and political plots, redefines Bellario's sexuality as categorically anomalous in that she is female, heterosexual, yet committed to a life of unfulfilled desire in a world where the consummated heterosexual union of the prince and princess is the ideal. In *The Honest Man's Fortune* the girl-page figure Veramour is used to expose quite openly some of the more subversive possibilities of the transvestite convention; the audience is invited to recognise that the relationship between a character's given gender within the dramatic narrative and the true sex of the boy actor may be actively in play, and thus to acknowledge that gender identity may be as much to do with constructed roles as with inherent tendencies. At the same time, the gaps in our understanding of the meanings of the maid-in-male-disguise on the stage in this period must be taken into account; and they render it possible that, since in this play the character, Laverdine, who is most erotically attracted to Veramour, and the only one who persists almost to the end in his delusion about Veramour's true sex, is a ridiculous city fop, the play's final statement is that everyone should recognise gender as biologically determined. This is unquestionably the case in *Love's Cure* where the transvestite siblings cast off their borrowed gender roles as the accretions of custom, and are, with some instruction, eventually enabled to right 'wrong'd nature' and behave in accordance with society's conventional expectations of their biological sexes.

The experimental spirit of *Philaster* and *The Honest Man's Fortune* is exceptional rather than usual in Beaumont and Fletcher's treatment of gender roles. In plays featuring mannish women there are evident boundaries demarcating the acceptable limits of gender behaviour, boundaries which are, predictably, more severely enforced for women. In *The Double Marriage*, Juliana, the true wife, may be praised for a 'masculine spirit' and the demonstration of 'more than woman's virtues', but only because her strength is mustered to support, and not, like that of the false wife, Martia, to challenge, masculine prerogatives. Women who attempt to take over male roles or to regard themselves as self-sufficient, like the Amazonian community in *The Sea Voyage* become objects of satire and ridicule. Women who expose the workings of patriarchal ideology, like Martia or Rosellia, are demonised, and women who are too powerful, such as the Queens Bacha, Bonduca, and Brunhalt, are readily co-opted into the stereotype of the monstrous woman, and either tamed or eliminated. A common component of monstrosity is promiscuous or deviant sexual behaviour, such as the impulses to incest in Bacha or Lelia in *The Captain*, or the preference for lovers who are younger or of lower social status, as in Brunhalt. Nonconformist female sexuality may be threatening because it constitutes a refusal to admit any limits to desire. The vulnerability of men to female power, and the hideous 'fantasy of subjection to maternal malevolence'[4] are embodied in Brunhalt whose reckless appetites ruin her sons personally, destroy their political power, and result in her own death: 'a woman in her liberal will defeated'. Lelia, in a generically heterogeneous play with a comic ending, is punished by a penitential regime of solitary confinement and starvation until she is humbled into modesty and silence. Even in comedy female sexual energy requires severe regulation: the assertive Margarita in *Rule a Wife and Have a Wife*, who contracts a marriage as a cover for potential illicit liaisons, must also submit to a quasi-religious regime of humiliation devised by her husband from which she emerges purged of her 'base selfe'.

Conclusion

The stigmatising of women's claims to political or sexual power as deviant and monstrous is an aspect of the discourse of misogyny, within which it complements the valorising of chastity as a means of containing women's appetites. There is no contradiction between the ubiquity in the plays of Beaumont and Fletcher of women who are depicted as virtuous in the face of trial and persecution, resistant to tyranny, witty and intellectually resourceful, and the ubiquity of misogynist attitudes. In some contexts this misogyny quite directly reflects masculine sexual insecurity. This is predictably evident in plays featuring a type of the conventional stage misogynist, such as *The Woman Hater* or *The Captain*, where, although this figure is eventually reformed or defeated, social explanations are proffered for his bias (the bitter experience of a shrewish wife, or the fear of humiliation and rejection by unfeeling women). It is also present in the assumptions according to which gender relations are explored in a whole range of plays which do not feature a male character defined as a misogynist. In plays with a military context like *The Humorous Lieutenant* or *Bonduca* the identification of war with masculinity and valour, and peace with the predominance of feminine values not only privileges masculinity but makes available an equation between the feminine and degeneracy. The quasi-homoerotic feeling between the male military commanders on opposing sides decisively excludes Bonduca and her daughters and defines them as 'other'. They are transgressors by virtue of their attempt to enter the masculine domain of war, where, however apparently successful their tactics or courageous their behaviour, they can never achieve authenticity. In plays about courtship and marriage such as *The Scornful Lady* or *Rule a Wife and Have a Wife*, set in a realm to which the feminine can make some legitimate claims, misogynistic discourse remains common currency, not restricted to men who are sexually or socially incompetent, but acceptable as a regular mode of exchange between, for example, the gentlemanly brothers Elder and Younger Loveless. The system of gender-difference underlying those plays implicitly defines many socially desirable qualities as the prerogative of men: political power, financial independence, active sexuality. When women lay claim to any of these, by virtue of high social standing, wealth, energy, or intellectual resourcefulness, they constitute a threat. In comedy marriage is the main means by which this threat is neutralised in the interests of preserving patriarchalism, though the resources of misogyny may be recruited to perform some secondary discrediting operations on the women's reputations. In tragedy, transgressive women are demonised and eliminated.

Perhaps some caveat should be made here in relation to comedies which fantasise societies where the values of patriarchy are challenged by the claims of desire. In *The Scornful Lady*, *Wit Without Money*, and, to a lesser extent, *The Wild-Goose Chase*, the couples negotiate between themselves for terms on which marriage can be made acceptable, and the obligations to family and society are negligible or dispensable. By liberating the couples from the conventional apparatus of patriarchy represented in Shakespeare by importunate fathers or dynastic imperatives, Beaumont and Fletcher create opportunities to raise questions about the social functions of courtship and marriage, and the extent to which marriage resolves the problem of sexual desire. It is not exclusively male desire which is problematic and unruly: the Scornful Lady, Margarita, and Emilia in *The Two Noble Kinsmen* are women who at least initially resist the role of wife as in different ways constricting and unsatisfactory. The competing nature of men's and women's interests where marriage is concerned is handled so as to develop scenes of outstanding sexual vitality and aggressiveness. The fact that marriage is the conventional form of closure in comedy and that ultimately it is men's interests which are served by it does not obscure the recognition in these plays of significant contradictions within contemporary sexual ideology, contradictions which it may be said, have by no means been resolved even today.

In the current climate of close scrutiny of the relationship between politics and the Renaissance theatre, Beaumont and Fletcher's tyrant plays constitute an important body of work which has not yet been accorded the attention it deserves.[5] The recurrent situation of the tyrant whose illegitimate exercise of power is reflected in his attempts to lay claim to a woman to whom he has no right raises many issues around Jacobean absolutism, and in doing so politicises sexuality. In some instances it could perhaps be said that because the tyrant's victim is a woman any political critique of the doctrines of absolutism is defused, though I would argue that overwhelmingly this is not the case. In fact, the very focus on desire helps press the questions of the nature of the contract between subject and ruler and of the legitimate limits of a sovereign ruler's power. Naturally these were challenging but also very delicate issues which the playwrights were compelled to negotiate with care; and it is not surprising that some of the strategies they adopt appear evasive. Yet they consistently depict rulers who are tyrannous, though not technically usurpers, whose desires if enforced would directly violate accepted structures of order in the state and in the family. In the most extreme example, *A King and No King*, the King's irresistible desire for his sister can be satisfied only at the expense of his humanity, the play being based on the humanist postulate of reason or rational law as the heart of all social organisation; but in this instance the horrific image of anarchy is transformed by the revelation of the King's true identity. The critique of absolutism offered in *The Maid's Tragedy* and *Valentinian*, amongst other plays, does not necessarily extend to a critique of the patriarchal structures of society; and the tendency to fragmented and discontinuous dramatic structures discussed earlier makes difficulties for those wishing to uncover evidence of radical politics or to discern distinctive, let alone consistent, positions on questions of gender-relations. But the plays certainly extend our knowledge of the options available in this period for representing the politics of sexuality, and offer a distinctive dramaturgy in which this representation can take place.

Notes

Introduction

1. Clifford Leech, *The John Fletcher Plays* (London, Chatto & Windus, 1962), lists this number, as does Bentley in *JCS* III, 305–43. But C. Hoy in *Shares* 8 (1956), 129, states that the canon traditionally consists of fifty-two plays.
2. *Henry VIII* had appeared in the three Shakespeare Folios printed before 1679, and was probably not included for this reason; *A Very Woman* was attributed solely to Massinger in the seventeenth century, and not included in an edition of Beaumont and Fletcher until the Cambridge *Works*, ed. Bowers, VII (1989); *Barnavelt* did not exist in print at all until A. H. Bullen discovered the manuscript in the British Museum and published it in 1803.
3. See Bentley, *JCS* III, 305–433, for a discussion of *Cardenio, or The Double Falsehood*, *The Devil of Dowgate, or Usury Put to Use*, *The History of Madon, King of Britain*, *The Jeweller of Amsterdam or The Hague*, *Monsieur Perrolis*, and *A Right Woman*.
4. Eugene M. Waith drew attention to it in *The Pattern of Tragicomedy in Beaumont and Fletcher* (New Haven, CT, Yale University Press, 1952); perhaps the position has improved a little since then.
5. Arthur Kirsch, *Jacobean Dramatic Perspectives* (Charlottesville, VA, University Press of Virginia, 1972), p. 4.
6. Norman Rabkin, 'Problems in the study of collaboration, *RORD* 19 (1976), 10.
7. T. B. Tomlinson, *A Study of Elizabethan and Jacobean Tragedy* (Cambridge, Cambridge University Press, 1964), pp. 242, 252.
8. Mary Beth Rose, *The Expense of Spirit: Love and sexuality in English Renaissance drama* (Ithaca, NY, Cornell University Press, 1988), pp. 178, 180.
9. These quotations from Coleridge's criticism are cited from *Coleridge on the Seventeenth Century*, ed. Roberta F. Brinkley (Durham, NC, Duke University Press, 1955), pp. 657, 658, 668, 656.
10. From *Imagination and Fantasy*, 4th edn., 1871, quoted by Laurence B. Wallis, *Fletcher, Beaumont, and Company* (New York, Octagon, 1947; reprinted 1968), p. 73.
11. Margot Heinemann, *Puritanism and Theatre: Thomas Middleton and opposition drama under the early Stuarts* (Cambridge, Cambridge University Press, 1980), p. 38.
12. M. Mincoff, 'Fletcher's early tragedies', *Renaissance Drama*, 7 (1964), p. 74.
13. J. F. Danby, *Poets on Fortune's Hill: Studies in Sidney, Shakespeare, Beaumont and Fletcher* (London, Faber & Faber, 1952), p. 41. See Ch. 6 'Beaumont and Fletcher: Jacobean absolutists'.

14. R. Flecknoe, *A Short Discourse of the English Stage* (1664) in *Critical Essays of the Seventeenth Century*, 3 vols, ed. J. Spingarn, (Oxford, Oxford University Press, 1908–09), II, 94.
15. T. Rymer, *The Tragedies of the Last Age Consider'd* (1678) in *The Critical Works of Thomas Rymer*, ed. Curt A. Zimansky (New Haven, CT, Yale University Press, 1956), p. 42.
16. See Dryden, *Of Dramatic Poesy and Other Critical Essays*, 2 vols, ed. George Watson (London, Dent, 1962), p. 252. The quotations are from 'The Grounds of Criticism in Tragedy'.
17. R. D. Hume, '*The Maid's Tragedy* and censorship in the Restoration theatre', *Philological Quarterly*, 61 (1982), 484–90, is the most recent contribution. Hume finds no evidence of a formal prohibition on *The Maid's Tragedy*, and concludes that even if an informal ban existed it was probably not connected with the appearance of Waller's alternative version.
18. Wallis, *op.cit.*, n10, p. 136. Wallis devotes the first four chapters of his book to a survey of Beaumont and Fletcher's reputation.
19. Philip J. Finkelpearl, *Court and Country Politics in the Plays of Beaumont and Fletcher* (Princeton, NJ, Princeton University Press, 1990), and Rebecca W. Bushnell, *Tragedies of Tyrants: Political thought and theater in the English Renaissance* (Ithaca, NY, Cornell University Press, 1990). Bushnell provides a succinct and useful account of the way that criticism of Beaumont and Fletcher since Coleridge has 'indiscriminately mixed political, moral, and aesthetic categories' (p. 159).
20. Numerous books could be listed here. I am thinking particularly of J. W. Lever, *The Tragedy of State: A study of Jacobean drama* (London, Methuen, 1971; reprinted 1980); Stephen Orgel, *The Illusion of Power: Political theater in the English Renaissance* (Berkeley, CA, University of California Press, 1975); Leonard Tennenhouse, *Power on Display: The politics of Shakespeare's genres* (London, Methuen, 1986); Kathleen McLuskie, *Renaissance Dramatists* (Hemel Hempstead, Harvester Wheatsheaf, 1989); and Phyllis Rackin, *Stages of History: Shakespeare's English chronicles* (London, Routledge, 1991).
21. Rymer, *op.cit.*, n15, p. 35.
22. Flecknoe, *op.cit.*, n14, II, 94.
23. Charles Mills Gayley, *Francis Beaumont, dramatist: A portrait* (London, Duckworth, 1914), pp. 380, 383; E. H. C. Oliphant, *The Plays of Beaumont and Fletcher: An attempt to determine their respective shares and the shares of others* (New Haven, CT, Yale University Press, 1927), p. 57. See also Oliphant's comments on the 'hare-brained virgins and lascivious ladies' of Fletcher's comedies (p. 42). S. Schoenbaum, *Internal Evidence and Elizabethan Dramatic Authorship* (London, 1966), illustrates how the same view of Fletcher, that he suffered from 'impure thoughts' and 'want of just moral feeling', has been used to differentiate his contributions from Shakespeare's in *The Two Noble Kinsmen* and *Henry VIII* (p. 32).
24. Philip Edwards, 'The danger not the death: the art of John Fletcher', in *Jacobean Theatre*, eds. J. R. Brown and B. Harris (London, Arnold, 1960), p. 171; Robert Ornstein, *The Moral Vision of Jacobean Tragedy* (Madison, WI, University of Wisconsin Press, 1960), p. 163.
25. L. C. Knights, *Drama and Society in the Age of Jonson* (1962), p. 296, as quoted in M. Cone, *Fletcher without Beaumont: A study of the independent plays of John Fletcher*, Salzburg Studies in English Literature, Jacobean Drama Studies (Salzburg, Institut für Englische Sprache und Literatur, Universität

Salzburg, 1976). Cone makes a valiant attempt to exonerate Fletcher from many of the standard charges, asserting, quite correctly, that his independent plays were not any bawdier than either the collaborative productions or certain plays of Shakespeare.
26. Finkelpearl, *op.cit.*, n19, p. 115, and elsewhere. See my discussion *supra*, pp. 79, 97, 172n5
27. Lawrence Venuti, 'The marginalization of Philip Massinger's plays', in *Our Halcyon Dayes: English prerevolutionary texts and postmodern culture* (Madison, WI, University of Wisconsin Press, 1989), p. 57.
28. *Ibid.*, p. 69.
29. The quoted expressions come respectively from M. C. Bradbrook, *The Growth and Structure of Elizabethan Comedy* (Harmondsworth, Penguin, 1955, 1963), p. 187; Una Ellis-Fermor, *The Jacobean Drama* (London, Methuen, 1936, revised 1958), p. 206; George Herndl, *The High Design: English Renaissance tragedy and the natural law* (Lexington, KY, University Press of Kentucky, 1970), p. 230. Comparisons between Shakespeare's profound moral values and Beaumont and Fletcher's superficial ones may be found (among many other places) in Leech, *op.cit.*, n1, pp. 5, 87–8, 142; John Greenwood, *Shifting Perspectives and the Stylish Style: Mannerism in Shakespeare and his Jacobean contemporaries* (Toronto, University of Toronto Press, 1988), pp. 105, 139; Rabkin, *op.cit.*, n6, p. 12.
30. Brinkley, *op.cit.*, n9, p. 664.
31. Waith, *op.cit.*, n4, pp. 25, 41.
32. Joseph W. Donohue, Jr, *Dramatic Character in the English Romantic Age* (Princeton, NJ, Princeton University Press, 1970), pp. 20, 24.
33. Catherine Belsey, *The Subject of Tragedy: Identity and difference in Renaissance drama* (London, Methuen, 1985), p. 49. Belsey's whole discussion of dramatic interiority in Ch. 2, 'Unity', is highly illuminating.
34. G. E. Bentley, *The Profession of Dramatist in Shakespeare's Time, 1590–1642* (Princeton, NJ, Princeton University Press, 1971), p. 199.
35. Walter Cohen, *Drama of a Nation: Public theater in Renaissance England and Spain* (Ithaca, NY, Cornell University Press, 1985), p. 174.
36. Ian Fletcher, *Beaumont and Fletcher* (London, Longmans, 1967), p. 9. Leech, *op.cit.*, is thinking similarly when, at the end of his chapter on tragedy, he says that Fletcher, in comparison with Shakespeare or Webster, could not write the profoundest tragedy because 'there is no sign in Fletcher's work that he needed to be alone' (p. 143).
37. A. R. Humphreys, (ed.), *Henry VIII* (Harmondsworth, Penguin, 1971), p. 20.
38. Cyrus Hoy, 'Critical and aesthetic problems of collaboration', *RORD* 19 (1976), 6.
39. Jeffery A. Maslen, 'Beaumont and/or Fletcher: collaboration and the interpretation of Renaissance drama', *English Literary History* 59 (1992), 342.
40. Many critics have remarked on the similarity of the Beaumont and Fletcher tragedies to tragicomedies. See, for example, Waith, *op cit.*, p. 14, on *Cupid's Revenge*.
41. The quoted phrase is from Lee Bliss, 'Tragicomic romance for the King's Men, 1609–1611: Shakespeare, Beaumont, and Fletcher', in *Comedy from Shakespeare to Sheridan*, eds. A. R. Braunmuller and J. Bulman (Newark, NJ, University of Delaware Press, 1986), p. 162. Robert K. Turner, 'Collaborators at work: *The Queen of Corinth* and *The Knight of Malta*', in *Shakespeare: Text,*

language, criticism, eds. B. Fabian and K. Tetzeli von Rosador (Hildesheim, Olms-Weldmann, 1987), pp. 315–30, is also useful on this subject.
42. Edwards, *op.cit.*, n24, is interesting on the importance of 'strong scenes'.
43. See C. H. Herford and Percy Simpson (eds.), *Ben Jonson*, 11 vols (Oxford, Clarendon Press, 1925–52), IV, 351. On Jonson's suppressed works, see Richard Dutton, *Ben Jonson: To the First Folio* (Cambridge, Cambridge University Press, 1983), pp. 11–12.
44. G. E. Bentley, *The Profession of Dramatist in Shakespeare's Time, 1590–1642* (Princeton, NJ, Princeton University Press, 1971), p. 209.
45. Quoted from *Massinger: The critical heritage*, ed. Martin Garnett (London, Routledge, 1991), p. 2. See Garnett's discussion of Massinger's collaborative work, pp. 1–2, 10.
46. See *supra*, p. 12.
47. See A. Gurr's discussion of the contemporary confusion over the authorship of *Philaster* in his edition for the Revels Plays (Manchester, Manchester University Press, 1969), p. xix. See also Wallis, *op.cit.*, n10, pp. 4–6.
48. Bentley, *JCS* III, 415–17.
49. It also contributed to his early reputation. John Taylor, the Water-Poet, in *The Praise of Hemp-Seed* (1620) praises Massinger, with Fletcher and others, as one of the best living writers in print; Massinger's first known non-collaborative work dates from 1621 at the earliest. See *Massinger: The critical heritage*, ed. M. Garnett, pp. 54–5.
50. Quoted from *Massinger: The critical heritage*, p. 72. See also T. A. Dunn, *Philip Massinger: The man and the playwright* (London, Thomas Nelson, 1957), pp. 26–7.
51. The prefatory matter from the Folio is cited from *The Works of Francis Beaumont and John Fletcher*, eds. Arnold Glover and A. R. Waller, 10 vols (Cambridge, Cambridge University Press, 1905–12), I, lxx, xxii, xxxv, xxxv–vi.
52. See, for example, the tributes by William Cartwright in the Folio. Moseley's references in his prefatory address to Beaumont's 'strong and searching brain' and 'judicious wit' imply this idea. Dryden, in 'Of Dramatic Poesy: An essay' (1668) notes Jonson's admiration for Beaumont's skills as an editor (*Of Dramatic Poesy and Other Critical Essays*, ed. George Watson, I, 68). Aubrey in *Brief Lives* records the view that Beaumont's 'maine Businesse' was to prune 'Mr Fletcher's luxuriant Fancy and flowing Witte', *Aubrey's Brief Lives*, ed. Oliver Lawson Dick (Harmondsworth, Penguin, reprinted 1982), p. 128.
53. For the ascriptions, see Hoy, *Shares* 11 (*Beggar's Bush* and *The Coxcomb*), 9 (*The False One*).
54. Gurr, *op.cit.*, n46, p. xxv.
55. See Neil Carson, 'Collaborative playwriting: the Chettle, Dekker, Heywood syndicate', *Theatre Research International*, 14 (1989), 13–23. Carson's detailed and closely argued account of a specific collaborative partnership challenges earlier views of the rigidity of the process, but also shows, by implication, how different the Beaumont and Fletcher partnership was from the norm of 'casual' arrangements, 'loose partnerships or syndicates which worked together for short periods, and then broke up or reformed into other alliances' (p. 22).
56. *Aubrey's Brief Lives*, p. 128. In Shadwell's *Bury-Fair* (1689), Oldwit reminisces about Fletcher in rather similar terms. See Bentley, *JCS* III, 307.
57. R. K. Turner, *Works*, I, xxvii.

58. See J. C. Reed, 'Humphrey Moseley, publisher', *Proceedings and Papers of the Oxford Bibliographical Society*, 2 (1927–30), 57–142; and L. B. Wright, 'The reading of plays during the Puritan Revolution', *Huntington Library Bulletin* 6 (1934), 73–108.
59. For a discussion of the dating problems of this play, see *supra*, pp. 171n11, 173n38.
60. This is the claim put forward by J. H. Astington in 'The popularity of *Cupid's Revels*', *SEL* 19 (1979), 219.
61. In the preface 'To the Reader' of *The White Devil*.
62. See Bentley, *The Profession of Dramatist*, p. 209.
63. Bentley, *JCS* III, 408.
64. Bentley, *JCS* I, 29. See his comment on the benefits derived by the King's Men from their ownership of the plays.
65. J. Q. Adams (ed.), *Dramatic Records of Sir Henry Herbert* (New Haven, CT, Yale University Press, 1917), p. 58.
66. Difficulties of dating make it impossible to be quite certain here, but *The Scornful Lady* at any rate and possibly *The Coxcomb* came later.
67. See Martin Butler, *Theatre and Crisis 1632–1642* (Cambridge, Cambridge University Press, 1984), p. 101, and Ch. 4 'The Caroline audience'.
68. For discussions of the audience from a range of viewpoints see Wallis, *op.cit.*, A. Harbage, *The Cavalier Drama* (New York, Russell & Russell, 1936), and *Shakespeare and the Rival Traditions* (New York, Columbia University Press, 1952); P. J. Finkelpearl, 'The role of the court in the development of Jacobean drama', *Criticism*, 24 (1982), 138–58, and *Court and Country Politics*, pp. 50–4.
69. Butler, *op.cit.*, p. 100.
70. Ashley H. Thorndike, *The Influence of Beaumont and Fletcher on Shakespeare* (Worcester, MA, O. B. Wood, 1901); Gayley, *op.cit.*, n23; A. W. Upton, 'Allusions to James I and his court in Marston's *The Fawn* and Beaumont's *The Woman Hater*', *PMLA* 44 (1929), 1048–65; Baldwin Maxwell, *Studies in Beaumont, Fletcher, and Massinger* (Chapel Hill, NC, North Carolina Press, 1930).
71. The comment appears in Tucker Brooke, 'The royal Fletcher and the loyal Heywood', in *Elizabethan Studies and other Essays in Honour of George F. Reynolds* (Boulder, CO, University of Colorado, 1945), p. 192.
72. Leech, *op.cit.*, p. 13; R. Y. Turner, 'Responses to tyranny in John Fletcher's plays', *Medieval and Renaissance Drama in England* 4 (1988), 140.
73. Bentley, *JCS* III, 416. For *The Jeweller of Amsterdam*, see *JCS* III, 350–51.
74. Upton, *op.cit.*, n69, p. 1048.
75. Finkelpearl, *Court and Country Politics*, p. 74.
76. Annabel Patterson, *Censorship and Interpretation: The conditions of writing and reading in early modern England* (Madison, WI, University of Wisconsin Press, 1984). See especially Ch. 2.
77. See James J. Yoch, 'The Renaissance dramatization of temperance: the Italian revival of tragicomedy and *The Faithful Shepherdess*', in *Renaissance Tragicomedy: Explorations in genre and politics*, ed. Nancy Klein Maguire (New York, AMS Press, 1987). Maguire's introduction to this collection, and all the articles in the second half of it deal with the politicisation of pastoral. See also Finkelpearl and Patterson, nn 75 and 76.
78. William W. Appleton, *Beaumont and Fletcher: A critical study* (London: Allen and Unwin, 1956), p. 63. Appleton also mentions *Bonduca* and *The False One* as plays that may have alluded to the Ralegh affair.

79. See *Works*, III, 115–17. Baldwin Maxwell, *op.cit.*, n69, pp. 147–65, also discusses topical allusions in *The Noble Gentleman*.
80. J. E. Savage, 'The "gaping wounds" in the text of *Philaster*', *Philological Quarterly* 28 (1949), 443–58; R. K. Turner, *Works*, I, 381–86; Gurr, *op.cit.*, pp. lxxv–lxxviii. On the other hand Janet Clare in '*Art made tongue-tied by authority*': *Elizabethan and Jacobean dramatic censorship* (Manchester, Manchester University Press, 1990), while not accepting Savage's argument in its totality, does consider that the first quarto is scarred by theatrical censorship' in some respects. Her view that *Philaster* is one of those texts which 'acquired greater political significance after its composition' (p. 184) is relevant here.
81. Gurr, *op.cit.*, p. lii. He here regards *The Woman Hater* as by Beaumont alone.
82. *Ibid.*, pp. lv–lvi; G. M. Adkins, 'The citizens in *Philaster*: their function and significance', *Studies in Philology* 43 (1946), 203–12; P. Davison, 'The serious concerns of *Philaster*', *English Literary History* 30 (1963), 1–15.
83. Clare, *op.cit.*, n79, pp. 165–7. Craik does admit in a footnote that Amintor's words to Evadne in the play's last scene,

> and to augment my woe
> You now are present, stained with a King's blood
> Violently shed (V, iii, 145–47)

were omitted from Q1 'probably because of their vivid reference to regicide' (p. 190).
84. Fredson Bowers, *Elizabethan Revenge Tragedy 1587–1642* (Princeton, NJ, Princeton University Press, 1940), p. 172.
85. For fuller discussion of this point, and of *The Maid's Tragedy*, see below Ch. 5 'Sex and tyranny'.
86. See Michael Neill, '"The simetry which gives a poem grace": masque, imagery and the fancy of *The Maid's Tragedy*', *Renaissance Drama* 3 (1970), 111–35; William Shullenberger, '"This for the most wrong'd of women": a reappraisal of *The Maid's Tragedy*', *Renaissance Drama* 13 (1982), 131–56; and Finkelpearl, *Court and Country Politics*, pp. 182–206.
87. Finkelpearl, *Court and Country Politics*, p. 199.
88. For example, by Finkelpearl, *Court and Country Politics*, Chs 8–10.
89. See Jean-Pierre Teissedou, 'L'absolutisme en question dans *A King and No King*', in *Coriolan: Théâtre et politique*, eds. Jean-Paul Debax and Yves Peyre (Toulouse, Université de Toulouse – Le Mirail, 1984); Michael Neill, 'The defence of contraries: skeptical paradox in *A King and No King*', *SEL* 21 (1981), 319–32; Rebecca W. Bushnell, *Tragedies of Tyrants: Political thought and theater in the English Renaissance*, pp. 159–71; and Finkelpearl, *Court and Country Politics*, Ch. 9.
90. Butler, *op.cit.*, p. 69. He discusses the significance of Pembroke's sponsorship of the play at court on p. 62.
91. See L. Hotson, *The Commonwealth and Restoration Stage* (Cambridge, MA, Harvard University Press, 1928), Ch. 1; Wallis, *op.cit.*, p. 252. Hotson also notes, without comment, a reference in a pamphlet, *A Discourse Between a Citizen and a Country Gentleman* (1642), to a play done at the Guildhall: 'some say it was called *A King or no King, or King Careo*' (p. 6).
92. Jean E. Howard and Marion F. O' Connor (eds), *Shakespeare Reproduced: The text in history and ideology* (London, Methuen, 1987), p. 11.

93. Rymer, *op.cit.*, ed. Zimansky, p. 74.
94. Valerie Traub, 'Desire and the differences it makes', in *The Matter of Difference: Materialist feminist criticism of Shakespeare*, ed. Valerie Wayne (Hemel Hempstead, Harvester Wheatsheaf, 1991), p. 107.
95. This quesion is considered in several essays in the collection, *Erotic Politics: Desire on the Renaissance stage*, ed. Susan Zimmerman (New York and London, Routledge, 1992).
96. Stephen Greenblatt, *Shakespearean Negotiations: The circulation of social energy in Renaissance England* (Oxford, Clarendon Press, 1988), p. 6. The phrases subsequently quoted appear on pp. 6–7.
97. The phrase in this instance is from Greenblatt, *op.cit.*, p. 7.
98. See Richard Levin, 'Women in the Renaissance theatre audience', *SQ* 40 (1989), 164–74.
99. *The Woman Hater*, not included in the First Folio, was published in a second quarto soon afterwards. The existence of two title pages for separate issues of this quarto illustrates the confusion over the play's authorship. In the words of the Cambridge editor, George Walton Williams, 'The earlier issue (1648) exhibits on the title-page: "Written by John Fletcher Gent." The second issue, released in 1649, cancelled the old title-leaf and substituted a single fold in its place. The new title-page ascribes the play to "Francis Beaumont and John Fletcher Gent."' (*Works*, I, 148).
100. Coleridge, *op.cit.*, n9, ed. Brinkley, p. 670.
101. See, for example, Finkelpearl, *Court and Country Politics*.
102. Flecknoe, *op.cit.*, ed. Spingarn, II, 94. Lamb, discussing *The Faithful Shepherdess*, observes that 'female lewdness at once shocks nature and morality' (*Lamb as Critic*, ed. Roy Park (London, Routledge, 1980), p. 134).
103. Ann Thompson gives a brief, clear account of the problems created by such programmatic critical activity in 'Shakespeare and Feminist Criticism' in *The Shakespeare Myth*, ed. Graham Holderness (Manchester, Manchester University Press, 1988), pp. 76–80.

Chapter 1

1. See Mary Beth Rose, *The Expense of Spirit: Love and sexuality in the English Renaissance* (Ithaca, NY, Cornell University Press, 1986), pp. 12–42, pp. 93–131, and Lawrence Stone, *The Family, Sex, and Marriage in England, 1500–1800* (New York, Harper & Row, 1977). The view that was to be superseded is well expressed by Aquinas in *Summa Theologiae*:

> Virginity seeks the soul's good in a life of contemplation *mindful of the things of God*. Marriage seeks the body's good – the bodily multiplication of the human race – in active life in which the husband and wife are *mindful of the things of this world*. Without doubt then the state of virginity is preferable to that of even continent marriage. *Summa Theologiae. A Concise Translation*, ed. Timothy McDermott, (London, Methuen, 1989) p. 430.

See also David Norbrook, *Poetry and Politics in the English Renaissance* (London, Routledge, 1984), p. 251 on *Comus*.
2. *Astrophel and Stella*, 71.

Notes

3. See Philippa Berry, *Of Chastity and Power: Elizabethan literature and the unmarried Queen* (London, Routledge, 1989), pp. 9–37.
4. *Apius and Virginia* in *Three Tudor Interludes*, ed. Peter Happé (Harmondsworth, Penguin, 1972) p. 288.
5. Berry, *op.cit.*, p. 82.
6. *Ibid.*, p. 87.
7. Peter Stallybrass, 'Patriarchal territories: the body enclosed', in *Rewriting the Renaissance: The discourses of sexual difference in early modern Europe*, eds. Margaret W. Ferguson, Maureen Quilligan, and Nancy J. Vickers, (Chicago, IL, University of Chicago Press, 1986), p. 129.
8. John Lyly, *Euphues and His England*, in *The Complete Works*, ed. R. W. Bond, 3 vols (Oxford, Oxford University Press, 1902), II, 208–11.
9. See Simon Shepherd, *Amazons and Warrior Women: Varieties of feminism in seventeenth century drama* (Brighton, Harvester, 1981).
10. Stallybrass, *op.cit.*, p. 127.
11. Peter Stallybrass, 'Reading the body: *The Revenger's Tragedy*', *Renaissance Drama* 18 (1987), p. 131.
12. Rose, *op.cit.*, p. 17.
13. Mikhail Bakhtin, *Rabelais and His World*, trans. Helene Iswolsky, (Bloomington, IN, Indiana University Press, 1984) p. 26.
14. See Gail Kern Pastor, 'Leaky vessels: the incontinent women of city comedy', *Renaissance Drama* 18 (1987).
15. Gonzalo in *The Tempest* (I, i, 48) calls the ship 'leaky as an unstanched wench'.
16. Pastor, *op.cit.*, p. 222.
17. Susan J. Wiseman, '*'Tis Pity She's a Whore*: representing the incestuous body', in *Renaissance Bodies*, eds Lucy Gent and Nigel Llewellyn (London, Reaktion Books, 1990), p. 186.
18. For example, by Clifford Leech, *The John Fletcher Plays* (London, Chatto & Windus, 1962) in his discussion of *The Faithful Shepherdess*, pp. 156, 158, 160, and by Nancy Cotton Pearse, *John Fletcher's Chastity Plays: Mirrors of modesty* (Lewisburg, PA, Bucknell University Press, 1973), *passim*.
19. For discussion, see below, pp. 33 and 168n38.
20. In particular, in Ch. 4 'Sex and tyranny', but also in Ch. 2 'Gender'.
21. See David Norbrook, *op.cit.*, n1, especially Ch. 5; and Philippa Berry, *op.cit.*, n3.
22. E. K. Chambers's dating for *The Woman Hater* (*c.* 1606) and *The Knight of the Burning Pestle* (1607) is generally accepted. See *ES* III, 219–21. *Love's Cure* presents tricky problems, summarised by George Walton Williams, *Works*, III, 3–7. See also Ch. 2 note 11 below. For *Cupid's Revenge* see J. H. Astington, 'The popularity of *Cupid's Revenge*', *SEL* 19 (1979), 215–27, and James E. Savage, 'The date of Beaumont and Fletcher's *Cupid's Revenge*', *English Literary History*, 15 (1948), 186–94.
23. This definition comes from Louise George Clubb, 'Shakespeare's comedy and late cinquecento mixed genres', *New York Literary Forum*, 5–6 (1980), 138. See also her more extended treatment of the concept in Ch. 1 'Theatregrams' in *Italian Drama in Shakespeare's Time* (New Haven, CT, Yale University Press, 1989) which contains an account of the development of Italian tragicomedy through 'construction by contamination, the premeditated and usually explicit combination of pre-texts' (p. 6) relevant to *The Faithful Shepherdess*.
24. See Hoy, *Works*, III, 485.

25. In his consolatory poem to Fletcher, published with *The Faithful Shepherdess*. See *Works*, III, 493.
26. See *The Complete Poems of John Milton*, eds. J. Carey and A. Fowler (London, Longmans, 1968), pp. 170–1.
27. See P. J. Finkelpearl, *Court and Country Politics in the Plays of Beaumont and Fletcher* (Princeton, NJ, Princeton University Press, 1990), p. 114.
28. For a succinct and witty account of Guarini's prolix drama, see John Shearman, *Mannerism* (Harmondsworth, Penguin, 1967), pp. 91–6.
29. On this point, see Pearse, *op.cit.*, n18, p. 68. She ascribes Fletcher's popularity to the 'soothing, wish-fulfilling reassurance' his plays provided to 'audiences indoctrinated with a horror of wifely unchastity and the dishonour it brought to the husband'.
30. Kathleen McLuskie, *Renaissance Dramatists* (Hemel Hempstead, Harvester Wheatsheaf, 1989), p. 202.
31. See G. K. Hunter, *Dramatic Identities and Cultural Tradition* (Liverpool, Liverpool University Press, 1978), p. 141. Hunter thinks the unpopularity of *The Faithful Shepherdess* in its first production due in part to a perceived lack of seriousness in the genre.
32. See, for example, the essays in *Renaissance Tragicomedy: Explorations in genre and politics*, ed. Nancy Klein Maguire (New York, AMS Press, 1987), and Annabel Patterson's discussion of pastoral in *Censorship and Interpretation: The Conditions of Writing and Reading in Early Modern England* (Madison, WI, University of Wisconsin Press, 1984).
33. James J. Yoch, 'The Renaissance dramatization of temperance: the Italian revival of tragicomedy and *The Faithful Shepherdess*', in *Renaissance Tragicomedy*, ed. Maguire, p. 116.
34. Fletcher in his address to the Reader specifically mentions that his shepherds were 'such, as all the ancient Poets and modern of understanding have received them: that is, the owners of flockes and not hyerlings' (*Works*, III, 497).
35. Berry, *op.cit.*, pp. 90–5, has a discussion of the iconography of the wild man, as featured in courtly entertainments for Elizabeth, which is relevant here.
36. Finkelpearl, *op.cit.*, n27, p. 110.
37. Marco Mincoff, '*The Faithful Shepherdess*: a Fletcherian experiment', *Renaissance Drama*, 9 (1960), 170. Leech, *op.cit.*, n18, pp. 44–5, citing the views of Gayley and Greg that Fletcher adopted a cynical attitude towards chastity, finds comic not only the behaviour of Cloe, but also that of Perigot and Amoret.
38. First printed in 1613 but probably written and performed in 1607. See the discussion of the date in Lee Bliss, *Francis Beaumont* (Boston, MA, Twayne, 1987), pp. 40–1. The appearance of this motif in a play in which Fletcher is almost unanimously thought to have had no hand is significant for the collaboration, since scenes featuring the wounded woman in the collaborative plays (*Cupid's Revenge*, *Philaster*, and *The Maid's Tragedy*) are usually ascribed to Fletcher.
39. Finkelpearl, *op.cit.*, pp. 85–7.
40. *Ibid.*, p. 87.
41. For a fuller discussion of these and other transvestite roles, see Ch. 2 'Gender'.
42. Urania's story, like some other elements of *Cupid's Revenge*, derives from Sidney's *Arcadia*. Beaumont and Fletcher conflate two characters, Urania, a shepherdess, lover of Strephon (Book I, Chs 1 and 2) and, more importantly,

Notes 169

Zelmane, daughter of the wicked King Plexirtus, who loves Pyrocles and serves him disguised as a page. She discloses her identity to him only when she is dying (Book 2, Chs 22 and 23).

43. The phrase comes from Lotte van de Pol and Rudolf M. Dekker, *The Tradition of Female Transvestism in Early Modern Europe* (Basingstoke, Macmillan, 1989), p. 45, from a discussion of legends of transvestite female saints.
44. R. Huebert in '"An artificial way to grieve": the forsaken women in Beaumont and Fletcher, Massinger, and Ford', *English Literary History* 44 (1977), 601–21, regards Aspatia's death as a kind of victory for her, and claims that 'in this society a woman may take decisive action only by assuming masculine qualities' (p. 610). He detects signs of 'latent feminism' in the play which are not evident to me, nor do I accept his view of Aspatia's death, which is the reverse of self-affirming. The implications of her men's clothes are counteracted by her gender: she cannot fight.
45. A typical statement of this view is to be found in Tasso, *Discorso della feminile e donnesca* (1582). See I. MacLean, *The Renaissance Notion of Woman* (Cambridge, Cambridge University Press, 1980), p. 61, for a summary of the ethical view of women in the Renaissance.
46. That there were alternative views of the appropriate course of action for a raped woman is acknowledged in the play in the arguments put by Aecius, especially in III, i, 213–31. See also Ian Donaldson, *The Rapes of Lucretia: A myth and its transformations* (Oxford, Clarendon Press, 1982), especially Chs 2 and 3. For a fuller account of *Valentinian*, see my Ch. 4 'Sex and tyranny'.
47. A fuller discussion of this play is given in Ch. 3 'Misogyny and manhood'. Its dating and authorship pose problems. It was printed in 1621, but Hoy supposes Beaumont to have been a collaborator, with Fletcher and Massinger, so that it must have existed in some form before 1613. See Hoy, *Shares*, and Robert K. Turner's introduction in *Works*, III, 365–6.
48. Probably one of the latest plays, accepted as solely the product of Fletcher's authorship and written in 1624. See Hoy, *Shares*, 8 (1956), 129–46.
49. This is an Augustinian view. See Donaldson, *op.cit.*, p. 31.
50. The view that Lucrece must have experienced some sexual pleasure during the rape is not uncommon in discussions of the story in the Renaissance period. See Donaldson, *op.cit.*, pp. 36–7.
51. Leech's account of the play, *The John Fletcher Plays*, pp. 100–6 is predicated on this assumption, and defends Evanthe's language on naturalistic grounds.
52. E. K. Chambers's view of the play as 'substantially Beaumont's' (*ES* III, 220) has been subject to some refinement in more recent studies of its authorship; Hoy traces Fletcher's hand in five scenes, including III, i and V, iv, in which the treatment of chastity motifs distinctively recalls other plays where Fletcher's contribution is undoubted. See Hoy, *Shares*, pp. 98–9. G. Walton Williams, *Works*, I, 150–2, finds even more evidence of Fletcher's contribution. The play is discussed more fully in Ch. 3 'Misogyny and manhood'.
53. On the sexual politics of the blazon, conventionally a rhetorical technique by means of which a male speaker describes a woman's body, see Patricia Parker, *Literary Fat Ladies: Rhetoric, gender, property* (London, Methuen, 1987), Ch. 7. Two women in Shakespeare who act as self-blazoners and may be compared with Oriana are Venus in *Venus and Adonis* and Olivia in *Twelfth Night*.

54. Oriana's words recall Angelo's to Isabella in *Measure for Measure* (1604) when he cites sexual stereotyping as a means of persuading her to sleep with him:

> Be that you are;
> That is, a woman. If you be more, you're none.
> (II, iv, 134–5)

The resemblance may be accidental, but the treatments of chastity, as well as the roles of the ducal figures in both plays, have much in common. The trial of Oriana's chastity in V, iv, when she is threatened with death if she will not sleep with Arrigo, also echoes Shakespeare.

55. *Monsieur Thomas* is dated by Chambers between 1610 and 1616 (*ES* III, 228) but H. W. Gabler, *Works*, IV, 417–18, thinks the earlier end of this spectrum the more probable. *The Loyal Subject* was licensed for performance in November 1618 when it was new and probably also topical. For a discussion of this see Ch. 2 'Gender'. *The Humorous Lieutenant* is usually dated *c.* 1619, though there is no specific evidence for this. See Bentley, *JCS* III, 346.

56. For a discussion of castle symbolism in relation to women's chastity, see Anne Lancashire, 'The emblematic castle in Shakespeare and Middleton', in *Mirror up to Nature: Essays in Honour of G. R. Hibbard* (Toronto, University of Toronto Press, 1984), pp. 223–41. Male virginity is rarely alluded to in plays of this period, and then more usually in comic terms. See *Wit at Several Weapons* (*Works*, VII) where Sir Perfidious Oldcraft is incredulous to hear that Sir Gregory Fop still has his maidenhead: 'A gentleman of your ranke ride with a Cloak-bag? / Never an hostesse by the way to leave it with? / Nor Tapsters sister?' (III, i, 25–27).

57. For date and attribution see Bentley, *JCS*, III, 376–9, and Hoy, *Shares*. Rowley not only collaborated on the play but also acted in it. The two major scenes which I discuss both occur in the portion of the play attributed to Fletcher.

58. See Dyce, *Works*, IX, 199–205. Quotations from *The Maid in the Mill* are taken from the edition by Glover and Waller, VII.

59. For the division of authorship in the final scene, see Hoy, *Shares*.

60. The same kind of subversion occurs in the alternative (and more conventional) ending to *Philaster* found in Q1, where to 'make all compleat' in Philaster's own words, Bellario is married off to a conveniently available courtier, rather than, as in Q2, living in perpetual virginity. Editors agree that Q2 is the more authentic text, but not as to the nature and origins of Q1. See Gurr's introduction to the Revels edition (Manchester, Manchester University Press 1969), pp. lxxiv–lxxxiii.

61. Dymphna Callaghan, *Woman and Gender in Renaissance Tragedy* (Hemel Hempstead, Harvester Wheatsheaf, 1989), p. 154, relates the idea that 'women are ...constructed through "excessive" discourses' to tragedy only, but the Beaumont and Fletcher plays demonstrate that it is not generically restricted.

Chapter 2

1. See, for example, Winfried Schleiner, 'Male cross-dressing and transvestism in Renaissance romances', *Sixteenth-Century Journal* 14 (1988), 605–19; Stephen Greenblatt, *Shakespearean Negotiations* (Oxford, Clarendon Press, 1988), Ch. 3,

'Fiction and friction'; *Playing with Gender: A Renaissance pursuit*, eds Jean R. Brink, Maryanne C. Horowitz, and Allison P. Coudert (Urbana and Chicago, IL, University of Illinois Press, 1991); Molly Smith, *The Darker World Within: Evil in the tragedies of Shakespeare and his successors* (London and Toronto: Associated University Presses, 1991), pp. 141–8; and David Underdown, 'The Taming of the scold: the enforcement of authority in early modern England', in *Order and Disorder in Early Modern England* (Cambridge, Cambridge University Press, 1985), pp. 116–36, where 'a crisis in gender relations in the years around 1600' is postulated (p. 122).
2. Phyllis Rackin, 'Androgyny, mimesis, and the marriage of the Boy Heroine on the English Renaissance stage', *PMLA* 102 (1987), 38.
3. See, for example, the evidence provided by Ian MacLean in *The Renaissance Notion of Woman: A study in the fortunes of scholasticism and medical science in European intellectual life* (Cambridge, Cambridge University Press, 1980), Ch. 1, especially pp. 27, 39.
4. See Jean E. Howard, 'Crossdressing, the theatre, and gender struggle in early modern England', *SQ* 89 (1988), 418–40; Natalie Zemon Davis, *Society and Culture in Early Modern France* (London, Duckworth, 1975), especially Ch. 5 'Women on top'.
5. Chambers, *ES*, IV, gives a number of examples of contemporary attacks on transvestism in the theatre in Appendix C. See also J. Rainoldes, *Th' Overthrow of Stage-Playes* (Middleburgh, 1599); K. Young, 'An Elizabethan defence of the stage', *Shakespeare Studies by Members of the Department of English of the University of Wisconsin* (Madison, WI, University of Wisconsin, 1916); J. W. Binns, 'Women or transvestites on the Elizabethan stage? An Oxford controversy', *Sixteenth-Century Journal* 5 (1974), 95–120; A. F. Kinney, *Markets of Bawdrie: The dramatic criticism of Stephen Gosson* (Salzburg, Institüt für Englische Sprache und Literatur, Universität Salzburg, 1974).
6. See Linda Woodbridge, *Women and the English Renaissance: Literature and the nature of womankind, 1540–1620* (Urbana, IL, University of Illinois Press, 1983).
7. See Sandra Clark, '*Hic Mulier, Haec Vir*, and the controversy over masculine women', *SP* 82 (1985), 157–83; Mary Beth Rose, *The Expense of Spirit: Love and sexuality in English Renaissance drama* (Ithaca, NY, Cornell University Press, 1988), Ch. 2.
8. Rackin, *op.cit.*, p. 102.
9. Kathleen McLuskie, *Renaissance Dramatists* (Hemel Hempstead, Harvester Wheatsheaf, 1989), p. 101. See also her article, 'The Act, the role, and the actor', *New Theatre Quarterly*, 3, 10 (1987), pp. 120–30.
10. Howard, *op.cit.*, p. 435.
11. The dating of *Love's Cure* is problematic. There are no contemporary performance records, and no text before F1. Parts of it are early, in all probability close to 1605, but the Spanish source for the transvestite siblings plot was not in print before 1625. See M. Erickson, 'A review of scholarship dealing with the problem of a Spanish source for *Love's Cure*', in *Studies in Comparative Literature*, ed. Waldo F. McNeir (Baton Rouge, LA, Louisiana State University, 1962), pp. 102–19; J. Loftis, *Renaissance Drama in England and Spain: Topical allusion and history plays* (Princeton, NJ, Princeton University Press, 1987), pp. 253–6.
12. Juliet Dusinberre, *Shakespeare and the Nature of Womankind* (London, Macmillan, 1975), p. 241.

13. For the stage history of *Philaster* see Andrew Gurr's edition, Revels Plays (Manchester, Manchester University Press, 1969), pp. lxxi–lxxiv.
14. See Schleiner's illuminating article, cited above, n1, for more detail.
15. See James E. Savage, 'Beaumont and Fletcher's *Philaster* and Sidney's *Arcadia*', *English Literary History* 14 (1947), 184–206. He provides a good account of how the materials of *Arcadia* as a source-text are filtered through *Cupid's Revels* into *Philaster*. See also Gurr's introduction to the Revels edition of *Philaster op.cit.*, p. xxv, where the contribution of Sidney's influence to Beaumont and Fletcher's pre-Restoration popularity is strongly rated.
16. Sidney, *Arcadia*, ed. Maurice Evans (Harmondsworth, Penguin, 1977), p. 367.
17. *Ibid.*, p. 133. Foucault, discussing the ethics of sexuality in classical Greece, notes the distinction between active and passive partners, and the moral opprobrium attached to the adult free male who took on the role normally associated with 'women, boys, slaves' (*The Use of Pleasure: The history of sexuality* (Harmondsworth, Penguin, 1987), II, 47). See also Lisa Jardine, *Still Harping on Daughters: Women and drama in the age of Shakespeare* (Brighton, Harvester, 1983), p. 19.
18. This is the view of Aspatia taken by Ronald Huebert, '"An artificial way to grieve": the forsaken woman in Beaumont and Fletcher, Massinger, and Ford', *English Literary History* 44 (1977), 601–21.
19. I exclude The *Roaring Girl* from discussion here because Moll, based on a real-life transvestite, does not assume her disguise for purposes of intrigue, nor is anyone in doubt as to her true sex.
20. The disguised Alathe in *The Nightwalker* (*c.* 1611) is the nearest equivalent in the Beaumont and Fletcher canon.
21. Violett's uncertainty as to the nature of this garment may be a clue here. She tells Philippa, 'The slaves had stript him to the very shirt, mistress; / I think it was a shirt; I know not well, / For gallants wear both now-a-days' (III, iii, 26–8). The sexual ambivalence of the shirt/smock is commented on explicitly in *More Dissemblers*, I, iv.
22. Again, Alathe in *The Nightwalker* is exceptional here.
23. Schleiner gives several examples from episodes in romances where a cross-dressed man is regarded as very beautiful, and attracts the attentions of both men and women. But these, although sometimes characterised as very young, are not page figures, and play different and far more active roles in the narrative than Beaumont and Fletcher's disguised pages.
24. In some iconographical traditions Cupid is represented as a youth rather than an infant, and associated with musical instruments, representing the idea of Love the conqueror. See James Hall, *Dictionary of Subjects and Symbols in Art*, revised edn (London, John Murray, 1979), p. 88. Hylas, Adonis, and Apollo, to whom Megra refers, are often portrayed as beautiful effeminate youths, and Apollo, of course, as patron of poetry and music has the lyre as his instrument.
25. Philaster's lines recall Pyrocles' description of Zelmane's extraordinary fidelity when serving as his page. See *Arcadia*, ed. Evans, p. 367.
26. I follow here the Q2 reading preferred by Gurr in the Revels edition, although R. K. Turner in *Works*, I reads 'try' from Q3. As Gurr notes, 'tire' puns on the meanings 'be sufficient clothing for' and 'make weary'. In the context the idea of nakedness disclosing truth, and substituting for the protective disguise of clothing, makes 'tire' a richer reading.
27. All quotations are taken from *Works*, eds Glover and Waller, X. For a

discussion of the authorship of this play, see Hoy, *Shares*, and ed. J. Gerritsen, *The Honest Man's Fortune* (Groningen, Djakarta, 1952).
28. See J. F. Danby, *Poets on Fortune's Hill: Studies in Sidney, Shakespeare, Beaumont and Fletcher* (London, Faber & Faber, 1952), Chs 6 and 7; and Gurr's discussion of Danby in his introduction to *Philaster*, I,ii.
29. See for example Dekker, *The Honest Whore*, Part I, IV, i; Middleton, *More Dissemblers Besides Women*, I, ii; and Laxton's view of Moll in Middleton and Dekker's *The Roaring Girl*.
30. I quote here from the MS version of the speech, which Dyce gives in a footnote (*The Works of Beaumont and Fletcher*, III, 450) in preference to the F1 version which omits the words 'madame I took that habit'. The pun on 'habit' suits the play's verbal and theatrical self-consciousness in this scene.
31. McLuskie, *op.cit.*, n9, p. 159.
32. See Rose, *op.cit.*, n7, p. 61.
33. See the excellent account of this in L. Bliss *Francis Beaumont* (Boston, MA, G. K. Hall, 1987), Ch. 3.
34. See Rose, *op.cit.*, p. 58; Woodbridge, *op.cit.*, n6, Ch. 7.
35. By Jonathan Dollimore in 'Subjectivity, sexuality, and transgression', *Renaissance Drama* 17 (1986), 72.
36. For example, in *Haec Vir: or The Womanish-Man* (1620), sig. B3r.
37. See Simon Shepherd, *Amazons and Warrior Women: Varieties of feminism in seventeenth-century drama* (Brighton, Harvester, 1981), p. 89. He discusses the play in the light of the *Hic Mulier* and *Haec Vir* pamphlets, though the difficulties over dating the play (mentioned on p. 171n11) render this a debatable procedure.
38. The close resemblance between this part of the play (and especially Vitelli's aside about the horror of men's sexual enslavement to an unworthy woman) and *The Dutch Courtesan* argues strongly for an early date for it. It also highlights the fuller involvement of Marston's play with the theme of sexuality.
39. See Dollimore, *op.cit.*, for a differently focused discussion of this point.
40. *Ibid.*, p. 72. He relates the sword-phallus metaphor to the play's critique of masculine honour.
41. Woodbridge, *op.cit.*, p. 152, calls the pairing of the effeminate man with the virago 'a prominent literary device' in this period.
42. For discussions of the Amazons' bad press in Elizabethan drama, see Woodbridge, *op.cit.*, pp. 164–5; Shepherd, *op.cit.*, especially pp. 14–17. See also Morose's exclamations about Epicoene and her 'Amazonian impudence' (III, ii). Celeste Turner Wright's article, 'The Amazons in Elizabethan literature', *SP*, 37 (1940), 433–56, remains the major source of information on this subject. This play is quoted from *Works*, eds Glover and Waller, IX.
43. Shepherd, *op.cit.*, p. 135, contrasts the effect of these lines with that of Isabella's lines in *Women Beware Women* (I, ii, 169–76) which he calls 'shocking', though it could be argued that Isabella's position too is undermined.
44. Crocale's description of Clarinda in II, ii distantly derives from *Aeneid*, VII, 804–17.
45. See Shepherd, *op.cit.*, Ch. 13. Quotations from this play are taken from *Works*, eds Glover and Waller, VI.
46. Shepherd, *op.cit.*, p. 183.
47. See also Lisa Jardine, *Still Harping on Daughters: Women and drama in the age of Shakespeare* (Brighton, Harvester, 1982), p. 71, whose discussion of the

relation between majesty and suffering in the female hero in *The Duchess of Malfi* is relevant here.
48. For example, III, i, Glover and Waller, VI, 368, where Pandulpho, Virolet's father, expresses his admiration at his first sight of Martia with the words, 'What Masque is this?'
49. Shepherd, *op.cit.*, p. 183.

Chapter 3

1. Kathleen McLuskie, *Renaissance Dramatists* (Hemel Hempstead, Harvester Wheatsheaf, 1988), p. 213. Nancy Cotton Pearse, *John Fletcher's Chastity Plays: Mirrors of modesty* (Lewisburg, PA, Bucknell University Press 1973), p. 40, claims that misogynist characters 'abound' in the plays, but does not demonstrate this. Linda Woodbridge, *Women and the English Renaissance* (Urbana, IL, University of Illinois Press, 1983), p. 276, calls Algripe in *The Nightwalker* (?1611) a misogynist, but this is a very secondary aspect of the character. For useful accounts of misogyny in the period see Woodbridge, *op.cit.*, especially Chs 10 and 11, and *passim*; Valerie Wayne, 'Historical differences: misogyny and *Othello*' in *The Matter of Difference: Materialist feminist criticism of Shakespeare*, ed. Valerie Wayne (Hemel Hempstead, Harvester Wheatsheaf, 1991).
2. See Woodbridge, *op.cit.*, especially pp. 81–110, 300–22.
3. Wayne, *op.cit.*, pp. 153–80.
4. There are uncertainties over the dating of both these plays, though most recent critics (see, for example, Lee Bliss, *Francis Beaumont* (Boston, MA, G. K. Hall, 1987), pp. 122, 146; P. J. Finkelpearl, *Court and Country Politics in the Plays of Beaumont and Fletcher* (Princeton, NJ, Princeton University Press, 1990), p. 115) are inclined to accept the conjectures of Baldwin Maxwell, *Studies in Beaumont, Fletcher and Massinger* (Chapel Hill, NC, University of North Carolina Press, 1939), pp. 17–28, and put *The Woman's Prize* at *c.* 1611 and *The Scornful Lady* shortly before.
5. Finkelpearl, *op.cit.*, p. 115, mentions the subject in a footnote. He regards 'a mixture of traditional anti-feminine material and pure perversity in the character of ladies' as hallmarks of Beaumont's plays, and finds 'far greater sympathy for women' in Fletcher. Although the playwrights have often been differentiated on the basis of their respective attitudes to women, there has been no consistent line of argument. Finkelpearl's view represents the antithesis to that of Gayley, some seventy-five years earlier (*Francis Beaumont, Dramatist: A portrait*, London, Duckworth, 1914), who found much of Fletcher's work morally repulsive (he ascribes to Fletcher those sections of *The Coxcomb* and *The Scornful Lady* 'that are carnal, trivial, or unnatural', p. 383) but championed Beaumont's greater 'purity'. More recently, Robert Ornstein, *The Moral Vision of Jacobean Tragedy* (Madison, WI, University of Wisconsin Press, 1965), Ch. 6, objected to the moral ambivalence with which Fletcher depicts his heroines and to his 'ethical frivolity' generally. W. W. Appleton writes of 'misogynistic abuse of women' as a 'commonplace' in Fletcher's later work: see his *Beaumont and Fletcher: A critical study* (London, Allen & Unwin, 1956), p. 12.
6. Finkelpearl, *op.cit.*, p. 70.
7. Hoy, *Shares* (III), 11 (1958), 98–9, thinks that the play as originally staged

was Beaumont's, and that Fletcher's contribution was made later. See also G. Walton Williams, *Works*, I, 150–3; Bliss, *op.cit.*, pp. 19, 143. Walton Williams finds significant evidence of Fletcher's hand in III, i, 1–153, III, ii, IV, ii, 1–271, and V, ii, iv, and further traces of it in III, iii, IV, ii, 272–361, and V, i. The interesting prologue to the play published in the Second issue of the First Folio (1649; in *Works*, I, 236–7) assumes it to be the sole work of Fletcher, and begs the women in the audience not to object to it because 'His Muse beleev'd not, what she then did write' and elsewhere Fletcher wrote more flatteringly of women, citing the characters of Evadne, Aspatia, Arathusa, and Panthea.

8. Like, for example, *The Malcontent* (1602–3), Sharpham's *The Fleire* (1605), Middleton's *The Phoenix* (c. 1604), and *Measure for Measure*.
9. McLuskie, *op.cit.*, p. 214.
10. The play was not printed before the 1647 Folio, and although it is possible that the original version was by Fletcher alone, there is evidence in the printed text for the presence of a collaborator. Hoy thinks this was Beaumont (see *Shares* 14 (1961), 46), but Beaurline (*Works*, I, 544–6) is less certain.
11. Woodbridge, *op.cit.*, pp. 279–81, briefly discusses the association between soldiers and misogyny. But her point, that soldiers like Benedick and Jacomo leave behind their profession for the 'sane hermaphrodism' of the civilian world, is simplistic.
12. I have been influenced in this account by Finkelpearl, *op.cit.*, Ch. 5, who sees the ending of *The Captain* as a celebration of manly energies, and the play itself as an exploration of the dilemma of would-be heroes in an unheroic age.
13. Scenes in which a disguised father confronts a prostitute daughter are not uncommon and occur, for example, in *The Honest Whore* Part 1, Middleton's *Michaelmas Term*, and Sharpham's *The Fleire*; Fletcher's scene capitalises on the potential for irony in this situation in having Lelia solicit her father.
14. One version is Hamlet's scene with Gertrude (IV, iii) which is imitated in *The Maid's Tragedy* (IV, i). Greene's *A Disputation, Betweene a Hee Conny-catcher, and a Shee Conny-catcher* (1592) includes the story of the prostitute reformed by a would-be client (pp. 75–9), adapted from Erasmus, *Colloquia*.
15. S. Shepherd, *Amazons and Warrior Women* (Brighton, Harvester, 1981), pp. 144–5, notes a number of references to Bonduca/Boadicea in this tradition, and also connects her with notions of Puritan virtue. The adaptation of the play by George Powell, *Bonduca: or, The British Heroine, A Tragedy* (1696) treats Bonduca more conventionally and enhances the theme of female heroism in the character of Claudia, her elder daughter.
16. David Farley-Hills, *Jacobean Drama: A critical survey of the professional drama, 1600–25* (Basingstoke, Macmillan, 1988), pp. 190–1, relates Fletcher's account of Roman values in this play to that of the near-contemporary *Coriolanus* (1608). This speech strongly recalls Aufidius's in IV, v.
17. On the Renaissance identification of spinning as 'woman's work' see Merry E. Weisner, 'Spinsters and seamstresses: women in cloth and clothing production' in *Rewriting the Renaissance: The discourses of sexual differences in early modern Europe*, eds Margaret W. Ferguson, Maureen Quilligan, and Nancy J. Vickers (Chicago, University of Chicago Press, 1986).
18. See also the account of sexual politics in *Bonduca* by Paul D. Green, 'Theme and Structure in Fletcher's *Bonduca*', *SEL* 22 (1982), 305–16. Farley-Hills, *op.cit.*, pp. 191–2, considers that the play reveals a 'deep-seated feeling of woman's "otherness"', well beyond 'the usual Jacobean anti-feminism', which

has gone 'out of control'. Clifford Leech, *The John Fletcher Plays* (London, Chatto & Windus, 1962), p. 165, thinks that the 'revulsion from the idea of sexual union' displayed in *Bonduca* is in part due to Fletcher's over-dependence on *Cymbeline*.
19. The quotation is from Terence, *Eunuchus*, l. 105.
20. For further discussion of *Bonduca* on these lines see Shepherd, *op.cit.*, pp. 145–50.
21. Bowers, *Works*, II, 331, suggests 1607–8; John Astington, 'The popularity of *Cupid's Revenge*', *SEL* 19 (1979), 215–27, presents a good argument which supports this date, and suggests that the play influenced Shakespeare in *Cymbeline*.
22. Catherine Belsey, *The Subject of Tragedy: Identity and difference in Renaissance drama* (London, Methuen, 1985), p. 149.
23. Finkelpearl, *op.cit.*, Ch. 6, sees a political dimension in Leucippus's 'tired nobility', and suggests that it reflects the 'confused idealism' of Jacobean cavaliers betrayed by a false sense of chivalry into loyalty to such hollow absolutes as divine right.
24. There is no evidence for dating the play's composition other than the likelihood of Massinger's having collaborated on it with Beaumont and Fletcher. This in itself is indecisive since the date at which Massinger began to emerge as a dramatist, 1613, is also the date at which Beaumont withdrew from writing. Finkelpearl, *op.cit.*, p. 251, following a dating proposed by Fleay, groups it *c.* 1617 with *Rollo, Duke of Normandy* as another play about fratricide, but the date of *Rollo* is also disputable, and 1617 would, of course, rule out Beaumont's collaboration. It also resembles *A Wife for a Month* in certain ways; *A Wife for a Month*, dated 1624, is one of Fletcher's last plays.
25. This point confirms Wayne's view of the relation between the value accorded to female chastity, and misogyny (Wayne, *op.cit.*, nl, p. 159).
26. Belsey, *op.cit.*, p. 165, gives other examples of these particular female stereotypes.
27. Chambers, *ES* III, 229, dates the play between 1613 and 1616, though as Finkelpearl, *op.cit.*, p. 115, points out this cannot be right if Beaumont was a collaborator; he accepts Baldwin Maxwell's suggestion of *c.* 1608–10. This suits his argument, since it makes *The Scornful Lady* more or less contemporary with *The Woman's Prize*, but it also accords with Oliphant's suggestion of 1610 (E. M. C. Oliphant, *The Plays of Beaumont and Fletcher: An attempt to determine their respective shares and the shares of others* (New Haven, CT, Yale University Press, 1927), pp. 208–9).
28. Finkelpearl, *op.cit.*, p. 115 n.
29. Hoy allots to Beaumont only I, i, II, i, and V, ii in *The Scornful Lady*, and it is generally accepted that Beaumont's part in the play is not large. But the complexities of the collaboration make such author-based distinctions difficult to sustain.
30. The play was not printed before the Folio of 1647; its prologue speaks of Fletcher in the past tense. It was performed at Court in November 1633, after censorship of 'Oaths, prophaness, and ribaldrye' had taken place on the orders of Sir Henry Herbert, who noted in his Office Book that 'in former time the poetts tooke greater liberty than is allowed by mee'. The change in moral climate since the play's composition may perhaps be due to the influence of Henrietta Maria and her circle; and the prologue's author, in addressing the play to ladies, may have had an eye on this audience. Herbert noted that the play was 'very well likt' when done at Court on 28 November 1633, two days

after *The Taming of the Shrew*, which was only 'likt'. The date of composition is uncertain; *c.* 1611 is accepted by many critics (see, for example, Maxwell, *op.cit.*, pp. 29–45; Leech, *op.cit.*, pp. 50–1; Finkelpearl, *op.cit.*, p. 251); but Oliphant suggests a date of 1603, supported by a reference to the siege of Ostend and a series of plays on women and marriage at other theatres at this time (*op.cit.*, p. 153), and though this seems too early, Bowers in *Works*, IV, 3, says the play was 'composed early' in Fletcher's career but acted in 1611.
31. See the discussion in McLuskie, *op.cit.*, pp. 214–18.
32. Lisa Jardine, *Still Harping on Daughters* (Brighton, Harvester, 1983), discusses the tongue as metonymic of female sexuality, pp. 121–4.
33. Significantly, they are present in the Folger manuscript, generally regarded as a revision of the play cut for performance.

Chapter 4

1. For a discussion of Beaumont and Fletcher's reputation see above, Ch. 1.
2. Rebecca Bushnell, *Tragedies of Tyrants: Political thought and theater in the English Renaissance* (Ithaca, NY, Cornell University Press, 1990), p. 163.
3. See Bushnell, *op.cit.*, Ch. 1; W. A. Armstrong, 'The Elizabethan conception of the tyrant', *Review of English Studies* 22 (1946), 161–81.
4. R. Y. Turner, 'Responses to tyranny in John Fletcher's plays', *Medieval and Renaissance Drama in England* 4 (1989), 123.
5. See Armstrong, *op.cit.* 'Dynastic nationalism' is his phrase.
6. See J. N. Figgis, *The Divine Right of Kings* (London, Cambridge University Press, 1896; 2nd edn. 1922), pp. 96–106.
7. See C. H. McIlwain (ed.), *The Political Works of James I* (Cambridge, MA, and London, Harvard University Press, 1918), pp. 66, 67.
8. See Bushnell's acute discussion of this, *op.cit.*, pp. 141–2.
9. *An Apology for Poetry* (1595), ed. G. Shepherd (Manchester, Manchester University Press, 1965), pp. 117–18.
10. For example, by Walter Cohen, *Drama of a Nation: Public theater in Renaissance England and Spain* (Ithaca, NY, Cornell University Press, 1985); T. W. Craik, introduction to the Revels edition of *The Maid's Tragedy* (Manchester, Manchester University Press, 1988), p. 13; and A. C. Kirsch, *Jacobean Dramatic Perspectives* (Charlottesville, VA, University Press of Virginia, 1972), Ch. 3. Janet Clare, *'Art made tongue-tied by authority': Elizabethan and Jacobean dramatic censorship*, (Manchester, Manchester University Press, 1990), who also regards the play as politically significant although evasive in its treatment of regicide, supports her view with evidence that it had been censored in a few small instances to dilute the brutality of some references to regicide (p. 166).
11. F. T. Bowers, *Elizabethan Revenge Tragedy 1587–1642* (Princeton, NJ, Princeton University Press, 1940) pp. 169–76.
12. See Clare, *op.cit.*, p. 167, and D. H. Wilson, *King James VI and I* (London, Jonathan Cape, 1956), pp. 279, 367, to which she refers.
13. See Craik's edition of *The Maid's Tragedy*, *op.cit.*, pp. 2–3.
14. See A. A. Bromham and Zara Bruzzi, *The Changeling and the Years of Crisis 1619–1624* (London, Pinter Press, 1990), p. 194.
15. See McIlwain (ed.), *Political Works*, *op.cit.*, Appendix B, pp. lxxxvii–lxxxix.
16. See R. K. Turner, in *Works*, IV, 389–90 for a note on the probability that the song 'Care-charming sleep' was adapted to suit the circumstances of the

death of Prince Henry in November 1612, which the composition of the play therefore pre-dates.
17. For example, L. B. Wallis, Ch. 7, *Fletcher, Beaumont and Company: Entertainers to the Jacobean gentry* (New York, Octagon, 1947; rpt, 1968), Bushnell, *op.cit.*, pp. 166–8; Finkelpearl, *Court and Country Politics*, p. 199.
18. See McLuskie, *Renaissance Dramatists*, p. 194. She does, however, go on to argue that such 'precise ideological readings' are not the point of this (or any other Beaumont and Fletcher) text, since ideas are subject to theatrical 'play' and thus 'shaped and modulated' by stage representation.
19. Bushnell, *op.cit.*, p. 53.
20. This is a commonplace, but see especially H. Neville Davies, 'Beaumont and Fletcher's *Hamlet*', in *Shakespeare: Man of the theatre*, eds. K. Muir, J. L. Halio, and D. J. Palmer (Newark, NJ, University of Delaware Press, 1983).
21. Tennenhouse, *Power on Display* (London, Methuen, 1986) p. 122, makes this point in contrasting *Valentinian* as a typical Jacobean tragedy of female punishment and Elizabethan plays about rape. But I cannot accept his argument that the politics of the female body are differently represented in Jacobean and Elizabethan texts, nor that the polarities of gender are 'dissolved' (p. 123) in Jacobean drama into purely political themes.
22. In later rape plays, such as *The Queen of Corinth* and *The Spanish Gipsy* (by Middleton and Rowley), the meaning of the rape is modified by its conditions; the victim is an unmarried woman, and the rapist is socially recuperated by being able to marry her. See S. Gossett, '"Best men are molded out of faults": marrying the rapist in Jacobean drama', *English Literary Review*, 14 (1984).
23. See Shepherd, *Amazons and Warrior Women* p. 174, who refers to Livy.
24. Another difference from D'Urfé, which Shepherd, *op.cit.*, does not mention, is that the story of Valentinian and Isidore (Lucina) is narrated by a character with pronounced royalist views. He expresses horror at the murder of the Emperor: 'Had I been neere his person at that time, doubtless I had dyed in defence of him: For though the act which he had committed against Isidore was wicked; yet there can be no cause whatsoever for lifting up a hand against a Soveraine' (quoted from the English translation of 1657, vol. I, p. 416). The authority of this character, Ursaces, is by no means reproduced in the expressions of royalism given to Aecius in Fletcher's text.
25. Compare James I, 'A Speech to the Lords and Commons of the Parlaiament at Whitehall' (1610), in McIlwain (ed.), *Political Works*, p. 310: 'As to dispute what God may doe, is Blasphemie . . . So is it sedition in subiects, to dispute what a King may doe in the height of his power.'
26. Shepherd, *op.cit.*, p. 174. In this connection it is interesting to consider the politicisation of the Lucrece myth as discussed by Zara Bruzzi in Bromham and Bruzzi, *op.cit.*, n14, pp. 190–4, and E. P. Kuhl, 'Shakespeare's Rape of Lucrece', *Philological Quarterly* 20 (1941), 352–60. See also, I. Donaldson, *The Rapes of Lucrece* (Oxford, Clarendon Press, 1982). Fletcher by handling the story in this way seems also to avoid any identification of Lucina as a figure of Protestant resistance.
27. Finkelpearl, *Court and Country Politics*, p. 204.
28. McLuskie, *Renaissance Dramatists*, pp. 194–8; R. Y. Turner, *op.cit.*, n4, p. 133.
29. Danby, *Poets on Fortune's Hill* (London, Faber & Faber, 1952), p. 17. Compare Finkelpearl, who calls Aecius 'a narrow fanatic', *op.cit.*, p. 214.
30. For other accounts which share this view, see Wallis, *op.cit.*, pp. 215–17.

31. For *The Maid's Tragedy*, see Inga-Stina Ewbank, '"These pretty devices": a study of masques in plays', in eds, T. J. B. Spencer and S. W. Wells, *A Book of Masques in Honour of Allardyce Nicoll* (Cambridge, Cambridge University Press, 1967), especially p. 418.
32. Clare, *op.cit.*, n10, p. 169.
33. For an account of the play's allusions to contemporary court scandal and to religious controversy, see Anne Lancashire's introduction to her Revels Plays edition (Manchester, Manchester University Press, 1978), especially pp. 43–4, and her account of the censorship of the play, Appendix A, pp. 275–81.
34. Dating and authorship are both uncertain. Bentley, *JCS* III, 401–7, suggests ?1617, with possible revision 1627–30. For a discussion of the authorship, distributed between four playwrights, see Hoy, *Shares*; Bertha Hensman, in the introduction to her edition, *The Bloody Brother: A tragedy by John Fletcher and Nathan Field* (New York, Vintage Press, 1991).
35. See Bentley, *JCS* I, 30, 109, and III, 401–7, for accounts of seventeenth-century performances. Edward Howard, Preface to *The Woman's Conquest* (1671) ranked it with *Catiline*, *The Maid's Tragedy*, *The Cardinal*, and *The Traitor* as the best of English tragedy. Langbaine, *An Account of the English Dramatick Poets* (1691), p. 207, says it was then 'much in request'; Dryden in the *Essay of Dramatic Poesy* admires it for 'uniformity and unity of design' and 'truth of history'; Rymer analyses it at length and calls it one of 'the choicest and most applauded English Tragedies of this last age' along with *A King and No King*, *The Maid's Tragedy*, *Othello*, *Julius Caesar*, and *Catiline*. John Jump in the introduction to his edition, *Rollo, Duke of Normandy* (Liverpool, Liverpool University Press, 1969), p. xxxi, calls it 'one of the most popular plays of the seventeenth century'.
36. According to Bentley, it was especially popular in the 1630s and early 1660s. A surreptitious performance in 1648 was interrupted by soldiers (Wright, *Historia Histrionica*, quoted in *JCS* II, 695).
37. Coleridge thought the tyranny of Rollo too generalised an image of 'outrageous Wickedness' not 'philosophically intelligible'. See R. Brinkley (ed.), *Coleridge on the Seventeenth Century* (Durham, NC, Duke University Press, 1955), p. 661.
38. For example, by Finkelpearl, p. 237.
39. Like *Rollo, Duke of Normandy*, *A King and No King* was performed during the interregnum, in October 1647. L. Hotson, *The Commonwealth and Restoration Stage* (New York, Russell & Russell, 1926; reprinted 1962), p. 26, says that 'the choice of the play *A King and No King* was in itself an affront to the Parliament'.
40. R. K. Turner (ed.), *A King and No King*, Regents Renaissance Drama Series (Lincoln, NE, University of Nebraska Press, 1963), p. xxv.
41. See Bushnell, *op.cit.*, pp. 159, 161 ff., and her discussion of criticism of the 'decadence' of Beaumont and Fletcher. Mizener in his influential article, 'The high design of *A King and No King*', *Modern Philology*, 38 (1940–41), pp. 133–54, is in the same tradition, contrasting the lack of 'fundamental seriousness' in Beaumont and Fletcher's 'sense of the world' with Shakespeare's abundance of it.
42. R. K. Turner, 'The morality of *A King and No King*', *Renaissance Papers* 1958–1960 (1961), p. 103.
43. Jean-Pierre Teissedou, L'Absolutisme en question dans *A King and No King*' in *Coriolan: Théâtre et politique*, eds Jean-Paul Debax and Yves Peyre (Toulouse, Université de Toulouse - Le Mirail, 1984). Teissedou also notes

the extraordinary frequency of terms for royalty in the play; 'king' occurs nearly fifty times, and there are regular uses of queen, majesty, grace, royal, throne, tyrant and tyranny.

44. Michael Neill, 'The defence of contraries: skeptical paradox in *A King and No King*', *SEL* 21 (1981), 332.
45. See Tucker Brooke, 'The royal Fletcher and the loyal Heywood', in *Elizabethan Studies and Other Essays in Honour of George F. Reynolds* (Boulder, CO, University of Colorado, 1945), pp. 192–4, who contrasts the plays in Heywood's favour. Tucker Brooke admires the treatment of loyalty to the monarch in Heywood, which he calls 'God's special invention against Judgement Day'; predictably he finds Fletcher's play 'hollow'. He comments with surprise and implied distaste, on the 'abnormally low quality of the kings' in the Beaumont and Fletcher plays (p. 192). No text of the play exists before 1637, but S. Schoenbaum and S. Wagonheim, *Annals of English Drama 975–1700*, revised edn (London and New York, Methuen, 1989), date it in 1602.
46. The contrast with the Restoration version of the play, *The Faithful General* by 'M. N.' is significant in this connection. The transvestite disguise of Alinda (the Artemisia-figure, but actually a boy) has been abandoned, and the duke-figure, Emperor Galerius, lusts strongly after Artemisia, his general's daughter. He twice threatens to rape her when she refuses his advances.
47. See, for example, Finkelpearl, *Court and Country Politics*, p. 219; Tucker Brooke, *op.cit.*
48. See Robert Lacey, *Sir Walter Ralegh* (London, Weidenfeld & Nicolson, 1973), pp. 379–82; Stephen J. Greenblatt, *Sir Walter Ralegh: The Renaissance man and his roles* (New Haven, CT, and London, Yale University Press, 1973), p. 180, n23, where a list of contemporary accounts of Ralegh's execution is given.
49. See Lacey, *op.cit.*, p. 328.
50. W. W. Appleton, *Beaumont and Fletcher: A critical study* (London, Allen and Unwin, 1956), p. 63. The seizure of the treasure may however reflect a similar incident in Heywood's play.
51. See Lacey, *op.cit.*, pp. 366–7. Appleton, *op.cit.*, p. 88, thinks the treacherous Septimus in *The False One* (*c.* 1620) also alludes to Stukeley.
52. See the introduction by Albert J. Schmidt, *Of the Rus Commonwealth*, Folger Shakespeare Library (Ithaca, NY, Cornell University Press, 1966).
53. See James I's discussion of the concept of the king as overlord of his subjects' lands and property, *The trew Law of Free Monarchies* in McIlwain (ed.), *Political Works*, pp. 62–3.
54. Bushnell, *op.cit.*, p. 165.
55. Eugene Waith, for example, in his discussion of the play in *The Pattern of Tragicomedy in Beaumont and Fletcher* (New Haven, CT, Yale University Press, 1952), recalls Rymer's comment about Beaumont and Fletcher being unable to depict an honourable woman 'without somewhat of the Dol Common in her' (p. 163), and censures Evanthe for lacking the decorum proper to 'the courtly heroine' (p. 165). Leech, *op.cit.*, makes a case on psychological and dramaturgical grounds for the necessity for Evanthe to be 'self-assertive' (pp. 104–6).
56. See Ch. 1 'The price of virtue: chastity plays'.
57. See H. Blau, 'The absolved riddle: sovereign pleasure and the baroque subject in the tragicomedies of John Fletcher', *New Literary History* 17 (1985–6), 539–54, especially p. 547.

58. This rather different image of tyranny is probably the creation of Massinger, thought to be the author of the play's first act.
59. See the discussion of Martia in Ch. 3 'Misogyny and manhood', pp. 75–7.
60. McLuskie, *Renaissance Dramatists*, p. 194.

Chapter 5

1. For the dating of *The Woman's Prize*, see Ch. 3 'Misogyny and manhood', n30.
2. For the dating of *The Scornful Lady*, see Ch. 3 'Misogyny and manhood', n27; for *Wit Without Money*, see E. K. Chambers, *ES* III, 229, and H. W. Gabler in *Works*, VI, 4–5. *The Wild-Goose Chase* and *Rule a Wife and Have a Wife* were performed at court in 1621 and 1624 respectively, and it has always been assumed that they were then new.
3. McLuskie, *Renaissance Dramatists*, p. 222.
4. A. S. W. Rosenbach, 'The curious-impertinent in English dramatic literature before Shelton's translation of *Don Quixote*', *Modern Language Notes*, 17 (1962), 357–67, briefly mentions *The Coxcomb*, but considers *The Second Maiden's Tragedy* (1611) to be the first play in English undoubtedly influenced by Cervantes. See also Lee Bliss *Francis Beaumont* (Boston, MA, G. K. Hall, 1987), pp. 122–3.
5. See Bliss's account in *op.cit.*, Ch. 3.
6. See Rosenbach, *op.cit.*, p. 364. Field's play, which is theatrically very self-conscious, may also of course have been influenced by *The Coxcomb*; he collaborated with Fletcher on several plays, including the lost play, *The Jeweller of Amsterdam* (see Bentley, *JCS* III, 350–1), *The Knight of Malta*, and *The Queen of Corinth*. Quotations from *Amends for Ladies* are taken from the edition of A. Wilson Verity in *Nero and Other Plays*, ed. Herbert P. Horne et al. (London, T. Fisher Unwin; New York, Charles Scribner's Sons, 1917). For another handling of this motif in a play of the same year, see the subplot of *The Second Maiden's Tragedy*.
7. See Rose, *The Expense of Spirit*, Ch. 3 'The heroics of marriage in Renaissance tragedy'.
8. Ann Thompson, *Shakespeare's Chaucer: A study in literary origins* (Liverpool, Liverpool University Press, 1978), p. 178, compares the relationship with accounts of female friendships in *A Midsummer Night's Dream*, III, ii, 203–14, and *As You Like It*, I, iii, 69–72.
9. Compare, for example, the opening scene of *Amends for Ladies*. Woodbridge, *Women and the English Renaissance*, Ch. 9, discusses the 'maid/wife/widow debate'.
10. Thompson, *op.cit.*, p. 182, notes that 'the heavily ironical stress on the men's friendship' just before the entrance of Emilia is not present in *The Knight's Tale*, the play's source.
11. Richard Abrams, in 'Gender confusion and sexual politics in *The Two Noble Kinsmen*', in *Drama, Sex, and Politics: Themes in drama* 7 (1985), 69–76, assumes the dialogue between Emilia and her woman in this scene to be specifically lesbian. The scene could be played this way, no doubt, but a heterosexual slant is most immediately obvious. Abrams considers the play's unpopularity to be due in part to its 'sexual–political content'; that is, the privileging of homosocial over heterosexual bonding.
12. For example, Plato, *Phaedrus*, 246A, and Vergil, *The Georgics*, 1. 512–14. In Chaucer, the horse stumbles because it is frightened by a monster sent by the god Saturn.

13. For a discussion of the generic relationship between the two plots in different terms, see Lois Potter, 'Topicality or politics: *The Two Noble Kinsmen*', in *The Politics of Tragicomedy: Shakespeare and after*, eds. Gordon McMullan and Jonathan Hope (London, Routledge, 1992), pp. 88–90.
14. In the RSC production of 1986 the director chose to make a parallel between Emilia and the Jailor's Daughter, juxtaposing them in a final tableau both as reluctant brides. But the text is sufficiently open-ended (or, it might be said, bedevilled by the problems of a collaboration that did not tie up all the loose ends) to allow for the reading of the subplot which I propose. Rose, *The Expense of Spirit*, also sees the play in this way. The contrast with Davenant's Restoration version, *The Rivals* (1668), is instructive. Here, the Jailor's daughter is socially elevated (her father is now a Provost) and in the end she marries one of the kinsmen.
15. Greenblatt's account of courtship in *Twelfth Night* (in *Shakespearean Negotiations*, pp. 68–70) is suggestive here.
16. A. Leggatt, *Citizen Comedy in the Age of Shakespeare* (Toronto, University of Toronto Press, 1973), p. 151.
17. T. B. Leinwand, *The City Staged: Jacobean comedy, 1603–1613* (Madison, WI, University of Wisconsin Press, 1986), p. 145.
18. Finkelpearl, *Court and Country Politics*, p. 118, n7.
19. M. D. Bristol, *Carnival and Theater: Plebeian culture and the structure of authority in Renaissance England* (London, Methuen, 1985), p. 164.
20. N. Rigaud, *Femme mythifiée, femme de raison: La veuve dans la comedie Anglaise au temps de Shakespeare 1600–1625* (Aix-en-Provence, Université de Provence, 1986), p. 143.
21. Rigaud, *op.cit.*, p. 144, suggests that this stratagem is required because the virtuous widow herself cannot be allowed to initiate intrigue: 'Elle peut etre point de depart d'une action en ce qu'elle attire ... mais elle-meme n'agit pas directment.'
22. Charles R. Forker, '*Wit Without Money*: A Fletcherian antecedent to *Keep the Widow Waking*', *Comparative Drama* 8 (1974), 178. The lost play, *Keep the Widow Waking* (1624), by Dekker, Ford, Rowley, and Webster was in all probability based on the true story recounted in the pamphlet.
23. Although R. K. Turner, *Works*, VI, 301–2, agrees with Hoy and Lake that the play is essentially Middleton and Rowley's, his feeling that 'Fletcher's ghost lingers' is strong enough to warrant the play's inclusion in the Cambridge edition. The prologue, written for a revival, attributes at least 'an Act, or two' solely to Fletcher.
24. See Bentley, *JCS* III, 425–9.
25. Cf. the commonplace, 'For men have marble, women waxen minds', *The Rape of Lucrece*, 1240. See R. Howard Bloch's interesting discussion of the role played by the form/matter distinction in the discourse of misogyny in 'Medieval Misogyny', *Representations* 20 (1987), 10–11.
26. C. Hoy, 'Fletcherian Romantic Comedy', *RORD* 27 (1984), 3.
27. D. Farley-Hills, *Jacobean Drama: A critical survey of the professional drama, 1600–25* (Basingstoke, Macmillan, 1988), p. 187.
28. See K. McLuskie, 'John Fletcher', in *The Revels History of Drama in English*, IV, ed. Philip Edwards *et al.* (London, Methuen, 1981) pp. 194–6. She considers that Mirabel's agreeing to marry the disguised Oriana at the end of the play reveals 'the connections between sex, money, and power', because he thinks he is marrying a rich woman. In my view she takes insufficient account

of the effect and meaning of Oriana's disguise which makes the ending more ambiguous.
29. See Edward M. Wilson, '*Rule a Wife and Have a Wife* and *El Sagaz Estacio*', *Review of English Studies*, 24 (1948), 187–94, for an account of the relationship between the texts, citing some close verbal parallels.
30. C. Kahn, 'Whores and wives in Jacobean drama', in *In Another Country: Feminist perspectives on Renaissance drama*, eds. D. Kehler and S. Baker (Metuchen, NJ, Scarecrow Press, 1991), p. 253.
31. Discussed at greater length in Ch. 3 'Misogyny and manhood'.
32. See McLuskie, *Renaissance Dramatists*, p. 215.
33. Hoy, *RORD* 27, p. 3. See also W. W. Appleton, *Beaumont and Fletcher: A critical study* (London, Allen & Unwin, 1956), p. 78, where, at the conclusion of his account of *Rule a Wife*, Appleton finds Leon guilty of bullying and humiliating Margarita, but explains it on the grounds of 'the overwhelmingly male nature of the Jacobean drama'.
34. Leinwand, *op.cit.*, n17, pp. 153–4.
35. G. Sorelius, '*The Giant Race Before the Flood*': *Pre-Restoration drama on the stage and in the criticism of the Renaissance* (Acta Universitatis Upsaliensis, Uppsala, 1966), p. 81, includes *The Scornful Lady*, *Wit Without Money* and *Rule a Wife* with *The Spanish Curate* and *The Beggars' Bush* among the most popular of the Beaumont and Fletcher plays on the Restoration stage.
36. See Rose, *The Expense of Spirit*, especially Ch. 1.

Conclusion

1. The extraordinary proliferation of articles in the last ten or so years on, for example, Middleton and Dekker's *The Roaring Girl* makes this point. There is also a considerable increase of interest in domestic tragedies such as *Arden of Faversham* and *A Woman Killed with Kindness*. In terms of the Beaumont and Fletcher canon *Love's Cure* and to a lesser extent *The Sea Voyage* are achieving a new prominence.
2. See Introduction, nn 31 and 32.
3. Valerie Traub, 'Desire and the difference it makes' in *The Matter of Difference: Materialist feminist criticism of Shakespeare*, ed. Valerie Wayne, (Hemel Hempstead, Harvester Wheatsheaf, 1991), p. 104.
4. Janet Adelman, '"Born of woman": fantasies of maternal power in *Macbeth*' in *Cannibals, Witches, and Divorce*, ed. Marjorie Garber, Selected Papers from the English Institute, 1985, 11 (Baltimore, Johns Hopkins University Press, 1987), p. 97.
5. Rebecca Bushnell, *Tragedies of Tyrants: Political thought and theater in the English Renaissance* (Ithaca, NY and London, Cornell University Press, 1990) is an important exception here.

Bibliography

Primary sources

Aubrey, John, *Aubrey's Brief Lives*, ed. Oliver Lawson Dick (Harmondsworth, Penguin, reissue, 1982).

Beaumont, Francis and Fletcher, John, *Comedies and Tragedies written by Francis Beaumont and John Fletcher, Gentlemen* (London, 1647).

Beaumont, Francis and Fletcher, John, *Fifty Comedies and Tragedies ... All in one volume* (London, 1679).

Beaumont, Francis and Fletcher, John, *The Dramatic Works in the Beaumont and Fletcher Canon*, General Editor, Fredson Bowers (Cambridge, Cambridge University Press, 1966– 8 vols to date).

Beaumont, Francis and Fletcher, John, *The Works of Beaumont and Fletcher, with Notes and a Biographical Memoir*, ed. A Dyce, 11 vols (London, Edward Moxon, 1843–46).

Beaumont, Francis and Fletcher, John, *The Works of Francis Beaumont and John Fletcher*, eds Arnold Glover and A. R. Waller, 10 vols (Cambridge, Cambridge University Press, 1905–1912).

Beaumont, Francis and Fletcher, John, *The Bloody Brother: A Tragedy by John Fletcher and Nathan Field (written 1616–17) and Refurbished by Philip Massinger (written 1630) as Rollo, Duke of Normandy*, ed. Bertha Hensman (New York, Vintage Press, 1991).

Beaumont, Francis and Fletcher, John, *The Maid's Tragedy*, ed. T. W. Craik, Revels Plays (Manchester, Manchester University Press, 1988).

Beaumont, Francis and Fletcher, John, *Philaster*, ed. A. Gurr, Revels Plays (Manchester, Manchester University Press, 1969).

Beaumont, Francis and Fletcher, John, *Rollo, Duke of Normandy, or, The Bloody Brother*, ed. John Jump, Regents Renaissance Plays (Liverpool, Liverpool University Press, 1969).

Brinkley, Roberta ed., *Coleridge on the Seventeenth Century* (Durham, NC, Duke University Press, 1955)

Cokain, Sir Aston, *Small Poems of Divers Sorts* (1658).

Dryden, John, *Of Dramatic Poesy and Other Critical Essays*, ed. George Watson, 2 vols (London, Dent, 1962).

Field, Nathan, *Amends for Ladies* (1611) in ed. Herbert P. Horne et al. *Nero and Other Plays* (London, T. Fisher Unwin).

Flecknoe, Richard, *A Short Discourse of the English Stage* (1664) in ed. J. Spingarn, *Critical Essays of the Seventeenth Century*, 3 vols (Oxford, Clarendon Press, 1908–1909).

Fletcher, Giles, *Of the Rus Commonwealth* (1591), ed. Albert J Schnisdt, Folger University Library (Ithaca, NY, Cornell, 1966).
Fletcher, J. and Massinger, Philip, *Sir John van Olden Barnavelt*, Malone Society Reprints (Oxford, Malone Society, 1979; 1980).
Guarini, Giambattista, *The Faithful Shepherdess* (1590) in ed. B. Penman, *Five Italian Renaissance Comedies* (Harmondsworth, Penguin, 1978).
Horne, Herbert P. ed., *Nero and Other Plays* (London, T. Fisher Unwin; New York, Charles Scribner's Sons).
Jonson, Ben, *Ben Jonson*, ed. C. H. Herford and Percy and Evelyn Simpson, 11 vols (Oxford, Clarendon Press, 1925–52).
Leech, Clifford ed., *The Two Noble Kinsmen, Titus Andronicus, and Pericles*, ed. S. Barnet (New York, New American Library, 1966).
Lyly, John, *The Complete Works*, ed. R. W. Bond, 3 vols (Oxford, Oxford University Press, 1902).
Marston, John, *The Plays of John Marston*, ed. H. Harvey Wood, 3 vols (Edinburgh, Oliver & Boyd, 1934–9).
McIlwain, Charles Howard ed., *The Political Works of James I* (Cambridge, MA, Harvard University Press, 1918).
Middleton, Thomas, *The Works of Thomas Middleton*, ed. A. H. Bullen, 8 vols (London, John C. Nimmo, 1885–6).
Milton, John, *The Complete Poems of John Milton*, eds. J. Carey and A. Fowler (London, Longmans, 1968).
Park, Roy ed., *Lamb as Critic* (London, Routledge, 1980).
Rainoldes, John, *Th'Overthrow of Stage-Playes* (Middleburgh, 1599).
Rymer, Thomas, *The Critical Works of Thomas Rymer*, ed. Curt A. Zimansky (New Haven, CT, Yale University Press, 1956).
The Second Maiden's Tragedy, ed. Anne Lancashire, Revels Plays (Manchester, Manchester University Press, 1978).
Sidney, Sir Philip, *An Apologie for Poetry* (1595), ed. G. Shepherd (Manchester, Manchester University Press, 1965).
Sidney, Sir Philip, *Arcadia*, ed. Maurice Evans (Harmondsworth, Penguin, 1977).

Secondary sources

Abrams, Richard, 'Gender Confusion and Sexual Politics in *The Two Noble Kinsmen*' in *Drama, Sex, and Politics: Themes in drama 7* (1985), pp. 69–76.
Adams, J. Q. ed., *Dramatic Records of Sir Henry Herbert* (New Haven, CT, Yale University Press, 1917).
Adelman, Janet, '"Born of woman": fantasies of maternal power in *Macbeth*' in *Cannibals, Witches and Divorce*, ed. Marjorie Garber *Selected Papers from the English Institute*, 1985, 11 (Baltimore, MA, Johns Hopkins University Press, 1987).
Adkins, M. G. M., 'The citizens in *Philaster* their function and significance', *Studies in Philology* 43 (1946), pp. 203–12.
Agnew, J. C., *Worlds Apart: The market and the theatre in Anglo-American thought, 1550–1750* (Cambridge, Cambridge University Press, 1986).
Albright, E. M., *Dramatic Publication in England, 1580–1640* (New York, Modern Language Association of America, 1927; reprinted 1971).
Amussen, Susan, *An Ordered Society: Gender and class in early modern England* (Oxford, Blackwell, 1988).

Appleton, W. W., *Beaumont and Fletcher: A critical study* (London, Allen & Unwin, 1956).
Aquinas, St Thomas, *Summa Theologiae: A Concise Translation*, ed. Timothy McDermott (London, Methuen, 1989).
Armstrong, W. W., 'The Elizabethan conception of the tyrant', *Review of English Studies* 22 (1946), pp. 161–81.
Armstrong, W. W., 'The influence of Seneca and Machiavelli on the Elizabethan tyrant', *Review of English Studies* 24 (1948), pp. 19–35.
Astington, J. H., 'The popularity of *Cupid's Revenge*', *SEL* 19 (1979), pp. 215–27.
Baines, Barbara and Williams, Mary C., 'The contemporary and classical anti-feminist tradition in Jonson's *Epicoene*', *Renaissance Papers* (1977), pp. 43–58.
Bakhtin, Mikhail, *Rabelais and his World*, trans. Helene Iswolsky (Bloomington, IN, Indiana University Press, 1984).
Barker, F., *The Tremulous Private Body: Essays on subjection* (London, Methuen, 1984).
Belsey, Catherine, *The Subject of Tragedy: Identity and difference in Renaissance drama* (London and New York, Methuen, 1985).
Bentley, G. E., *The Jacobean and Caroline Stage*, 7 vols (Oxford, Oxford University Press, 1940–1968).
Bentley, G. E., *The Profession of Dramatist in Shakespeare's Time, 1590–1642* (Princeton, NJ, Princeton University Press, 1971).
Bentley, G. E., *The Profession of Player in Shakespeare's Time, 1590–1642* (Princeton, NJ, Princeton University Press, 1984).
Berry, Philippa, *Of Chastity and Power: Elizabethan literature and the unmarried queen* (London and New York, Routledge, 1989).
Binns, J., 'Women or transvestites on the Elizabethan stage? An Oxford controversy', *Sixteenth Century Journal* 5 (1974), pp. 95–120.
Blau, Herbert, 'The absolved riddle: sovereign pleasure and the baroque subject in the tragicomedies of John Fletcher', *New Literary History* 17.3 (1986), pp. 539–54.
Bliss, Lee, 'Defending Fletcher's shepherds', *SEL* 23 (1983), pp. 295–310.
Bliss, Lee, *Francis Beaumont* (Boston, G. K. Hall, 1987).
Bliss, Lee, 'Tragicomic romance for the King's Men, 1609–1611: Shakespeare, Beaumont and Fletcher' in *Comedy from Shakespeare to Sheridan*, ed. A. R. Braunmuller and J. C. Bulman (Newark, DE, University of Delaware Press, 1986).
Bloch, R. Howard, 'Medieval Misogyny', *Representations* 20 (1987), pp. 1–24.
Bowers, Fredson, *Elizabethan Revenge Tragedy: 1587–1642* (Princeton, NJ, Princeton University Press, 1940).
Bradbrook, M., *The Growth and Structure of Elizabethan Comedy* (Harmondsworth, Penguin, 1955; 1963).
Bray, Alan, *Homosexuality in Renaissance England* (Viborg, Denmark, Gay Men's Press, 1982).
Brink, Jean R., Horowitz, Maryanne and Coudert, Allison P. eds, *Playing with Gender: A Renaissance Pursuit* (Urbana and Chicago, IL, University of Illinois Press, 1991).
Bristol, M. D., *Carnival and Theater: Plebeian culture and the structure of authority in Renaissance England* (New York and London, Methuen, 1985).
Brodwin, Leonora Leet, *Elizabethan Love Tragedy, 1587–1625* (London, University of London Press, 1972).
Bromham, A. H. and Bruzzi, Zara, *The Changeling and the Years of Crisis, 1619–1624* (London, Pinter Press, 1990).

Bibliography

Brooke, Tucker, 'The royal Fletcher and the loyal Heywood' in *Elizabethan Studies and Other Essays in Honour of George F. Reynolds*, (Boulder, CO, University of Colorado, 1945).
Burt, Richard A., '"'Tis writ by me": Massinger's *The Roman Actor* and the politics of reception in the English Renaissance theatre', *Theatre Journal* 40 (1988), pp. 332–46.
Bushnell, Rebecca W., *Tragedies of Tyrants: Political thought and theater in the English Renaissance* (Ithaca, NY and London, Cornell University Press, 1990).
Butler, M., *Theatre and Crisis, 1632–1642* (Cambridge, Cambridge University Press, 1984).
Callaghan, Dymphna, *Women and Gender in Renaissance Tragedy* (Hemel Hempstead, Harvester Wheatsheaf, 1989).
Carson, Neil, 'Collaborative playwriting: the Chettle, Dekker, Heywood syndicate', *Theatre Research International* 14 (1989), pp. 13–23.
Clare, Janet, *"Art made tongue-tied by authority": Elizabethan and Jacobean dramatic censorship* (Manchester, Manchester University Press, 1990).
Clark, Sandra, '*Hic Mulier, Haec Vir* and the controversy over masculine women', *Studies in Philology* 82 (1985), pp. 157–83.
Clubb, Louise George, *Italian Drama in Shakespeare's Time* (New Haven, CT and London, Yale University Press, 1989).
Cohen, Walter, *Drama of a Nation: Public theater in Renaissance England and Spain*. (Ithaca, NY and London, Cornell University Press, 1985).
Cone, M., 'Fletcher without Beaumont: a study of the independent plays of John Fletcher' *Salzburg Studies in English Literature, Jacobean Drama Studies* (Salzburg, Institüt für Englische Sprache und Literatur, Universität Salzburg, 1976).
Danby, J. F., *Poets on Fortune's Hill: Studies in Sidney, Shakespeare, Beaumont and Fletcher* (London, Faber & Faber, 1952).
Davies, H. Neville, 'Beaumont and Fletcher's *Hamlet*' in *Shakespeare, Man of the Theatre* eds. K. Muir, J. L. Halio and D. J. Palmer (Newark, NJ, University of Delaware Press, 1983).
Davis, Natalie Zemon, *Society and Culture in Early Modern France* (London, Duckworth, 1975).
Davison, P., 'The serious concerns of *Philaster*', *English Literary History* 30 (1963), pp. 1–15.
Dekker, R. M. and van de Pol, L. C., *The Tradition of Female Transvestism in Early Modern Europe* (Basingstoke and London, Macmillan, 1989).
Dollimore, J., 'Subjectivity, sexuality and transgression', *Renaissance Drama* 17 (1986), pp. 53–87.
Donaldson, Ian, *The Rapes of Lucretia: A myth and its transformations* (Oxford, Clarendon Press, 1982).
Donohue, Joseph W. Jr., *Dramatic Character in the English Romantic Age* (Princeton, Princeton University Press, 1970).
Dunn, T. A., *Philip Massinger: The Man and the playwright*, University College of Ghana (London, Nelson, 1957).
Dusinberre, Juliet, *Shakespeare and the Nature of Womankind* (London, Macmillan, 1975).
Dutton, Richard, *Ben Jonson: To the First Folio* (Cambridge, Cambridge University Press, 1983).
Edwards, P., 'The danger not the death: the art of John Fletcher' in *Jacobean Theatre*, Stratford-upon-Avon Studies 1 (London, Arnold, 1960).

Edwards, P., *The Revels History of Drama in English*, IV: *1613–60*, General Eds C. Leech and T. W. Craik (London, Methuen, 1981).
Ellis-Fermor, U., *The Jacobean Drama* (London, Methuen, 1936; revised edn 1958).
Eliot, T. S., *Selected Essays, 1917–1932* (London, Faber & Faber, 1932).
Erickson, Martin E., 'A review of scholarship dealing with the problem of a Spanish source for *Love's Cure*' in ed. Waldo F. McNeil *Studies in Comparative Literature* (Baton Rouge, Louisiana State University, 1962), pp. 102–19.
Ewbank, Inga-Stina, '"Those pretty devices": a study of masques in plays' in *A Book of Masques in Honour of Allardyce Nicoll*, eds T. J. B. Spencer and S. W. Wells (Cambridge, Cambridge University Press, 1967).
Farley-Hills, David, *Jacobean Drama: A critical survey of the professional drama, 1600–25* (Basingstoke, Macmillan, 1988).
Figgis, J. N., *The Divine Right of Kings* (London, Cambridge, 1896, 2nd edn 1922).
Finkelpearl, P. J., 'Beaumont, Fletcher and "Beaumont and Fletcher": some distinctions', *English Literary Renaissance* 1 (1971), pp. 144–64.
Finkelpearl, P. J., '"The comedians' liberty": censorship of the Jacobean stage reconsidered', *English Literary Renaissance* 16 (1986), pp. 123–38.
Finkelpearl, P. J., *Court and Country Politics in the Plays of Beaumont and Fletcher* (Princeton, NJ, Princeton University Press, 1990).
Finkelpearl, P. J., 'John Fletcher as a Spenserian playwright: *The Faithful Shepherdess* and *The Island Princess*', *SEL* 27 (1987), pp. 285–302.
Finkelpearl, P. J., 'The role of the court in the development of Jacobean drama', *Criticism* 24 (1982), pp. 138–58.
Fleay, F. G., *A Biographical Chronicle of the English Drama, 1559–1642*, 2 vols (London, Reeves & Turner, 1891).
Fletcher, I., *Beaumont and Fletcher* (London, Longmans, 1967).
Forker, C. R., '*Wit Without Money*: a Fletcherian antecedent to *Keep the Widow Waking*', *Comparative Drama* 8 (1974), pp. 172–83.
Forsythe, R. S., *The Relation of Shirley's Plays to the Elizabethan Drama* (New York, Blom, 1914).
Foucault, M., *The Use of Pleasure: The history of sexuality*, vol. 2 (Harmondsworth, Penguin, 1987).
Freer, C., *The Poetics of Jacobean Drama* (Baltimore, MA, Johns Hopkins University Press, 1981).
Freeman, V. O., *Disguise Plots in English Drama: A study in stage tradition* (New York, Blom, 1965).
Frost, D. L., *The School of Shakespeare: The influence of Shakespeare on English drama, 1600–1642* (Cambridge, Cambridge University Press, 1968).
Garber, M. ed., *Cannibals, Witches and Divorce: Selected papers from the English Institute* (Baltimore, MA, Johns Hopkins University Press, 1985).
Garnett, Martin ed., *Massinger: The critical heritage* (London and New York, Routledge, 1991).
Gayley, C. M., *Francis Beaumont, Dramatist: A portrait*. (London, Duckworth, 1914).
Gildersleeve, V. C., *Government Regulation of the Elizabethan Drama* (New York, Columbia University Press, 1908; reprinted 1961).
Goldberg, J., *James I and the Politics of Literature* (Baltimore, MA and London, Johns Hopkins University Press, 1983).
Goldberg, J., 'The politics of Renaissance literature: a review essay', *English Literary History* 49 (1982), pp. 514–42.

Gossett, S., '"Best men are molded out of faults": marrying the rapist in Jacobean drama', *English Literary Review* 14 (1984), pp. 305–27.
Gossett, S., 'Masque influence on the dramaturgy of Beaumont and Fletcher', *Modern Philology* 69 (1971–72), pp. 199–208.
Gossett, S., 'The term "masque" in Shakespeare and Fletcher and *The Coxcomb*', *SEL* 14 (1974), pp. 285–95.
Green, Paul D., 'Theme and structure in Fletcher's *Bonduca*', *SEL* 22 (1982), pp. 305–16.
Greenblatt, Stephen J., *Shakespearean Negotiations: The circulation of social energy in Renaissance England* (Oxford, Clarendon Press, 1988).
Greenblatt, Stephen J., *Sir Walter Raleigh: The Renaissance man and his roles* (New Haven, CT and London, Yale University Press, 1973).
Greenwood, John., *Shifting Perspectives and the Stylish Style: Mannerism in Shakespeare and his Jacobean contemporaries* (Toronto, University of Toronto Press, 1988).
Greg, W. W., *Pastoral Poetry and Pastoral Drama* (1906; reprinted New York, Russell & Russell, 1959).
Harbage, A., *Annals of English Drama 975–1700*, revised by S. Schoenbaum; 3rd edn revised by S. S. Wagonheim (London and New York, Routledge, 1989).
Harbage, A., *Cavalier Drama* (New York, Russell & Russell, 1936; 1964).
Harbage, A., *Shakespeare and the Rival Traditions* (New York, Columbia University Press, 1952).
Haselkorn, Anne M., *Prostitution in Elizabethan and Jacobean Comedy* (Troy, New York, Whitston Publishing Co., 1983).
Heinemann, M., *Puritanism and Theatre: Thomas Middleton and opposition drama under the Early Stuarts* (Cambridge, Cambridge University Press, 1980).
Hensman, Bertha, *The shares of Fletcher, Field and Massinger in twelve plays of the Beaumont and Fletcher canon*, 2 vols (Salzburg, Institüt für Englische Sprache und Literatur, Universität Salzburg, 1974).
Herndl, George, *The High Design: English Renaissance tragedy and the natural law* (Lexington, KY, University Press of Kentucky, 1970).
Hickman, A., '*Bonduca*'s two ignoble armies and *The Two Noble Kinsmen*', *Medieval and Renaissance Drama in England* 4 (1989), pp. 143–71.
Hotson, Leslie, *The Commonwealth and Restoration Stage* (New York, Russell & Russell, 1926; reprinted 1962).
Howard, Jean E., 'Crossdressing, the theatre, and gender struggle in early modern England', *SQ* 39 (1988), pp. 418–40.
Howard, Jean E. and O'Connor, Marion F. eds, *Shakespeare Reproduced: The text in history and ideology* (New York and London, Methuen, 1987).
Howard-Hill, T. H., 'Buc and the censorship of *Sir John Van Olden Barnavelt* in 1619', *Review of English Studies* n.s xxxix (1988), pp. 39–63.
Hoy, Cyrus, 'Critical and aesthetic problems of collaboration in Renaissance drama', *RORD* 19 (1976), pp. 3–6.
Hoy, Cyrus, 'Fletcherian romantic comedy', *RORD* 27 (1984), pp. 3–11.
Hoy, Cyrus, *The Hyacinth Room: An investigation into the nature of comedy, tragedy and tragi-comedy* (London, Chatto & Windus, 1964).
Hoy, Cyrus, 'Massinger as collaborator: the plays with Fletcher and others' in *Philip Massinger: A critical assessment*, ed. D. Howard (Cambridge, Cambridge University Press, 1985).
Hoy, Cyrus, 'The shares of Fletcher and his collaborators in the Beaumont and Fletcher canon', *Studies in Bibliography* 8–15 (1956–62).

Huebert, Ronald, '"An artificial way to grieve": the forsaken woman in Beaumont and Fletcher, Massinger, and Ford', *English Literary History* 44 (1977), pp. 601–21.

Hume, R. D., '*The Maid's Tragedy* and censorship in the Restoration theatre', *Philological Quarterly* 61, (1982), pp. 484–90.

Hunter, G. K., *Dramatic Identities and Cultural Tradition* (Liverpool, Liverpool University Press, 1978).

Jardine, Lisa, *Still Harping on Daughters: Women and drama in the age of Shakespeare* (Brighton, Harvester, 1983).

Jones, M., 'The Court and the Dramatists' in *Elizabethan Theatre*, Stratford-upon-Avon Studies 9 (London, Arnold, 1966).

Kahn, Coppélia, 'Whores and wives in Jacobean drama' in *In Another Country: Feminist perspectives on Renaissance drama*, eds Dorothea Kehler and Susan Baker (Metuchen, NJ and London, Scarecrow Press, 1991).

Kinney, A. F., *Markets of Bawdrie: The dramatic criticism of Stephen Gosson* (Salzburg, Institüt für Englische Sprache und Literatur, Universität Salzburg, 1974).

Kirsch, A. C., *Jacobean Dramatic Perspectives* (Charlottesville, VA, University Press of Virginia, 1972).

Knights, L. C., *Public Voices: Literature and politics with special reference to the seventeenth century* (London, Chatto & Windus, 1971).

Kuhl, E. P., 'Shakespeare's *Rape of Lucrece*', *Philological Quarterly* 20 (1941), pp. 352–60.

Lacey, Robert, *Sir Walter Ralegh* (London, Weidenfeld & Nicolson, 1973).

Laird, David, '"A curious way of torturing": language and ideological transformation in *A King and No King*', *Themes in Drama* 12 (1990), pp. 107–25.

Lancashire, Anne, 'The emblematic castle in Shakespeare and Middleton' in *Mirror up to Nature: Essays in honour of G. R. Hibberd* (Toronto, University of Toronto Press, 1984), pp. 223–41.

Leech, C., *The John Fletcher Plays* (London, Chatto & Windus, 1962).

Leggatt, A., *Citizen Comedy in the Age of Shakespeare* (Toronto, University of Toronto Press, 1973).

Leinwand, Theodore B., *The City Staged: Jacobean comedy, 1603–13* (Madison, WI, University of Wisconsin Press, 1986).

Lever, J. W., *The Tragedy of State* (London, Routledge, 1971).

Levin, Richard, 'Women in the Renaissance theatre audience', *SQ* 40 (1989), pp. 164–74.

Loftis, John, *Renaissance Drama in England and Spain: Topical allusion and history plays* (Princeton, NJ, Princeton University Press, 1987).

McKeithan, D. M., *The Debt to Shakespeare in the Beaumont-and-Fletcher Plays* (Folcroft, PA, Folcroft Press, 1969).

McKendrick, Melveena, *Woman and Society in the Spanish Drama of the Golden Age: A study of the Mujer Varonil* (Cambridge, Cambridge University Press, 1974).

Maclean, Ian, *The Renaissance Notion of Women: A study in the fortunes of scholasticism and medical science in European intellectual life*, Cambridge Monographs on the History of Medicine (Cambridge, Cambridge University Press, 1980).

McLuskie, Kathleen, 'The act, the role, and the actor: boy actresses on the Elizabethan stage', *New Theatre Quarterly* 3.10 (1987), pp. 120–30.

McLuskie, Kathleen, *Renaissance Dramatists* (Hemel Hempstead, Harvester Wheatsheaf, 1989).

McMullan, Gordon and Hope, Jonathan eds, *The Politics of Tragicomedy* (London, Routledge, 1992).

Maguire, N. K. ed., *Renaissance Tragicomedy: Explorations in genre and politics*. (New York, AMS Press, 1987).
Marcus, Leah, 'Shakespeare's comic heroines, Elizabeth I, and the political uses of androgyny' in *Women in the Middle Ages and the Renaissance: Literary and historical perspectives*, ed. Mary Beth Rose (Syracuse, NY, Syracuse University Press, 1986).
Maslen, Jeffrey A., 'Beaumont and/or Beaumont and Fletcher: collaboration and the interpretation of Renaissance drama', *English Literary History* 59 (1992), 337–56.
Maxwell, Baldwin, *Studies in Beaumont, Fletcher and Massinger* (Chapel Hill, NC, North Carolina Press, 1930).
Mincoff, M., '*The Faithful Shepherdess*: a Fletcherian experiment', *Renaissance Drama* 9 (1966), pp. 163–77.
Mincoff, M., 'Fletcher's early tragedies', *Renaissance Drama* 7 (1964), pp. 70–94.
Mincoff, M., 'Shakespeare, Fletcher and baroque tragedy', *SS* 20 (1961), pp. 1–14.
Mincoff, M., 'The social background of Beaumont and Fletcher', *English Miscellany* I (1950), pp. 1–30.
Mizener, A., 'The high design of *A King and No King*', *Modern Philology* 38 (1940–41), pp. 133–54.
Montrose, L. A., '"The place of a brother" in *As You Like It*: social process and comic form' *SQ* 32 (Spring 1981), pp. 28–54.
Neill, M., 'The defence of contraries: skeptical paradox in *A King and No King*', *SEL* 21 (1981), pp. 319–32.
Neill, M., '"The simetry which gives a poem grace": masque imagery and the fancy of *The Maid's Tragedy*', *Renaissance Drama* n.s. 3 (1970), pp. 111–35.
Norbrook, David, *Poetry and Politics in the English Renaissance* (London, Routledge, 1984).
Oliphant, E. H. C., *The Plays of Beaumont and Fletcher: An attempt to determine their respective shares and the shares of others* (New Haven, CT, Yale University Press, 1927).
Orgel, Stephen, *The Illusion of Power: Political theater in the English Renaissance* (Berkeley, CA, University of California Press, 1975).
Ornstein, R., *The Moral Vision of Jacobean Tragedy* (Madison, WI, University of Wisconsin Press, 1960).
Parker, Patricia, *Literary Fat Ladies: Rhetoric, gender, property* (London, Methuen, 1987).
Parry, G., *The Golden Age Restor'd: The culture of the Stuart court, 1603–42* (Manchester, Manchester University Press, 1981).
Paster, Gail Kern, 'Leaky vessels: the incontinent women of city comedy', in *Renaissance Drama as Cultural History: Essays from 'Renaissance Drama', 1977–1987*, ed. Mary Beth Rose (Evanston, IL, Northwestern University Press, 1990), 211–34.
Patterson, A., *Censorship and Interpretation: The conditions of writing and reading in early modern England* (Madison, WI, Wisconsin University Press, 1984).
Pearse, N. C., *John Fletcher's Chastity Plays: Mirrors of modesty* (Lewisburg, PA, Bucknell University Press, 1973).
Pol, Lotte van de and Dekker, Rudolf M., *The Tradition of Female Transvestism in Early Modern Europe* (London and Basingstoke, Macmillan, 1989).
Potter, Lois, *Secret Rites and Secret Writing: Royalist literature, 1641–1660* (Cambridge, Cambridge University Press, 1989).
Potter, Lois, 'Topicality or Politics: *The Two Noble Kinsmen*' in *The Politics of*

Tragicomedy, eds Gordon McMullan and Jonathan Hope (London, Routledge, 1992).

Rabkin, Norman, 'Problems in the study of collaboration', *RORD* 19 (1976), pp. 7–13.

Rackin, Phyllis, 'Androgyny, mimesis, and the marriage of the boy heroine on the English Renaissance stage', *PMLA* 111 (1987), pp. 29–41.

Rackin, Phyllis, *Stages of History: Shakespeare's English chronicles* (London, Routledge, 1991).

Radel, N. F., '"Then thus I turne my language to you": the transformation of theatrical language in *Philaster*', *Medieval and Renaissance Drama in England* 3 (1986), pp. 129–47.

Randall, D. B. J., *The Golden Tapestry: A critical survey of non-chivalric Spanish fiction in English translation, 1543–1657* (Durham, NC, Duke University Press, 1963).

Reed, J. C., 'Humphrey Moseley, Publisher', *Proceedings and Papers of the Oxford Bibliographical Society* 2 (1927–30), pp. 57–142.

Rigaud, N. J., *Femme Mythifiée, femme de raison: La veuve dans la comedie anglaise au temps de Shakespeare 1600–1625* (Aix-en-Provence, Publications-Diffusion, Université de Provence, 1986).

Rose, Mary Beth, *The Expense of Spirit: Love and sexuality in English Renaissance drama* (Ithaca, NY, Cornell University Press, 1986).

Rose, Mary Beth ed., *Women in the Middle Ages and the Renaissance: Literary and historical perspectives* (Syracuse, NY, Syracuse University Press, 1986).

Rogers, K. M., *The Troublesome Helpmate: A history of misogyny in literature* (Seattle, WA, University of Washington Press, 1968).

Rosenbach, A. S. W., 'The curious-impertinent in English dramatic literature before Shelton's translation of *Don Quixote*', *Modern Language Notes* 17 (1902), pp. 357–67.

Sage, J. W., 'The context of comedy: Lope de Vega's *El Perr del Hortelano* and related plays' in *Studies in Spanish Literature of the Golden Age Presented to Edward M. Wilson*, ed. R. O. Jones (London, Tamesis, 1973).

Savage, J. E., 'The date of Beaumont and Fletcher's *Cupid's Revenge*', *English Literary History* 15 (1948), pp. 286–94.

Savage, J. E., 'Beaumont and Fletcher's *Philaster* and Sidney's *Arcadia*', *English Literary History* 14 (1947), pp. 194–206.

Savage, J. E., 'The "gaping wounds" in the text of *Philaster*', *Philological Quarterly* 28 (1949), pp. 443–57.

Schleiner, Winfred, '"Divina virago": Queen Elizabeth as an Amazon', *Studies in Philology* 75 (1978), pp. 163–80.

Schleiner, Winfred, 'Male cross-dressing and transvestism in Renaissance romances', *Sixteenth Century Journal* 14 (1988), pp. 60–193.

Schoenbaum, S., *Internal Evidence and Elizabethan Dramatic Authorship: An essay in literary history and method* (London, Arnold, 1966).

Shearman, John, *Mannerism* (Harmondsworth, Penguin, 1967).

Shepherd, S., *Amazons and Warrior Women: Varieties of feminism in seventeenth century drama* (Brighton, Harvester, 1981).

Shullenberger, W., '"This for the most wronged of women": a reappraisal of *The Maid's Tragedy*', *Renaissance Drama* n.s. 13 (1982), pp. 131–56.

Smith, Molly, *The Darker World Within: Evil in the tragedies of Shakespeare and his successors* (London and Toronto, Associated University Presses, 1991).

Smuts, R. M., *Court Culture and the Origins of a Royalist Tradition in Early Stuart England* (Philadelphia, PA, University of Pennsylvania Press, 1987).

Sorelius, Gunnar, *'The Giant Race Before the Flood': Pre-Restoration drama on the stage and in the criticism of the Restoration* (Uppsala, Acta Universitatis Upsaliensis, 1966).
Sprague, A. C., *Beaumont and Fletcher on the Restoration stage* (Cambridge, MA, Harvard University Press, 1926).
Squier, Charles L., *John Fletcher* (Boston, G. K. Hall, 1986).
Stallybrass, Peter, 'Patriarchal territories: the body enclosed' in *Rewriting the Renaissance: Discourses of sexual difference in early modern Europe*, eds Margaret W. Ferguson, Maureen Quilligan and Nancy J. Vickers (London and Chicago, IL, University of Chicago Press, 1986), 123–42.
Stallybrass, Peter, 'Reading the body: *The Revenger's Tragedy*', *Renaissance Drama* 18 (1987), 121–48.
Stone, Lawrence, *Family, Sex and Marriage in England, 1500–1800* (New York, Harper & Row, 1977).
Stone, Lawrence, 'Social Mobility in England, 1500–1700', *Past and Present* 33 (1966), 16–55.
Taunton, Nina, 'Did John Fletcher the playwright go to University?', *Notes and Queries* 235 (n.s. 37) (1990), pp. 170–2.
Teissedou, Jean-Pierre, 'L'absolutisme en question dans *A King and No King*' in *Coriolan: Théâtre et Politique*, eds Jean-Paul Debax and Yves Peyre (Toulouse, Université de Toulouse – Le Mirail, 1984).
Tennenhouse, L., *Power on Display: The politics of Shakespeare's genres* (London, Methuen, 1986).
Thomas, P. W., *Sir John Berkenhead, 1617–1679: A royalist career in politics and polemics* (Oxford, Clarendon Press, 1969).
Thompson, Ann, 'Shakespeare and feminist criticism', in *The Shakespeare Myth*, ed. Graham Holderness (Manchester, Manchester University Press, 1988).
Thompson, Ann, *Shakespeare's Chaucer: A study in literary origins* (Liverpool, Liverpool University Press, 1978).
Thompson, S., *Motif Index of Folk Literature: A classification of narrative elements in folktales, ballads, myths etc.*, 6 vols, revised edn (Bloomington, IN, Indiana University Studies, 1955–58).
Thorndike, A. H., *The Influence of Beaumont and Fletcher on Shakespere* (Worcester, MA, Oliver B. Wood, 1901).
Tomlinson, T. B., *A Study of Elizabethan and Jacobean Tragedy* (Cambridge, Cambridge University Press, 1964).
Traub, Valerie, 'Desire and the differences it makes' in *The Matter of Difference: Materialist feminist criticism of Shakespeare*, ed. Valerie Wayne (Hemel Hempstead, Harvester Wheatsheaf, 1991).
Tricomi, A. H., 'Philip, Earl of Pembroke, and the analogical way of reading political tragedy', *JEGP* 85 (1986), pp. 332–45.
Turner, Robert K., 'Collaborators at work: *The Queen of Corinth* and *The Knight of Malta*' in *Shakespeare: Text, language, criticism*, eds B. Fabian and K. Tetzeli von Rosador (Hildesheim, Zurich, New York, Olms-Weidemann, 1987).
Turner, Robert K., 'The morality of *A King and No King*', *Renaissance Papers* 1958–1960 (1961), pp. 93–103.
Turner, Robert Y., 'Reponses to tyranny in John Fletcher's plays', *Medieval and Renaissance Drama in England* IV (1989), pp. 123–41.
Underdown, David, 'The taming of the scold: the enforcement of patriarchal authority in early modern England' in *Order and Disorder in Early Modern*

England, eds A. Fletcher and J. Stevenson (Cambridge, Cambridge University Press, 1985).
Upton, A. W., 'Allusions to James I and his court in Marston's *The Fawn* and Beaumont and Fletcher's *The Woman Hater*', *PMLA* 44 (1929), pp. 1048–65.
Venuti, Lawrence, 'The marginalisation of Philip Massinger's plays' in *Our Halcyon Dayes: English prerevolutionary texts and postmodern culture* (Madison, WI, University of Wisconsin Press, 1989).
Waith, E. M., 'Characterisation in John Fletcher's Tragicomedies', *Review of English Studies* 19 (1943), pp. 141–64.
Waith, E. M., *The Pattern of Tragicomedy in Beaumont and Fletcher* (New Haven, CT and London, Yale University Press, 1952).
Wallis, L. B., *Fletcher, Beaumont and Company: Entertainers to the Jacobean gentry* (New York, Octagon 1947; reprint 1968).
Wayne, Valerie, 'Historical differences: misogyny and *Othello*' in *The Matter of Difference: Materialist feminist criticism of Shakespeare*, ed. Valerie Wayne (Hemel Hempstead, Harvester Wheatsheaf, 1991).
Weisner, Merry E., 'Spinsters and seamstresses: women in cloth and clothing production' in *Rewriting the Renaissance: The discourses of sexual difference in early modern Europe*, eds Margaret W. Ferguson, Maureen Quilligan and Nancy J. Vickers (Chicago, IL, and London, University of Chicago Press, 1986).
Williams, Gwyn, *Person and Persona* (Cardiff, University of Wales Press, 1981).
Willson, D. H., *King James VI and I* (London, Jonathan Cape, 1956).
Wilson, Edward M., '*Rule a Wife and Have a Wife* and *El Sagaz Estacio*', *Review of English Studies* 24 (1948), pp. 189–94.
Wilson, John Harold, *All the King's Ladies: Actresses of the Restoration* (Chicago, IL, University of Chicago Press, 1958).
Wiseman, Susan J., '"'Tis Pity She's a Whore": representing the incestuous body' in *Renaissance Bodies*, eds Lucy Gent and Nigel Llewellyn (London, Reaktion Books, 1990), 180–7.
Wood, Harvey H., ed., *The Plays of John Marston*, 3 vols (Edinburgh, Oliver & Boyd, 1934–39).
Woodbridge, Linda, *Women and the English Renaissance: Literature and the nature of womenkind, 1540–1620* (Urbana, IL, University of Illinois Press, 1985).
Woodson, William C., 'The casuistry of innocence in *A King and No King* and its implications for tragicomedy', *English Literary Renaissance* 8 (1978), pp. 312–28.
Wright, Celeste Turner, 'The Amazons in Elizabethan literature', *Studies in Philology* 37 (1940), pp. 433–56.
Wright, L. B., 'The reading of plays during the Puritan Revolution', *Huntington Library Bulletin* 6 (1934), pp. 73–108.
Yoch, James J., 'The Renaissance dramatization of temperance: the Italian revival of tragicomedy and *The Faithful Shepherdess*' in *Renaissance Tragicomedy: Explorations in genre and politics*, ed. Nancy Klein Maguire (New York, AMS Press, 1987).
Young, K., 'An Elizabethan Defence of the Stage' in *Shakespeare Studies by Members of the Department of English of the University of Wisconsin* (Madison, WI, University of Wisconsin Press, 1916).
Zimmerman, Susan ed., *Erotic Politics: Desire on the Renaissance stage* (London, Routledge, 1992).

Index

Amadis de Gaul, 55
Amazons, 72–3, 76, 173n42
Apius and Virginia ('R.B.'), 24
Appleton, W. W., 18, 22
Arden of Faversham, 183n1
Aubrey, John,
    Brief Lives, 14

Bakhtin, Mikhail, 2
Beaumont, Francis, and Fletcher, John,
    attitudes to women, 6, 22–3, 34, 42,
        51–2, 71–7, 87–8, 90–1, 95, 97,
        99–100, 105, 138–9, 146–7, 152,
        156–7, 161n23, 174n5
    attribution issues, 11, 13–14
    canonical plays:
    Beggars' Bush, 13, 16, 183n3
    Bonduca, 15, 79, 85–8, 92
    The Captain, 78, 82–5, 88, 156, 157,
        175n10
    Cupid's Revenge, 11, 15, 27, 33, 34, 36,
        37, 55, 56, 79, 88–90, 103
    The Custom of the Country, 37, 103, 123
    The Double Marriage, 71, 74–7, 103, 104,
        125–7, 156
    The Faithful Shepherdess, 15, 16, 18,
        27–33, 34, 35, 37, 43, 47, 49, 50,
        155, 168n31
    The False One, 13
    Henry VIII (Fletcher with Shakespeare),
        2, 9, 160n2
    The Honest Man's Fortune, 63–6, 155, 156
    The Humorous Lieutenant, 43, 44–6,
        49–50, 51, 67
    The Jeweller of Amsterdam (Fletcher with
        Massinger and Field), 18, 181n6
    A King and No King, 2, 4, 16, 19, 103,
        116–20, 121, 122, 158, 165n9,
        179n39
    The Knight of the Burning Pestle, 2,
        11, 18, 27, 33, 66, 79, 95, 130,
        168n38

Love's Cure, 15, 27, 55, 66, 68–71, 72,
    79, 171n11, 173n38, 183n1
Love's Pilgrimage, 16
The Loyal Subject, 4, 16, 18, 43–4, 66–8,
    101, 103, 120–3
The Maid in the Mill (Fletcher with
    Rowley), 16, 48–51
The Maid's Tragedy, 2, 4, 5, 7, 11, 18, 19,
    20, 33, 34, 36–7, 55, 56, 88, 101,
    103, 104–7, 109–14, 115, 116,
    117, 118, 120, 122, 127, 158,
    169n44
Monsieur Thomas, 43, 46–8, 51, 155
The Nightwalker, 172n20, 174n1
The Noble Gentleman, 18
Philaster, 2, 3, 13, 16, 18, 19, 27, 33,
    34–6, 55, 56, 59–63, 65, 66, 89,
    155, 156
*Rollo, Duke of Normandy, or The Bloody
    Brother*, 4, 6, 16, 19–20, 101, 103,
    179n35, n36
Rule a Wife and Have a Wife, 16, 128,
    148–52, 156, 157, 183n29, n33,
    n35
The Sea Voyage, 55, 71, 72–4, 156, 183n1
The Scornful Lady, 16, 79, 95–6, 97, 128,
    135–9, 144, 157, 176n27, n29,
    183n35
Sir John Van Olden Barnavelt, 2, 11, 17,
    160n2
The Spanish Curate, 16, 183n35
Thierry and Theodoret, 38–9, 79, 90–5,
    155, 176n24
The Two Noble Kinsmen (Fletcher with
    Shakespeare), 2, 128, 129, 132–5,
    136, 158, 181n11, 182n14
Valentinian, 4–5, 37, 101, 103,
    104–8, 111, 112, 114, 115, 122,
    124
A Very Woman, 2, 160n2
A Wife for a Month, 5, 16, 38, 39–43, 67,
    103, 104, 123, 124, 180n55

195

196   Index

Beaumont, Francis, and Fletcher, John, (*continued*)
  The Wild-Goose Chase, 16, 128, 144–8, 152, 157–8
  Wit at Severall Weapons (Middleton and Rowley, possibly with Fletcher), 142–4
  Wit Without Money, 20, 128, 135, 136, 139–42, 144, 157
  The Woman Hater, 18, 23, 27, 43, 78, 79, 147, 157, 166n99, 169n52, 174n7
  The Woman's prize, 22, 26, 79, 97–100, 128, 129, 151–2, 176n30
  censorship, 18–19, 97, 99, 165n80, n83, 176n30, 177n10
  deaths, 12
  differences between, 6, 23, 27, 79, 97, 115, 161n23, 162n29, n52, 174n5
  First Folio, 10, 12–15, 17, 19, 22
  Royalist associations, 14–15, 16, 19–20
Beaurline, L. A., 18
Belsey, Catherine, 8, 89, 162n33
Bentley, G. E., 9, 11
Blackfriars Theatre, 17, 28
Bowers, Fredson, 19, 104
Bristol, Michael, 139
Brooke, Tucker, 17, 180n45
Buc, Sir George, 19
Bushnell, Rebecca, 5, 101, 161n19
Butler, Martin, 17, 19

Carr, Robert, 122
Cervantes, Miguel de, 130, 131, 181n4
Chapman, George, 14, 15, 28
Charles II, King of England, 5
chastity tests, 37, 38, 41–2, 43
Chaucer, Geoffrey,
  The Knight's Tale, 181n10, n12
city comedy, 136, 137, 152
Clare, Janet, 19, 113, 177n10
Clubb, Louise George, 27
Cohen, Walter, 9, 104
Cokaine, Sir Aston, 12
Coke, Sir Edward, 18
Coleridge, Samuel Taylor, 1, 2, 3, 6–7, 17, 23, 101, 127, 153
collaborative playwriting, 9–15, 51, 153–4, 162n36, 163n49, n55, 176n29, 181n58, 182n14
Cone, M., 161n25
Cotton, Charles, 12
Cowell, William,
  The Interpreter, 104

Danby, John, 4, 63, 111
Davenant, William, 16, 23
  The Rivals, 182n14
Dekker, Thomas, 16
  Keep the Widow Waking (with Ford and Rowley), 182n22
  The Roaring Girl (with Middleton), 25, 26, 141, 183n1
divine right, 18–19, 102, 107–8, 110, 111, 112, 114, 178n24
Dollimore, Jonathan, 71, 154
Donohue, Joseph, 8, 154
Dryden, John, 4, 5, 6
Dudley, Robert, Earl of Leicester, 25
D'Urfé, Honore
  L'Astrée, 108, 178n24

Edwards, Philip, 6
Eliot, T. S., 6, 7
Elizabeth I, Queen of England, 33, 102, 123
  cult of, 24–5, 27, 155
  portraits of, 26
El sagas Estacio marido examinado, 148, 183n29
Erasmus,
  Colloquia, 175n14

Fanshaw, Sir Richard, 28
Farley-Hills, David, 148
Field, Nathan,
  Amends for Ladies, 130, 131–2, 181n6
  as collaborator, 181n6
Finkelpearl, Philip, 5, 6, 17, 18, 33, 79, 97, 104, 138
Flecknoe, Richard, 4, 5, 6, 23
Fletcher, Giles,
  Of the Rus Commonwealth, 123
Fletcher, Ian, 9
Ford, John,
  'Tis Pity She's a Whore, 25, 26
Forker, Charles, 142
Foucault, Michel, 172n17

Gayley, C. M., 6, 17, 18
Globe theatre, 17
Greenblatt, Stephen, 21
Greene, Robert, 175n14
Guarini, Giambattista,
  Il Pastor Fido, 28
Gurr, Andrew, 13, 18

Habington, William, 14, 19
Harington, Henry, 22
Hazlitt, William, 4
Heinemann, Margot, 4
Henrietta Maria, Queen to Charles I, 16

Henslowe, Philip,
  Diary, 9, 10
Herbert, William, Fourth Earl of Pembroke,
  11, 16, 19, 165n90
Herodian,
  Roman History, 114
Heywood, Thomas, 16
  The Royal King and the Loyal Subject, 120,
  122, 123, 180n45
  A Woman Killed with Kindness, 183n1
Howell, James, 14
Hoy, Cyrus, 9, 147
Hume, R. D., 161n17
Humphreys, A. R., 9
Hunt, Leigh, 4

James I, King of England, 4, 17, 18, 122
  and absolutism, 102, 178n25, 180n53
Jones, Inigo, 16
Jonson, Ben, 10, 15, 129, 163n43
  The Alchemist, 137
  Catiline, 4
  Epicoene, 65
  Sejanus, 11

Kahn, Coppelia, 148
Kings' Men, the, 14, 16–17, 20, 164n64
Knights, L. C., 6

Lamb, Charles, 3
Langbaine, Gerard, 5
Lee, Sir Henry, 25
Leech, Clifford, 17
Leinwand, Theodore, 152
L'Estrange, Roger, 14
Lisle, Sir George, 12
Lovelace, Richard, 22
Lyly, John,
  Euphues, 25

Maine, Jasper, 13
Marston, John, 2
  The Dutch Courtesan, 26, 70, 82, 85, 148,
  173n38
  Jack Drum's Entertainment, 130–1
Maslen, Jeffery, 9
Massinger, Philip, 6–7
  as collaborator, 11, 12, 17–18, 163n49,
  181n58
  The Virgin Martyr, 109
Maxwell, Baldwin, 17
McLuskie, Kathleen, 30, 54, 82, 105, 127
Middleton, Thomas, 2, 129
  and city comedy, 52
  A Chaste Maid in Cheapside, 26
  Michaelmas Term, 175n13
  More Dissemblers Besides Women, 57, 58 9

No Wit, No Help like a Woman's, 56–7
The Revenger's Tragedy, 26
The Roaring Girl (with Dekker), 25, 26,
  141, 172n19, 183n1
The Widow, 57
Wit at Severall Weapons (with Rowley and
  possibly Fletcher), 142–4
Women Beware Women, 49, 173n43
military life and values, 78, 82, 83, 84,
  85–8, 92, 109, 111–12, 157,
  175n11
Milton, John,
  Comus, 28, 166n1
Mincoff, Marco, 4
The Mirrour of Knighthood, 55
misogyny, 26, 27, 40, Ch3 78–100, 140,
  147, 151, 157, 174n5, 175n18,
  176n25, 182n25
Montague, Walter, 16
Montemayor, Jorge de,
  Diana, 55
Moseley, Humphrey, 11–14, 22

'N.M.',
  The Faithful General, 180n46
Neill, Michael, 119–20

'Oatmeale, Oliver', 142
Oedipus Rex, 28
Oliphant, E. H. C., 6, 161n23
Ornstein, Robert, 6

Patterson, Annabel, 18
Pearse, Nancy Cotton, 6
Pettus, Sir John, 12
Powell, George,
  Bonduca: or, The British Heroine, 175n15
'pretend wanton' motif, 43–52, 80, 81, 153,
  154–5
Prince Henry, 177n16
Prynne, William, 16

Ralegh, Sir Walter, 18, 122, 164n78,
  180n48
  The History of the World, 122
rape, 37, 51, 107–8, 122, 123, 169n46,
  n50, 178n21, n22
  Lucrece story, 108, 178n26
Rigaud, Nancy, 141
Robinson, Humphrey, 12
Rochester, John Wilmot, Earl of,
  Valentinian, 5
Rymer, Thomas, 4, 5, 6, 20, 23, 114, 153,
  180n55

Savage, J. E., 18
Schoenbaum, Samuel, 161n23

Scott, Thomas,
  The Unhappy Kindness, 5
The Second Maiden's Tragedy, 19, 113–14, 179n33, 181n4, n6
Shakespeare, William, 1, 14, 15, 21, 129, 152
  comparison with Beaumont and Fletcher, 2, 3, 4, 6–8, 62–3, 162n36
  First Folio, 17
  As You Like It, 54, 55, 181n8
  Coriolanus, 175n16
  Cymbeline, 119, 176n18
  Hamlet, 106–7, 113, 120, 175n14
  Henry VIII (with Shakespeare), 2, 9, 160n2
  Julius Caesar, 4, 74
  King Lear, 87, 94
  Macbeth, 102, 103
  Measure for Measure, 49, 80, 170n54
  A Midsummer Night's Dream, 32, 181n8
  Much Ado About Nothing, 78, 128
  Othello, 4, 25–6, 78
  The Rape of Lucrece, 26, 182n25
  Richard III, 103, 115, 116
  The Taming of the Shrew, 97, 99, 128
  The Tempest, 73, 75, 76
  Titus Andronicus, 90
  Two Gentlemen of Verona, 46
  The Two Noble Kinsmen (with Fletcher), 2, 128, 129, 132–5, 136, 147, 158, 181n11, 182n14
  Twelfth Night, 54, 56, 62–3, 66, 155, 182n15
Sharpham, Edward,
  The Fleire, 175n13
Shaw, Bernard,
  Major Barbara, 143
Shepherd, Simon, 54–5, 77, 109, 154
Shirley, James, 17
Sidney, Sir Philip, 40
  The Apologie for Poesy, 17, 102–3
  Arcadia, 55, 56, 62, 63, 168n42, 172n15
  Astrophel and Stella, 24

Spenser, Edmund, 28, 29
  The Faerie Queene, 25, 32, 84, 85
  The Shepheardes Calendar, 32
Stallybrass, Peter, 25
Stanley, Thomas, 15
Stuart, Arabella, 18
Stukeley, Sir Lewis, 122–3, 180n51

Thorndike, Ashley H., 17
tragicomedy, 3, 10, 32, 134–5, 155, 162n40, 164n77, 167n23
transvestism, 33–4, 35, Ch2 53–77, 155–6, 169n44, 171n5, 172n21, n23
Traub, Valerie, 21
Turner, R. K., 14
Turner, R. V., 17, 18, 101, 117

Upton, A. W., 17, 18

Venuti, Lawrence, 6–7
Vergil
  Aeneid, 73
Villiers, George, Duke of Buckingham, 18
virginity, 24, 25, 28, 29, 30, 32, 36, 123, 155, 166n1
  male, 170n56

Waith, Eugene M., 7, 154, 160n4
Waller, Edmund,
  adaptation of *The Maid's Tragedy*, 5, 161n17
Wallis, L. B., 4, 5, 16
Wayne, Valerie, 78
Webster, John, 2, 15–16, 162n36
  Appius and Virginia, 109
  The Duchess of Malfi, 25
Wiseman, Susan, 26
Wit at Severall Weapons (Middleton, Rowley, and possibly Fletcher), 142–4, 182n23
Woodbridge, Linda, 78

Yoch, James J., 32

DATE DUE